THE VICTORIAN TITANIC
The loss of the S.S. *Schiller* in 1875

Keith Austin

HALSGROVE

First published in Great Britain in 2001

British Library Cataloguing-in-Publication Data
A CIP record for this title is available from the British Library

ISBN 1 84114 133 X

HALSGROVE
PUBLISHING, MEDIA AND DISTRIBUTION

Halsgrove House
Lower Moor Way
Tiverton, Devon EX16 6SS
Tel: 01884 243242
Fax: 01884 243325
email sales@halsgrove.com
website www.halsgrove.com

Printed and bound in Great Britain by MPG Ltd, Bodmin

Contents

Memorial at Old Town Church, St Mary's, Isles of Scilly, erected in memory of Louise Holzmaister of New York, who was lost in the wreck of the S.S. Schiller *on 7 May 1875.*

Introduction

In September 1995, I took a holiday with my wife on the Isles of Scilly. On our first morning there, we walked from the guest house where we were staying near Pelistry Bay on the Isle of St Mary's, around the coast towards Hugh Town. The weather was warm and fine, with the few white, puffy clouds almost motionless in the blue above. Under it, the scenery looked magnificent, with azure seas changing to pale-green at the shallows, and white-sand beaches leading the eye over rocky promontories blanketed in green and dotted with flowers of all colours and varieties. It was a scene definitely not conducive to thoughts of wild and stormy nights and tragic shipwrecks.

At Old Town Bay there is a little stone-built church with a small bell tower at one end, situated in a walled churchyard just beyond the beach. Exploring the old church-yard, with an eye to interesting inscriptions on the lichen-covered tombstones, we were gradually drawn upwards, crossing successive terraces by steps until we reached the top. There a tall stone obelisk surmounting a plinth stood behind cast-iron railings, the site almost secluded under overhanging trees.

The obelisk stood in memorial of Louise Holzmaister, a young woman from New York who lost her life in the wreck of the S.S. *Schiller* in May 1875. I had not heard of the vessel or her wreck before, having had up to that point only a mild interest in the subject of shipwrecks. Poor Louise struck a chord of sympathy though – probably because she was quite young, being only eight days short of her 24th birthday. Somewhere in the New York of 120 years ago people had grieved for her; people who would have lived out the remainder of their lives, however long, with her always fresh in their memories.

For the rest of that day, in spite of the new discoveries made in our first hours on St Mary's, Louise Holzmaister and the *Schiller* somehow kept returning to mind. I was intrigued by the scant details I had read on the memorial and wanted to know more about the vessel and how it was wrecked. That evening, we attended one of the slide shows and lectures that are held frequently throughout the tourist season for the benefit of visitors at Hugh Town, covering such topics as the flora and fauna, history, and sea life of the islands. This show was about wrecks around the Scillies, especially that of the *Association* – Sir Clowdisley Shovell's flagship of 1707. It was delivered by our host at the guest house where we stayed, Roy Graham, an ex-Royal Navy Lieutenant and member of the Naval Air Command Sub-aqua Club which first located the wreck of the *Association* during 1965.

Roy dealt fairly briefly with the wreck of the *Schiller* as one wreck among the many in his talk, but it was sufficient to whet my appetite for further information. Back at the guest house he was kind enough to loan me several books from his library which gave brief accounts of the wreck. None were as informative as I wanted, and there were some discrepancies among the details they provided. I yearned to discover still more about the ship, her captain and the passengers aboard her on that terrible night in May 1875. From this starting point, I began the process from which this book is the outcome.

Acknowledgements

During my research a number of people gave invaluable assistance, without which this story would not have been told. I would like to extend my grateful thanks to the following: Joyce Austin; Anne Armitage, The American Museum in Britain, Bath; Peter H. Blum, Archivist, The Stroh Brewing Company, Detroit; Herr Bollmann, Senat Der Freien Und Hansestadt Hamburg Staatsarchiv, Hamburg; R.L. Bowley, St Mary's; H.J. Capell; Public Relations, Hapag-Lloyd AG, Hamburg; Jean Condito, The Sturgis Library, Barnstable, Massachusetts; Klaus Fuest, Deutsches Shiffahrtsmuseum, Bremerhaven; Eckart Giedke, Kamp-Lintfort; Roy Graham, St Mary's, for information, encouragement and reading and correcting my initial efforts; Dr Grupp, Auswartiges AMT, Bonn; Susan Hendricks, Director, and Steve Meyer, Researcher, Blairstown Public Library, Iowa; Osbert Hicks; St Agnes; Gerda Kerkemeier-Knigge, interpreter, Buggingen, Baden; John Koza and Kathy Flynn, Peabody Essex Museum, Salem, Massachusetts; Ann Landers, Local & Naval History Librarian, Devon Local Studies Library; Richard Larn, Shipwreck & Marine, Charlestown, St Austell, for reading the manuscript and much good advice; Sandra Luse, Scott County, Iowa Genealogical Society; Marie Lore, South Street Seaport Museum Library, New York; Graham McCargo, for interpreting German books, and newspapers; Moira MacKay, Assistant Archivist, University of Glasgow. John Norton and Joan Lovero, Librarians, Jersey City Public Library; Steve Ottery and Barry Puttick, Isles of Scilly Museum Association; Dr Johannes Paulmann, German Historical Institute, London; Dr C. Prange, Museum fur Hamburgische Geschichte, Hamburg; Judith A. Simonsen, Curator of Research Collections, Milwaukee Historical Society; Brenda Wall, Trinity House Lighthouse Service; Alice O. Walker, Local History Librarian, Augusta-Richmond Public Library; Miss J.M. Wraight; National Maritime Museum, Greenwich; Harms Ziegler, Institut für Stadtgeschichte, Frankfurt am Main. I also extend my gratitude to the staff at the Cornish Studies Library, Redruth; Bristol Library; Glasgow Transport Museum; Liverpool Maritime Museum Library; Manchester Central Library; National Maritime Museum and Maritime Information Centre, Greenwich; Public Record Office, Kew; The British Library Newspaper Library, Colindale; The British Library Oriental & India Collections, London.

CHAPTER 1

◆

Bishop Rock

The sound of footsteps running downstairs roused James Daniel, senior keeper at Bishop Rock lighthouse, from his bunk. He had not slept since turning in at ten that night. The high-pitched peal of the lighthouse's fog bell, reverberating through the thick walls of the tower six times in every minute, was enough to keep him well awake. He sat up at the urgency of the footsteps and William Mortimer, the third assistant, burst through the doorway forthwith.

'There's a vessel on the rocks!' he said breathlessly.

Leaping from his bunk, Daniel's first thought was that something must have happened to the lamp to have caused a wreck. Without stopping to dress, he ran to the top of the tower's spiral staircase and out on to the parapet of the lantern, with Mortimer close behind him. Raising his telescope towards the south-east and peering through it into the thick fog, Daniel could just make out the masthead light, the green starboard light, and a long row of cabin lights of what appeared to be a large steamship. She was burning blue flares and firing roman candles and rockets into the air. Loud reports of signal guns could be heard. Daniel thought she was sinking. The time was 11.40pm.

The two men watched, horrified by the sight of the wrecked steamer and their own helplessness in the face of the pitiful plight of those so near on board her. They had no means of mounting any rescue nor the capability of alerting anyone on the adjacent Isles of Scilly about the wreck. At midnight, George Gould, the second assistant keeper, came up to relieve Mortimer and joined them in their melancholy vigil. With the fog drifting, sometimes obscuring the vessel and then uncovering it again, it seemed that her crew were firing guns when it closed in and flares and rockets when it lifted enough for them to be seen. But at 12.30 the fog rolled in so thick that it

Bishop Rock lighthouse in 1875.
GRAPHIC MAGAZINE

Bishop Rock lighthouse and the Western Rocks viewed from St Agnes, 1875 – as depicted by an Illustrated London News *artist.*

obliterated the ship completely; although her signal guns could still be heard for another hour afterwards.

Bishop Rock lighthouse stands at the extreme south-westerly point of the Isles of Scilly and the formidable groups of rocks and islets which surround or lie between them. The Isles themselves are 28 miles to the south-west of Land's End, the western-most tip of the British mainland. There are five main islands in the group, each one relatively low-lying but with rock-bound and rugged landscapes that are themselves the highlands and peaks of a single, large island which became submerged in prehis-toric times. St Mary's, the largest, is roughly 2½ by 1½ miles across, with its main centre of commerce and population, Hugh Town, adjacent to a harbour in a sheltered bay. To the south-west of St Mary's lies the much smaller but inhabited island of St Agnes: between it and the Bishop Rock are the most fearsome, jagged, saw-toothed rocks to be found anywhere around the coast of Great Britain.

Despite the dangers posed to unwary shipping, the islands were an important landfall in the days of pure sailing ships. They offered the chance to re-provision after long weeks at sea and shelter from the worst of Atlantic weather. They are also

Aground on the Scillies: one of over 300 recorded wrecks in and around the islands since 1700.

situated where many eastbound vessels would diverge to take either the Bristol or English Channels. A welcome sight to mariners about to negotiate a course towards one or the other would be the islanders' pilot cutters and gigs manned by men with intimate knowledge of the many rocks and shoals which abounded in those parts. Nevertheless, vessels claimed as victims by the craggy islands and their outposts of reefs were innumerable.

The islands' first lighthouse had been erected under the auspices of Trinity House on St Agnes in 1680. For the first 110 years of its existence it was lit by a coal brazier inside its lantern. The light thrown by it was minimal at times but it did valiant service in saving lives, with a more powerful source of illumination provided by oil lamp after 1790. However, on one black, stormy night in October 1707, the warning rays of the St Agnes light remained unseen by many lookouts in a fleet of 21 British Navy vessels returning from Toulon to England. They were commanded by Admiral

Sir Clowdisley Shovell. Of this fleet, Shovell's own flagship *Association*, three other warships and between 1600 and 2000 men, including Sir Clowdisley himself, were claimed by the Western Rocks – all of them within three or four miles of the St Agnes lighthouse.

It was in this area, on a rock then known as 'The Bishop and Clerks' that a new lighthouse was planned and built in the years 1847–50. Of 'screw-pile' construction, the living quarters and lantern were supported on top of cast-iron columns braced with wrought-iron rods that allowed the sea to pass through beneath. It did not survive a severe storm of 5 February 1850. Although entirely washed away it was complete only up to the lantern; and fortunately there were no keepers in residence.

A second structure was begun a year later, designed as was its predecessor by Trinity House engineer, James Walker. It was constructed by the Douglass family of engineers, this time of Cornish granite. The working season was March to October, when the weather was least likely to be unco-operative. Workmen housed in a hut village built specially on the nearby Western Rocks islet of Rosevear, laboured hard on Bishop Rock laying stone which had been dressed at St Mary's and shipped across. The ring of foundation stones alone took three years to complete; the coffer dam around the site being often inundated by waves 20ft high. Workmen laying them would only venture into the foundation pit if James Nicholas Douglass, assistant engineer to his father, would accompany them. On many occasions they were forced to crouch and cling desperately to iron bars while relentless seas swept over their heads leaving them exhausted or injured. Twice, they were all washed out of the pit entirely and only saved by the life-belts they wore and the boat which stood by at all times. Fortunately no man lost his life in the building of the lighthouse and on its completion, on 28 August 1857, the workmen held a dance for all the islanders at their isolated hut village on Rosevear. Its light was first exhibited on 1 September the following year.

The finished lighthouse was massively built. Each of its stones was bolted to its immediate neighbour and the whole tower securely keyed into the rock on which it stood. With a base diameter of just over 48ft – covering almost the whole of the rock – it rose 110ft from the high water mark tapering to 30ft in diameter beneath the lantern gallery. From the rock, up to 19ft above high water level, the tower was solid and from a doorway situated there it was almost solid except for the narrow central stairway leading to the living quarters, a further 26ft above. The accommodation

Bishop Rock lighthouse – after strengthening with added masonry and its height was increased in 1887.

consisted of five small rooms in which, apart from the space requirements of the three keepers and a regularly visiting mechanic, all the apparatus for maintaining the light, coals for heating, a loading crane and the clockwork mechanism for the fog bell had to be housed.

In spite of the solidity of its construction, the violent storms to which it was frequently subjected made the whole tower tremble so much that cups and plates would fall from shelves. Mountainous Atlantic rollers occasionally broke over the very top of its lantern, smashing the thick panes of glass. During one storm of particular fury, the five-hundredweight fog bell was wrenched from its anchorage beneath the gallery by an all-enveloping wave and lost to the deep.

Four keepers were assigned to the lighthouse; three being on duty and one off at any one time. Their tours of duty lasted for two months after which they had one month's leave. To embark or disembark to or from the tower meant securing a boat by grapnel at its base, with the keeper then being raised or lowered by means of the hoist. During one nine-week period of persistently bad weather the lighthouse door could not be opened at all to allow any changeover.

On 7 May 1875 the principal lighthouse keeper was on shore leave. In charge was senior keeper James Daniel, with George Gould his second assistant and William Mortimer the third, each taking turns on duty. A mechanic from Penzance, Thomas Cole, was also there to effect repairs. Each man's watch was four hours long. During this time the keeper was expected to remain by the lantern or on the gallery around it and to record the state of the weather on a meteorological form every three hours. There was also the 'Barometer Book' to be entered daily with details of the wind, weather and the heat of the lantern taken at lighting, midnight and on being extinguished. The forms were sent to Trinity House monthly and the Barometer Book annually.

Daniel's watch was from 4 until 8pm on the 7th. He recorded that there was thick fog all day, although, just as his watch was ending, the revolving white light of the old St Agnes lighthouse was still visible four miles off. Bishop Rock's own lamp was lit by Daniel 15 minutes before sunset and was burning at full power by 8pm. It had been fitted with a new burner during the previous year and with its powerful dioptric, fresnel lens was visible up to 18 miles away in good weather. Mortimer had come on duty at 8pm but because of the fog Daniel remained with him, giving him the order to wind up the clockwork fog bell mechanism which supplemented the light in such conditions, and to set it for six strokes per minute.

Stormy weather at Bishop Rock.

The fog bell hung below the south-east side of the lantern gallery. It was set going at 8.40pm, when the fog marks used for guidance became invisible. Its clockwork machinery was capable of ringing the bell, which sounded with a note like that of a siren, for just over an hour. Before he turned in to bed at 10pm, Daniel had helped Mortimer rewind it. His last words to his third assistant as he tended the lamp were to tell him to call a witness if anything occurred. Now, less than two hours later, he and his fellow lighthouse keepers were witnesses to an unfolding tragedy.

The sound of the guns fired by the stricken vessel was also heard by islanders on St Agnes, about three miles to the north-east of Bishop Rock. Stephen Hicks, a one-time ship's carpenter and for nineteen years a Trinity House pilot on the island, was awakened by the report of a gun at 12.30am. He got up from his bed, dressed and hurried from his house to a look-out place by the island's old lighthouse, hearing yet another gun go off while on his way there. When he arrived, several men there before him said they had heard six reports so far. They all strained to see the cause from their high vantage point, but the fog was far too thick to see anything at all.

The general opinion was that the guns were fired by a German steamship signalling her passing of the islands to the shipping company's agent on St Mary's. They had done this in the past, it was said, when the usual rockets and flares would not be

The lighthouse on St Agnes.

View of St Agnes and the Bishop Rock lighthouse, 1875.

GRAPHIC MAGAZINE

visible in foggy conditions. Hicks thought this was likely but was not entirely convinced. The use of guns in all but distress situations had been outlawed under an international agreement just two years before. He could not believe that this was just a passing ship using guns to make illegal signals. Instead of returning to bed when he got home, he lay on his sofa smoking a pipe and wondering if it really was a ship in trouble somewhere.

Two other St Agnes islanders were similarly affected. Stephen's brother Obadiah, also a Trinity House pilot, heard the guns from his house and concluded that a ship was in distress out on the Western Rocks. Another who heard, thinking the sound came from the direction of Bishop Rock, was retired pilot Jacob Deason. Both men decided independently that, what with the fog, the darkness and the sea being so rough, it was not prudent to go out there in the small boats which the island had; but they would set out at daybreak.

Three miles to the east of St Agnes, lies the main island of the Scillies grouping, St Mary's. On the night of 7 May, John Banfield, a Lloyd's agent and manager of the signal station there, had set a man on watch to a keep lookout for the *Schiller*, one of the German-based Eagle Line's ships. She had been due to pass the islands and dock at Plymouth earlier that day, while on passage from New York to Hamburg. Now, some hours overdue, she was expected to pass during the night. Her arrival off Scilly would be announced by her customary night signals of a blue light followed by a rocket and then a fireball. The watchman would then acknowledge her signals by firing off either a rocket or a roman candle.

At about 1am the watchman heard what might have been the report of a gun, but it was so faint he could not be sure. It might have been just the rattling of a window by the wind. However, he worried about it. Some time beforehand the captain of an Eagle Line steamship had reported the signal station for ignoring his signals and failing to telegraph ahead to Plymouth of his imminent arrival. The watchman was not sure what he should do.

Lloyd's Signal Tower, St Mary's; where John Banfield's nightwatchman awaited the Schiller's *passing signal on the night of 7 May.*
R.L. BOWLEY

CHAPTER 2

The Eagle Line – Boom and Bust

The Eagle Line began operating in the aftermath of the Franco-Prussian War of 1870–71 – the war that united the hitherto independent German states and loose-knit federations into one nation. Their victory celebrations, during which the Prussian King, Wilhelm, was proclaimed Emperor and his political adviser, Prince Bismarck, made Chancellor, heralded in a new sense of purpose. Confidence in Imperial Germany's international importance soon created an unprecedented expansion of trade. In its first three years more companies were launched than during the preceding twenty years. Tens of thousands of ordinary German citizens who never before dabbled in financial dealings, bought shares, their fever fanned by the prospect of unusually high dividends.

Once the hiatus in trade created by the war – when German ships remained in port for fear of capture by the formidable French navy – was finally ended, passenger and freight traffic between Germany and foreign ports soon resumed. On the North Atlantic routes the prime business of shipping lines was the emigrant trade; and people from Germany were once more clamouring to cross to the New World for a fresh start. Germans had to this date formed the largest group of emigrants to America, outnumbering both Irish and British among the multitudes – the yearly total of which had risen from 84 000 in 1840 to 380 000 by 1870. Most were drawn there by the opportunities to own land or earn higher wages for their artisan skills. Letters circulated in European countries, supposedly genuine, gave glowing accounts of life in America:

This is the country Jem… stated one, *employment of all sorts is going a-begging, and wages are capital. You only have to choose a trade, Jem, and be it…*[1]

Others had been impelled to go because of severe hardship or religious and political repression; the most poverty stricken undertaking the discomforts of a long, arduous voyage in the cramped and squalid quarters of a sailing packet ship's 'tween decks as steerage passengers.

Such transatlantic traffic was not entirely one-way; many who had settled and become prosperous in the land of opportunity made return visits to their homeland, often travelling first or second class rather than the steerage passage they had taken when emigrating. Others found that America was not paved with gold; the hardships there could be every bit as severe as at home. There were those who, having sold all they owned to finance emigration, later sold even the clothes they stood up in to pay for return tickets.

As the resumption of trade between Germany and the New World escalated following the war's end, the numbers of emigrants and others travelling between Hamburg and the United States rose dramatically. A generally held belief that this post-war boom in passenger and freight traffic would expand indefinitely, caused merchants and traders in Hamburg to cast a critical eye at the capacity of the main steamship line that represented them. They accused the Hamburg-Amerika Line of being ill-equipped to cope with this increasing demand, expressing fears that competitors from outside Germany would move in to take advantage of their lack of shipping tonnage. New lines were being set up all over Europe at the time – in Britain, Belgium, Holland, Norway, and at other ports in Germany.

Two groups were soon formed, each aiming to found a new Hamburg-based transatlantic steamship line. Both included local companies together with banking houses from inland whose interests had not previously incorporated shipping. Prominent in one group was a man with considerable experience of running a shipping company. This was Rob M. Sloman junior, owner of a Hamburg sailing packet line established by his grandfather in the late 1790s. He was keen to set up in direct opposition to Hamburg-Amerika for personal reasons.

When, in May 1847, the Hamburg-Amerika Line had been formed, their sailing packet ships competed directly with those of the Sloman Line. Sloman's father, Rob M. Sloman senior, met their challenge by attempting the change from sail to steam. In 1850 Sloman became the first German line to operate a steamship, having opted for its most modern form, iron hulled and screw driven. The venture was timely, for the iron screw steamers of the newly formed, Liverpool based, Inman Line had just begun to challenge the ten-year near-monopoly held by the wooden paddle steamers

Sloman line S.S. Helena Sloman, 800 tons; the first German transatlantic steamship, 1850.
ILLUSTRATED LONDON NEWS

owned by Cunard, the first truly successful transatlantic steamship line. Sloman's sojourn into steam was short-lived however, for his first steamship, *Helena Sloman*, was lost in November 1850 on only her third voyage to New York. When, in 1853, he ordered another iron screw steamship, Hamburg-Amerika promptly decided to switch from sail to steam and ordered two such steamships. Sloman then approached his River Elbe rivals, offering to run his new ship in a joint service with theirs, but they declined to co-operate. He did not forgive them for the snub he had received and when he died, in 1867, he left his son both the long-lived line of sailing packets and an inherited, bitter hostility towards Hamburg-Amerika.

Although trade was thriving by 1871, there was not enough to support a further two transatlantic steamship lines at Hamburg. When this was fully realised, the groups planning their formation made contact and amalgamated. At a meeting held between them on 16 January 1872, a new steamship line, named the Deutsche Transatlantische Dampfschiffahrts Gesellschaft (German Transatlantic Steamship Company) – but thereafter known as the Adler Linie (Eagle Line) from the symbol on its house flag – was inaugurated. Rob M. Sloman Jnr. was appointed Chairman of the Board of Directors. He aimed to better their rival on the River Elbe with bigger, more luxuriously appointed and faster steamships, and a weekly rather than fortnightly timetable.

The new company's founders estimated that a setting-up capital of 12 million thalers would be required and put up five million themselves. The remainder was

Hamburg-Amerika steamships in the River Elbe, c.1860.

raised by public subscription. In fact, such was the clamour for stock from people of all walks of life at the time, that on the first day's share issue, 19.5 million thalers were raised before trading ceased. It was said that Prince Bismarck himself speculated in the shares.

Eight new ships for the Eagle Line were soon on the order books of three Clydeside shipbuilders for British yards were then pre-eminent in the construction of iron steamships. Two of these vessels were to be built at the yard of Robert Napier & Sons, five were to be built by Alexander Stephen & Son and one more by J. & G. Thomson. They were to be almost identical: each one an iron-hulled screw steamship with a carrying capacity of 3000 tons cargo and up to 1000 passengers. Where they would differ most visibly was in the arrangement of their funnels. The Napier-built ships would have twin funnels while those from the Stephen and Thomson yards only one. Yet each ship was to be superior in all respects to the ships of their direct competitors on the North Atlantic run, with passenger accommodation unmatched for comfort and convenience and engines capable of turning out an extra knot in speed to shorten journey times. A German engineer, Ernst Voss – later joint founder of the Blohm and Voss shipyards at Hamburg – was appointed by the Eagle Line to oversee the construction of its new ships.

Robert Napier & Sons was first to receive contracts to build ships for the new German line. At that time the company had been in the shipbuilding business for almost fifty years. It was Napier himself who had advised Samuel Cunard and introduced him to Glasgow shipowners who were prepared to join his steamship venture back in 1840. Napier's had also constructed the first Cunard wooden paddle steamers' engines and during the 1860s, when iron hulls began to replace wood, built seven complete vessels for Cunard. By the arrival of the Eagle Line contracts, Robert Napier & Sons had an envied reputation for shipbuilding of all types, from small steam yachts to warships and ocean liners of 3000 tons or more, completing on average five large vessels per year.

The contract for the Eagle Line ships arrived on 28 March 1872. Each of the two large liners was to have a gross tonnage of over 3400, to measure 375ft long[2], have a beam of 40ft, and a depth of 33ft, 6ins from keel to gunwale. Passenger space was to be allocated for 71 in first-class staterooms, 78 in second class, and 796 on the steerage deck below them. Accommodation for 15 officers and engineers would be required, as would space for 104 seamen, firemen and other crew to be berthed. The liners were to be named *Goethe* and *Schiller*, after heroes of German literature, as were other transatlantic ships of the line. Napier was also contracted, on 12 September that year, to build the Eagle Line's River Elbe tender *Hoboken*, a 582-ton, single-deck paddle steamer for use as a passenger ferry.

First to have its skeletal, iron framework raised in the stocks at Napier's Govan, Glasgow yard was *Goethe*. Both *Goethe* and her sister ship *Schiller* each required over 1500 tons of ironwork, 240 tons of wood, and 75 tons of red lead and cement in the construction of their hulls alone, whilst during fitting out, a further 430 tons of smith-work, woodwork and other materials were added. The final price paid by the Eagle Line for each vessel was £107 580, which included £36 for expenses incurred during sea-trials and £115 for a Lloyd's special survey. Lloyd's awarded 100A1 certificates to both ships, their highest classification for iron vessels.

On completion, the Eagle Line ships were among the larger liners built for the North Atlantic, but by no means the largest – an honour long since held by I.K.

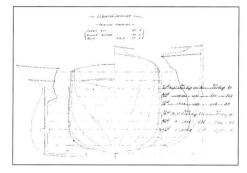

Hull plans for Schiller *and* Goethe *by Robert Napier & Co.*

GLASGOW UNIVERSITY ARCHIVES

Napier's specification and construction materials used for Schiller *and* Goethe.

GLASGOW UNIVERSITY ARCHIVES

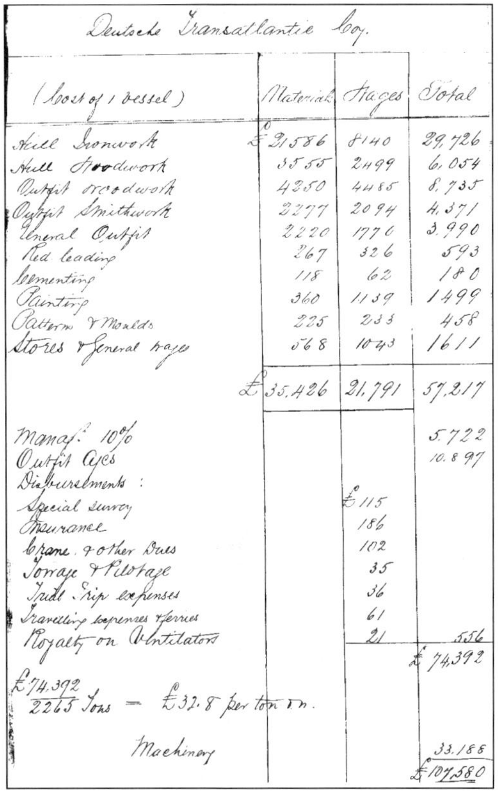

Below: *Scotch boiler.*

Left document (handwritten ledger):

Deutsche Transatlantic Coy.

(Cost of 1 vessel)	Material	Wages	Total
Hull Ironwork	£21,586	8,140	29,726
Hull Woodwork	3,555	2,499	6,054
Outfit woodwork	4,250	4,485	8,735
Outfit Smithwork	2,277	2,094	4,371
General Outfit	2,220	1,770	3,990
Red leading	267	326	593
Cementing	118	62	180
Painting	360	1,139	1,499
Pattern & Moulds	225	233	458
Stores & General wage	568	1,043	1,611
	£35,426	21,791	57,217

Manag.t 10%		5,722
Outfit &c		10,897
Disbursements:		
Special survey	£115	
Insurance	186	
Crane & other Dues	102	
Tonage & Pilotage	35	
Trial Trip expenses	36	
Travelling expences & ferries	61	
Royalty on Ventilators	21	556
		£74,392

£74,392
2265 Tons = £32.8 per ton r.m.

Machinery	33,188
	£107,580

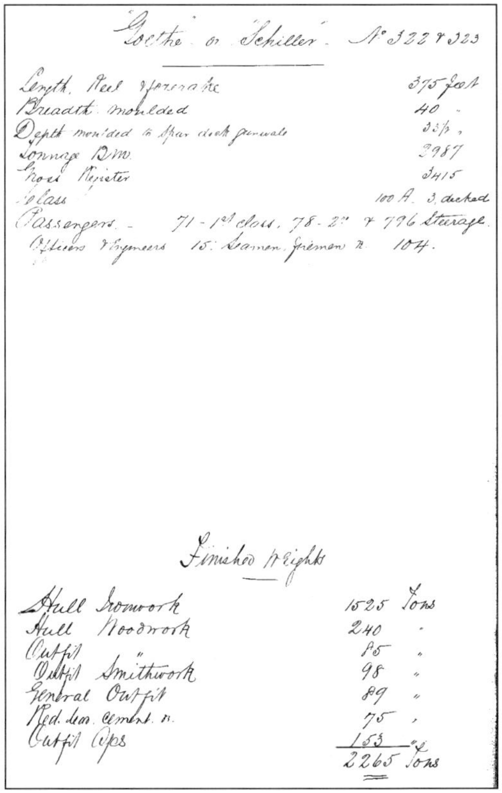

Right document (handwritten specification):

'Goethe' or 'Schiller'. No 322 & 323

Length, Reel &between	375 feet
Breadth moulded	40
Depth moulded to Spar deck gunwale	33½
Tonnage B.m.	2987
Gross Register	3415
Class	100 A 3 decked
Passengers – 71 1st class, 78 2nd & 776 Steerage.
Officers, Engineers 15, Seamen, firemen &c 104.

Finished Weights

Hull Ironwork	1525 Tons
Hull Woodwork	240 "
Outfit	85 "
Outfit Smithwork	98 "
General Outfit	89 "
Red lead cement &c	75 "
Outfit &c	153 "
	2265 Tons

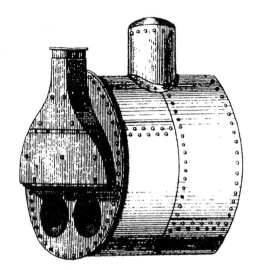

Brunel's *Great Eastern*, which at 20 000 tons and over 680ft long, would not be matched in size for a further quarter of a century. Yet there were several ships of over 4000 tons in service on the Atlantic, and White Star Line's 5000-ton liner *Britannic* was under construction at Harland & Wolff's yard in Belfast. However, of the German lines, Eagle Line ships had the edge in size over their rivals and in speed as well. While not destined to be contestants for the 'Blue Riband' – an honour held by White Star ships with speeds averaging 15 knots – the new Eagle Line vessels had the most up-to-date and fuel-efficient engines of their era, giving them a turn of speed around 14 knots.

Where earlier steamships were fitted with rectangular 'box' boilers and single cylinder engines, the Eagle Line vessels were fitted with 'Scotch' boilers and 'compound' engines. From around 1870 this combination had brought about a radical improvement. The cylindrically constructed Scotch boiler enabled steam pressures to be more than doubled – up to 70 pounds per square inch – and in a twin-cylinder

The ultimate in 'long ship' design; the White Star Line Britannic, *completed in 1874.*

Below: *Compound engine.*

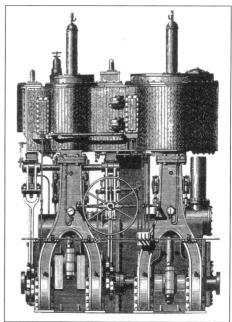

compound engine it was used twice; first being partially expanded in a small, high-pressure cylinder before passing to a large low-pressure cylinder, where the residual steam pressure was expanded further. The fuel efficiency of these engines was such that they could almost halve coal consumption and the much reduced bunker space provided a greater payload.

In style the new Eagle Line ships were modelled on the latest design features. During the early 1870s it was the White Star liner *Oceanic* that set new trends in steamship development. One of the first to have a compound engine, this was combined with a recently evolved hull design. Where the traditional relationship of beam to length in a ship was 8:1, the *Oceanic*'s was 10:1. The combination of this 'long ship' design and the compound engine maximised the advantages of the new engine's fuel efficiency. The hull design of both *Goethe* and *Schiller* approximated the new aspect ratio.

Another adopted feature pioneered by *Oceanic* was the fitting of stanchions and railings all around the upper 'spar deck' rather than raised, solid bulwarks. This allowed water shipped in heavy seas to run off immediately. Known as 'flush deck'

The White Star liner Oceanic *which pioneered the 'long ship' design.*

vessels, the Eagle liners had little superstructure, and the deckhouses and companions were only lightly constructed of iron with fluted 'Ionic' style columns for decoration. Below were two iron passenger decks, each with headroom of over 7ft, while the cargo holds and coal bunkers beneath them were 16ft deep. Six iron bulkheads divided the hull into seven watertight compartments.

As was usual on ships of their era, wind power provided assistance to the engine or could provide all the motive power should it break down, while the sails themselves aided stability. Both vessels were brig-rigged, with both fore and main masts of iron construction reaching to a height of 128ft above the spar deck, and braced in position by a 'standing rigging' made of wire. Each mast was rigged to carry three square sails on her yards, with staysails and trysails fore and aft.

While the new Eagle Line ships from the Napier and other yards were not distinguished by being the largest or fastest of ships, they did have a certain something. Their New York adverts were to include the phrase, 'elegant and full-powered Clyde-built steamships;' and they were certainly elegant, with long, sleek hulls having little superstructure to detract from their clean lines and just two masts when so many other vessels had three or four. Ships built on the Clyde, and by Napier & Sons in

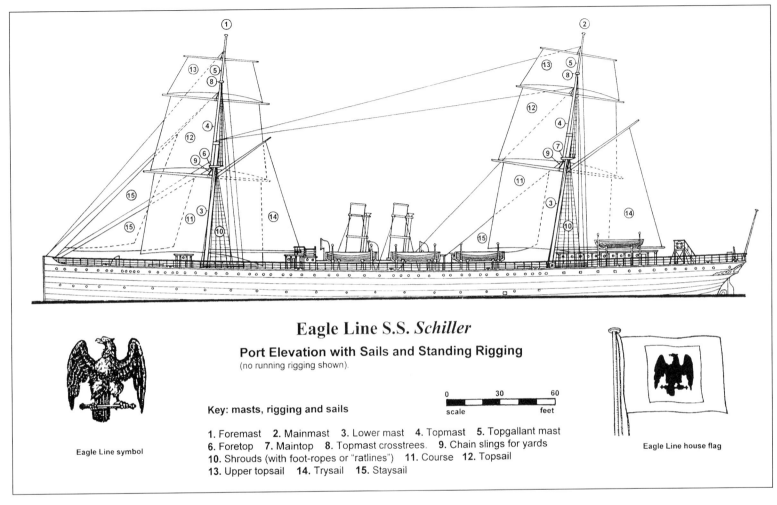

Eagle Line S.S. *Schiller*

Port Elevation with Sails and Standing Rigging
(no running rigging shown).

Eagle Line symbol

0   30   60
scale   feet

Key: masts, rigging and sails

1. Foremast   **2.** Mainmast   **3.** Lower mast   **4.** Topmast   **5.** Topgallant mast
6. Foretop   **7.** Maintop   **8.** Topmast crosstrees.   **9.** Chain slings for yards
10. Shrouds (with foot-ropes or "ratlines")   **11.** Course   **12.** Topsail
13. Upper topsail   **14.** Trysail   **15.** Staysail

Eagle Line house flag

particular, were considered then and for a long time afterwards in the highest regard by both British and European shipping lines.

Port elevation of Schiller.

Goethe was launched into the Clyde on 27 April 1873 and found capable of making 14 knots comfortably at her trials during August. Her maiden voyage, with 211 passengers on board, began on 12 September that year, but when only a day or two outward bound she lost a blade from her screw and was forced to make a diversion to Leith for repairs. Once these were completed she made a good passage, taking just ten days to cross to New York, where she tied up to the new, Eagle Line pier on 1 October.

Property for docks at Hoboken, New Jersey, had cost the company $600 000. This, at the foot of 1st Street, included a large bonded warehouse, freight houses, offices, a dry dock and a large shed covering almost all of a pier more than 80ft wide and 700ft long. *Goethe* remained tied up there for two weeks, a lengthy turn-around time during which the vessel was thrown open to public view for potential customers to examine her. The *New York Times* noted:

> *The accommodation for second and third class passengers is superior to that afforded in other steamships... All the newest improvements are introduced into the splendid appointments of the saloons and state rooms for first class passengers.*[3]

The ship made one more voyage in 1873, sailing direct to New York outward and calling at Plymouth and Cherbourg on the return, arriving back at Hamburg on 21 December.

Before 1873 was over, the Eagle Line took delivery of their Napier-built Elbe tender, *Hoboken*, which was launched on 16 August. The next launching planned was the *Schiller*, scheduled for Monday 25 August, eight months after her keel had been laid. The ceremony was to be performed by her newly appointed captain, George Thomas, and Mrs R.A. Napier. But with the River Clyde in a rather low state on the day, it had to be postponed. When late evening and overnight heavy rain brought the river into full flood, preparations were hastily made to launch the vessel at 3am, while the river was at its height. It was a particularly dark and wild night, a setting made even more Wagnerian in atmosphere by vivid flashes of lightning which lit the sky. As soon as Mrs Napier had christened the ship with champagne and the newly dubbed *Schiller* left the slipway, it appeared to all who witnessed the launch that the vessel was struck by lightning at the very moment she entered the water. It was an ominous beginning.

A Napier engineer's remarks on the launching of Schiller, *26 August 1873.*
GLASGOW MUSEUM OF TRANSPORT

S.S. Schiller.
GRAPHIC MAGAZINE

Schiller was ready to begin her transatlantic duties early in 1874. Departing from Hamburg on 5 February that year, spirits on board were high in spite of the low passenger numbers, only two in cabin class and a further 67 in steerage. Passing the eastward-bound Hamburg-Amerika *Westphalia* in mid-Atlantic on the 11th, Captain Thomas signalled with the Eagle Line's night signals, a blue light and a rocket followed by a fireball, as if proud to show their Hamburg rivals who they were. But the return to the Elbe on 14 March was an ignominious one for the new commander – in thick fog he ran his equally new ship aground at Krautsland.

The damage was severe. A diver's report showed the rudder to be broken below the water line, while the hull itself was leaking, especially in her coal bunkers and after compartments. But there was no dock large enough for the *Schiller* at Hamburg. With the rudder patched and the steam bilge pumps operating throughout the journey, she was sailed to Wilhelmshaven for the repairs. There it was discovered that the damage was more extensive than first thought – the stern post was broken. It needed replacing entirely; work which could only be undertaken at Napier's yard in Govan. Having departed from Glasgow proudly in his pristine vessel on New Year's day that year, Captain Thomas brought the crippled ship limping back up the Clyde on 14 April for a six-week stay to have her stern rebuilt. A Lloyd's survey at the end of June passed her once more as 100 A1.

In the meantime, other Eagle Line ships had become casualties. The *Herder*, built by Alexander Stephen & Son, had her second voyage ended prematurely in late February when violent Atlantic gales damaged her hull and washed away several lifeboats. Forced to turn back for Queenstown (now Cobh) in southern Ireland, her passengers were disembarked to await transfer to *Goethe*, while she was taken on to Glasgow for leaks to be repaired. Soon afterwards, *Goethe* herself became a casualty in two separate incidents, both while negotiating the Elbe. Leaving Hamburg on 16 April, she ran aground by Gluckstadt, damaging a cylinder in the process. When refloated, she put back to Brunshaven for repairs and did not sail for New York until mid-May. Then, on returning to the Elbe a month later, she grounded just below Blankenese and a tug employed in bringing her off struck her stern and broke the blades of her screw. As repair work was prolonged beyond her next departure date, her cargo and passengers were transferred to *Schiller,* which arrived back at Hamburg from her own repairs at Glasgow on 30 June, just in time to take over.

The line's misfortunes continued throughout 1874. The Stephen-built *Lessing* went ashore at Blankenese during her trials in the Elbe, but was refloated undamaged and began her maiden voyage on schedule, taking 247 passengers to New York on 28 May. At Hoboken, like *Goethe* before her, she was then proudly thrown open for a week of public inspection. But homeward-bound, she was damaged in a collision with a sailing ship off the coast of Cornwall, although able to continue on to Plymouth and Hamburg. *Lessing*'s scheduled third voyage was ended abruptly after leaving Hamburg on 13 November, when she was run down by the Hamburg-Süd Line's *Bahia* and a 10ft hole made in her bow. Her cargo and passengers were then disembarked for a five-day wait for the next brand-new Eagle Line vessel to appear on the scene. This was *Klopstock*, the only J. & G. Thomson vessel built for the line. She had

Advert for the Eagle Line, August 1874.
HAMBURG BORSENHALLE

a good first Atlantic crossing and unlike any of her predecessors, returned to Hamburg on 24 December without incident.

On 8 December Captain Thomas and *Schiller* arrived back in the mouth of the Elbe, where the ship was confronted by such heavy ice and thick fog that she could not proceed to Hamburg. There, at their Brooktor Strasse offices, the Eagle Line's directors were counting the costs of operations. Having had to cancel several scheduled departures during 1874, their ships had completed only 20 voyages. The five operating Eagle Line steamships had carried altogether 6064 outward-bound passengers and 2400 on return passages – an average of just over 200 passengers per trip and less than a quarter of each vessel's total capacity. The best outward-bound numbers were achieved on *Schiller,* when in August she conveyed 696 passengers. Freight figures were, at 2000 tons per trip average, about two-thirds capacity. The company directors could only report:

> *None of the voyages last year yielded any gains and on several occasions we suffered considerable losses.*[4]

The Eagle Line's offices, corner of Brooktor Strasse and St Annen Square, Hamburg.
HAMBURG STAATSARCHIV

In their original plans the Eagle Line had aimed to outdo their Hamburg rival's fortnightly timetable by offering weekly sailings, but after just one year and three months in service the Line was in serious trouble. Two further vessels built in the Alexander Stephen yard, *Wieland* and *Gellert*, were launched, fitted out and delivered during the latter half of 1874, with *Weiland*'s maiden voyage advertised for 1 October. But neither ship was to sail for the Eagle Line, that year or any other.

To counteract the shortfall in passengers, the outward-bound – direct to New York – passage was changed and in 1875 Eagle liners called at Cherbourg on the outward as well the homeward leg. The new year began badly though. For the first week in January *Schiller* was still unable to reach Hamburg because the Hamburg-Amerika *Cimbria* was aground and blocking the river. In the meantime her Napier-built sister *Goethe*, arriving at New York on the 7th, was struck and damaged by a pilot boat. Then *Lessing*, returning to her home port on the 14th, ran aground in the Elbe and was not floated off for three days. *Klopstock*, the only vessel to have survived two voyages undamaged, caught up with fate in March, when on her third voyage she had to put in at Halifax, Nova Scotia, short of coal and leaking through a long battle with ice on the way over.

Despite such problems the line was able to keep to its scheduled fortnightly sailings as the year progressed. Yet passenger figures were not improving. The Eagle

The same building (as above) *in 1908.*
HAMBURG STAATSARCHIV

Deutsche transatlantische Dampfschifffahrts-Gesellschaft.

DIE am **2. Januar 1875** fälligen Zins-Coupons der Prioritäts-Obligationen I. Emission werden **vom 2. Januar an** in den üblichen Geschäftsstunden im Bureau der Gesellschaft, **St. Annen Platz No. 1,** eingelöst. Die Coupons sind mit arithmetisch geordnetem Nummern-Verzeichniss einzureichen und geschieht die Zahlung nach Wahl der Inhaber entweder per Bank oder per Cassa.

Hamburg, 24. December 1874.

Der Verwaltungsrath.

Line was not alone in this situation. Both Hamburg-Amerika and the North-German Lloyd Lines were having difficulty in filling their ships as passenger bookings and freight handling dwindled. The much vaunted escalation of trade between the old and new worlds had, apart from a transient flare-up, fizzled out. Passengers from Hamburg declined from 60 000 in 1872 to 48 000 one year later, while North-German Lloyd figures showed a similar reduction at Bremen. The Eagle Line had entered the transatlantic trade with its brand-new fleet just when the post-war boom was about to bust.

Drastic measures were called for and taken – primarily by the Eagle Line directors under Rob M. Sloman. It was they who led out in a savage price-cutting war. The ticket price for a steerage passage to New York had been reduced by almost half by 1875, as also were cargo rates. Both Hamburg-Amerika and North-German Lloyd were forced to follow suit in spite of arriving at a position where receipts did not cover costs.

First of the shipping lines to fail in this cut-throat market was the old-established transatlantic sailing packet line belonging to Sloman. Soon, as the account books of the steamship lines sank further into the red, cutbacks in services were made. North-German Lloyd and Hamburg-Amerika both laid up some of their vessels. The Eagle Line sought another solution to its financial problems – a merger with its deadly rivals. This had been first suggested – and firmly rejected by Hamburg-Amerika directors – as early as March 1874. When another, similar proposal was turned down flat in September, the Eagle Line's directors offered to sell the company outright to their competitors, but their price was considered too high. By February 1875 the Eagle Line was fast approaching bankruptcy: work on their eighth and last steamship, *Theodore Korner*, still on the stocks at Alexander Stephen's Clydeside yard, was stopped because of unpaid bills. With the collapse of the Eagle Line imminent, Hamburg-Amerika's directors at last responded to the overtures of their rivals.

In the negotiations which followed, the two companies first agreed to amalgamate. The proposed new line was to be titled either 'Hamburg-Amerikan Packet and Eagle Line' or 'Eagle Line and Hamburg-Amerika Steamship Company.' In the event, ex-Eagle Line ships were absorbed into Hamburg-Amerika's fleet, for the Eagle Line was ultimately bought out by them, with only the docks at Hoboken remaining to be sold off to outside interests by the original owners. Their fleet of ships (except *Theodore Korner*, which eventually became P & O *Nepaul*), the docks and offices in Hamburg, plus goodwill, were acquired for an agreed sum of 12.5 million marks. Some Hamburg-Amerika shareholders quibbled that it was both expensive and unnecessary, considering they had no need of extra tonnage or dock property in the current slump, but it was argued that in the event of the Eagle Line's bankruptcy some outside competitor might buy up the line cheaply and then pose an even greater threat to their operations.

The price paid was so high that Hamburg-Amerika almost bankrupted themselves by their purchase. Yet their chairman insisted that the buy-out was the best solution for the Hamburg community as a whole, where other important interests were involved. The ex-chairman of the Eagle Line's board of directors, Rob M. Sloman, probably appreciated such consideration in this bitter hour of defeat by his father's old enemy. He had aimed to better his rival on the River Elbe with bigger, more luxuriously appointed and faster steamships, and a weekly rather than fortnightly timetable. However, post-war optimism had caused the Eagle Line's directors and investors to seriously over-estimate the normal capacity of the emigrant market. During its short, problematic career, the Eagle Line's steamships had, by 24 April 1875 – the date of the takeover agreement – completed only 29 voyages between them: *Goethe*'s total was ten; *Herder*'s six; *Klopstock*'s three; while *Lessing* and *Schiller*, still at sea, were on their sixth and seventh respectively.

NOTES

[1] Charles Dickens: *American Notes and Reprinted Pieces*, Chapman & Hall, London, 1894.

[2] Length was 375ft between perpendiculars (386ft from stem to stern) but was probably lengthened to 380ft (391ft) during repairs in June 1874.

[3] *New York Times*, 8 October 1873.

[4] *New York Tribune*, 10 May 1875.

CHAPTER 3

·◆·

Cabin Boy to Captain

The *Schiller* had soon become one of the most popular of the Eagle Line vessels. There was a regular coterie of Atlantic travellers who would sail on no other ship. One reason for this was her renowned punctuality in arriving at port on timetable. Another reason was Captain Thomas himself. By many accounts well-educated and scientifically inclined, he was also a highly personable and sociable man, a great favourite with passengers of both sexes. He was equally liked and respected by those who served under him, being a strict, but not harsh, disciplinarian as were some in other ships. At 39 years of age and unmarried, often taken to be a much younger man despite his fashionable heavy moustache and bushy side-whiskers, he cut a dashing and attractive figure.

Minna Kleeberg, a lady with literary pretensions, from Louisville, Kentucky, found Captain Thomas much to her liking. Travelling home from Germany on the west-bound *Schiller* between 1 and 14 April 1875, she admired both the way he ran the ship and the manner in which he cared for his passengers. He seemed selfless and unde-manding of his own needs, willing always to serve others first, she thought. During conversations, he told her much about his life at sea and that he had been to every trading coast on earth except California. Taking advantage of his amiable nature, she asked why he remained unmarried. 'The ship is my bride,' he joked, but then, more seriously, added that he had no intention of tying up the fate of a wife and family to the unstable nature of the seaman's life.

Yet beneath that affable, still youthful exterior, Minna Kleeberg had detected a streak of melancholy, perhaps even a grim foreboding of what fate could bring him. In a conversation about the wreck of the French liner, *Ville de Havre*, sunk by collision in November 1873 with 226 dead, she asked him whether the crew were at fault. His answer reflected both the feelings of responsibility that the position of captain had brought him and the universal fatalism of the ordinary sailor,

'When a ship has an accident it's always the fault of the captain. Yes, it's luck! It's luck!'[1]

Generally though, it was the good-humoured side of George Thomas's character which surfaced most in his dealings with passengers. His popularity, in a job where he was the principal representative of the shipping company while at sea, should have been a considerable asset to his future career prospects. His background, having risen from cabin boy to ship's master, showed him to be a man of unbounded ambition.

Born at Frankfurt on the Main, Germany, on 23 February 1836, he had been christened Johannes Georg after his father, Johannes Thomas. The elder Johannes (1793–1863) had spent nine years studying art in Paris and Italy, returning to his home city of Frankfurt in 1826 to work with considerable success as a painter, lithographer and teacher. He was later one of the founder members of the city's Art Society. Deeply pious, he turned his hand to writing books on religious subjects during the 1850s.

Young Johannes Georg was raised with four sisters in a home where the Catholic religion took some prominence, a large, ivory cross dominating their living room. The whole family, father, mother and five children, were frequent visitors at homes of other artists in the local community. Yet in spite of such strong influences on the choice of a career for the younger Johannes, or Georg as he was known, the tools of his father's trade held no particular appeal nor did the cross and Bible influence his decision. It was the sea rather than the painter's muse or religious fervour that had captured his imagination, and the chart and sextant which were to guide his future. In December 1851, at the age of 15, he signed on for service before the mast on a sailing vessel at Bremen. It was in this ship, *Livonia*, that he first entered New York harbour.

He was a cabin boy or apprentice on *Livonia*, but signed on as an ordinary seaman on his second sailing vessel, *Aeolus*, in August 1852. From June 1854, he was classed as able seaman. In these capacities, he shared the crew's quarters in the ship's forecastle and work that was harsh and physical – keeping the vessel 'shipshape' or clambering aloft with the rest of his watch at any significant change in the weather to set or reef sails. He was conscientious in his work and as a 'common sailor' in 1856 was commended for his 'watchfulness, sobriety and sociability'. He was also diligently applying himself to the task of learning seamanship. A certificate of competency as 'under mate' was granted him at Bremen a little later, and in July 1857 he proudly sailed from that port as second mate of the *Meridian*. After a year with her, he then joined the *Achilles* in the rank of first mate on 16 February 1859. He had by this date served in eight sailing ships on voyages ranging from three to 18 months long, two of them aboard the *Livonia*, and had travelled to many parts the world.

Georg Thomas's experience on the *Achilles,* a full-rigged, three-masted ship, marked a turning point in his career. Leaving Bremen that February, bound for New Orleans via the north of Scotland, she encountered a fierce hurricane on 12 March. With all sails except the foresail blown clean away from her yards by the force of the wind, the ship was driven hard ashore near Fitfull Head on the Shetland Islands; a very exposed part of the coastline. Georg acquitted himself well during the disaster, in which all the crew were saved. He was paid off from the ship – later refloated – on 8 April, but soon after returning to Germany, he set off for London.

While Georg had been serving in German sailing ships, his eldest sister, Elizabeth, had met and married an Englishman, Charles H. Martin; a man later to become quite prominent as a broker in the City of London. It was on the advice of his new brother-in-law that Georg – soon to sign himself in the Anglicised version, 'George' – travelled to England that May and sought work in the British Merchant Marine Service.

From his lodgings at the Sailors Home in Wells Street, London Docks, George first went to the Local Marine Board offices at Cornhill on 26 May and applied to be examined for a British first mate's certificate. For this he was required to have served two years as an officer of the watch and to sit an examination in the subjects of navigation, seamanship and commercial codes of signals. As a German citizen, with over five years certified service in German sailing ships and a German under mate's certificate, but only about 14 months actual experience as an officer, his request was granted by 'special application'. He passed the examination and was awarded a Board of Trade certificate of competency as first mate on 1 June. By this date, George had left the Sailors Home and moved in with his sister and her husband at Strinton Place, Blackheath, in south-east London.

His first new appointment took him to Calcutta, where on 29 July 1859 he became second mate on H.M. Bengal brig *Kedgeree,* a 220-ton vessel in the Bengal Pilot Service. *Kedgeree* served the Hughli river pilots, men whose long apprenticeships as 'licensed leadsman' on the river's notoriously shifting shoals qualified them for this highly paid and privileged occupation. George Thomas served there under Captain Mitchell for over five months, during which he was made up to first mate.

From January 1860 he seems not to have served on any ship until 25 June 1861, when he was appointed as fourth officer on the Peninsular & Oriental Line *Hindostan*, then in reserve at Calcutta. *Hindostan*, a wooden-built paddle steamer of over 2000 tons, was one of a pair of ships with which P & O had first opened up the sea route from Suez to Calcutta back in 1842. Passengers bound from England to the furthest outposts of Empire in India would journey by sea from Southampton to Alexandria in Egypt, change to River Nile steamers until Cairo was reached, cross 100 miles of desert to Suez in mule-drawn carriages, and complete the remainder of the journey in either *Hindostan* or her sister ship *Bentinck*. When George Thomas joined *Hindostan* in 1861, her days of elegant travel filled with the sahibs and memsahibs of the British Raj were almost over, for just one year later she was converted to a cargo sailing ship. However, it was the beginning of an association with P & O that was to last him for the next 11½ years of his life.

George Thomas's first steamship, P & O Line paddle steamer Hindostan.

George Thomas's sojourn with *Hindostan*, his first steamship, was only a few weeks, for on 17 July that year he became supplementary fourth officer on the P & O screw ship *Nubia*, remaining with her for two years on the Suez to Calcutta run. Then, after a period of leave taken in England during the July of 1863, he returned to India and, ranked as third officer, joined *Singapore*; one of the last of P & O's large paddle steamers, which operated on the monthly, Bombay–Galle (Ceylon)–Hong Kong–Shanghai route. He was soon transferred again, this time to the *Simla*, returning to the

On board the P & O paddle steamer Singapore.
ILLUSTRATED LONDON NEWS

Suez–Calcutta run in March 1864. Less than four months were to pass before he became *Simla*'s second officer.

As an officer of the P & O company, George Thomas would have had to live up to the high standards of efficiency, reliability and courtesy expected of its employees at all times. The Company had a reputation for providing the very best for its passengers and arriving at ports punctually. The passengers themselves travelled mostly first class; any in second-class accommodation were generally the servants of the former. There was no provision for a steerage class. While discipline was tight on board, with everyone from captain down to the lowliest deck-hand subject to detailed written instructions on behaviour and dress, on and off duty, conditions and pay were good. The company was generally perceived by its employees as a stern but benevolent master.

Dining first class on a P & O steamship in the 1870s.

ILLUSTRATED LONDON NEWS

The *Simla*, one of P & O's largest iron screw steamships, was to be George Thomas's ship for over two years. During his service with her he applied for a master's certificate at Calcutta, obtaining it on 28 November 1865. Further promotion followed in August 1866, when he became chief officer on the *Golconda*. After less than two years with this vessel, again on the Suez–Calcutta run, he arrived back in England on 12 May 1868

Lodging once more with his sister Elizabeth and her husband at Blackheath, George Thomas used part of his leave to study for the Board of Trade examination as an ordinary master. His master's certificate from Calcutta had probably left him insufficiently qualified for the Board of Trade's purposes. The certificate of competency as master, which he obtained on 28 September 1868, was overwritten, 'Passed in Commercial Code of Signals' – as if that part alone needed to be taken.

From late January to the early April of 1869 he was supplementary first officer of the screw steamship *Poonah* on P & O's Southampton to Alexandria service. But he was back in Calcutta by 24 May, having travelled overland – the journey lasting 37

P & O steamship Poonah.

GRAPHIC MAGAZINE

days. After a short voyage to Galle, Ceylon, in an unknown ship during August, he became the chief officer of *Mongolia*, a screw-driven steamer of just under 3000 tons. She was the largest of the P & O Line vessels with which he would be associated; one which carried 120 passengers in her first-class-only accommodation. The ship's captain was John S. Castle, hero of an epic struggle to extinguish a fire on board an earlier command, *Sarah Sands*, when serving as a troopship during the Indian Mutiny.

With the opening of the Suez Canal in 1869, the journey from Britain to India was made both easier and of shorter duration. A rail journey of 70 hours from London would bring passengers to Brindisi in southern Italy, from where the *Mongolia* began her regular service. She then sailed via the new canal direct to Bombay, usually arriving after a 17-day passage. With most of her passengers travelling on British Empire business, speed was important; and the British Government paid the line £25 for each day cut from the timetabled journey time.

By November 1871, when George Thomas left *Mongolia* for the post of chief officer on *Tanjore*, plying the Southampton–Marseilles–Alexandria route, he had served almost all of his ten years with P & O travelling the Red Sea and Indian Ocean. It would have been debilitating for some constitutions. While accommodation and food aboard ship were excellent, there was no escaping the extremely hot and humid conditions, particularly in the Red Sea, where ships would sometimes put about if the slightest breeze blew from astern, in an attempt to ventilate the below decks. Aware that cabins on the side away from the sun were coolest, passengers often demanded 'port out, starboard home' passages – and were duly recorded by P & O as travelling P.O.S.H.

P & O screw steamship Mongolia, *on which George Thomas served as first officer 1869–71.*
NATIONAL MARITIME MUSEUM, LONDON

During his six years in the rank of chief or first officer he would have been second only to the captain in the ship's hierarchy. In practice he was the captain's deputy; the man who not only passed on his every order, but who also ensured they were carried out to the letter and as quickly as possible. It was the first officer's duty to ensure that the maintenance and day-to-day running of the vessel were correct. As an experienced navigator, he was expected to assist or deputise the captain at noonday checking of the ship's position, either by 'shooting the sun' if it was visible, or from 'dead reckoning' on the chart table if it was not. He had also to measure the speed of

George Thomas, late 1860s, from a photo taken at a photographer's studio at Ryde, Isle of Wight.

ILLUSTRATED LONDON NEWS

the vessel by heaving the log, and, if in coastal waters, take soundings with the lead-line to check the depth of water beneath the keel. Where on some ships the lower ranking officers shared cabins, as first officer he would have enjoyed the privilege of having his own.

Yet despite this success in having attained such high rank from his humble beginnings as a cabin boy, George Thomas's ambition was thwarted. He seems to have become increasingly dissatisfied with his P & O existence. To a friend, he later said that he had found the climate of the east to be undermining his health. Another, possibly greater reason for this discontent, was the feeling that after six years as a chief officer and having held his master's certificate for about the same duration, he was overdue for promotion to the rank of captain. Promotion in P & O was by seniority rather than merit; a matter of waiting until those higher up in the ranks dropped out or died in their posts. George Thomas was not just ambitious, he was also comparatively young: it could have been a long wait to fill some 'dead man's shoes'.

His excellent record had not gone unnoticed. P & O had every confidence in his abilities and were in no doubt that he would one day command one of their vessels. Shipowners in the land of his birth were equally impressed by his reputation, for P & O officers were considered the 'cream' of the merchant marine. When the Eagle Line was inaugurated Thomas was soon offered the command of one of their new steamships. With the prospect of a change of hemispheres and a ship of his own as well, he resigned from P & O on 9 December 1872 and arrived at Southampton on 10 January in the new year.

As the first of the Eagle Line's new ships was not due for completion for several months and the opening of their service to New York later still, George Thomas had time to familiarise himself with the North Atlantic seaways. To do this with the thoroughness that his new responsibilities deserved, he took a passage to New York that April on the Hamburg-Amerika *Holsatia*, sailing under Captain James. He was allocated the engineer's stateroom on board, and he shared it with a New York lawyer named Daniel I. Baker on the return passage.

Soon after leaving New York on this passage, the *Holsatia* was engulfed in a fog which lasted for three days. It became so dense eventually that visibility was down to around six yards. On 24 April, when in 42° N latitude, 61° W longitude – about 600 miles out and south of Newfoundland's notorious Grand Banks – there came looming suddenly upon them through the swirling mists the grey shape of another, large steamship. She passed westbound at a distance so close that passengers on the

Holsatia could see people on its decks quite clearly. With the utmost relief and the most heartfelt thanksgiving at having so narrowly escaped destruction, passengers on both vessels cheered each other wildly. The incident was over in a minute before the other ship, Inman Line's *City of Limerick*, was lost to sight completely in the depths of the fog.

It was an incident which impressed George Thomas considerably. He confessed to Daniel Baker:

> *There was no danger which caused him so great concern, when afloat, as fog, and no occasion on which he felt himself to be more at a loss as to know how to prepare in advance for probable danger.*[2]

It was a feeling which, he told Baker, that all sea-going men with the responsibility of the ship's safety shared, and one which he still had, having passed from the lowest subordinate position aboard a vessel to the highest.

Shortly afterwards, George Thomas was sent to Glasgow to supervise in the construction of the Eagle Line's brand-new iron screw steamship *Schiller* – which was to be his new – and first – command.

On Monday evening, 26 April 1875, Captain Thomas attended a very special occasion at Seignhörtner's Restaurant in Lafayette Place, New York. He joined around 200 of New York's leading German and American figures, diplomats, financiers, businessmen and merchants among them, in welcoming the arrival of the gold-buttoned and braided figure of a venerable-looking sea captain. Their cheers and hurrahs as the elderly captain entered the brilliantly lit dining room were followed by much congratulatory handshaking, as everyone sought the hand that had so many times piloted a huge iron steamship on a 7000-mile voyage. The honoured guest of the evening, Captain H.F. Schwensen, was celebrating his hundredth such voyage, commanding ships of the Hamburg-Amerika Line across the Atlantic Ocean.

It was on his behalf that the restaurant was decked out with flags and flowers. Upon its walls the stars and stripes of the United States alternated with the black cross and eagle of the new German Empire, each one interlaced with ribbon bearing the blue and white colours of the Hanseatic City of Hamburg. In the main dining area, tables laden for the forthcoming banquet were decorated with brightly coloured floral arrangements while above them hung photographs of Captain Schwensen, his officers, and ships of the Hamburg-Amerika Line; each framed with trailing plants and more flowers. Most extravagant of all was the centrepiece that stood on the table in front of the celebrated guest's chair; a large ship modelled in the choicest and most gaily coloured blooms.

With the banqueting completed, Hamburg-Amerika's New York agent rose to congratulate Schwenson, concluding with a toast to the good captain's health. Schwensen briefly acknowledged the compliment from behind the floriferous ship model, and then the toasting began in earnest. 'The German Flag', proposed by the German Ambassador to Washington, was followed with a second draining of glasses honouring 'America,' both of which brought a rousing response from all present.

The remaining hours of the evening were to be in the form of a 'serenade' by a string band, all tuned up in an ante-room and ready to perform. Before they began, Schwensen was the recipient of several awards. First, on behalf of the German Emperor, the Order of the Red Eagle was conferred upon him, then he was presented with a valuable ring by American merchants and insurers. Finally, a representative of the Marine Underwriters of New York arose to congratulate Captain Schwensen on achieving his one-hundredth Atlantic crossing and to present him with an illuminated address. It was, he said:

In appreciation of the faithful fulfilment of his duties during a long career that had been singularly free of disaster.

Seated among the top-table dignitaries in Seignhörtner's that night, the gleaming buttons on his gold-braided uniform embossed with the symbol of an eagle, Captain Thomas must surely have felt ill at ease. The takeover deal between the Eagle and Hamburg-Amerika lines had been finalised on 24 April, just three days before. Beginning the next afternoon, the passage from New York to Hamburg was to be his seventh and last as master of a vessel belonging to the line which had given him his first command. Quite possibly it would be his final journey as master of the *Schiller*; for once it was absorbed into the Hamburg-Amerika fleet – what then? Clearly the new owners had an over-capacity of ships and men to sail them – so what did the future hold for him or the *Schiller*?

The *Schiller* was timetabled to arrive at Plymouth on 7 May. On that day the unification of the Hamburg-Amerika and Eagle Lines was to officially come into force – Eagle Line ships still at sea would be taken over when they reached their home port of Hamburg. Captain Schwensen was also bound for the usual trio of ports, departing on 29 April in the 3382-ton *Pommerania* to complete the final leg of his century of voyages. Yet Captain Schwensen and Captain Thomas were destined never to be colleagues under the blue and white house flag of Hamburg-Amerika. The Eagle Line captain and his command the *Schiller* had another appointment to keep on the 7th of that fateful month.

NOTES

[1] Letter in *Journal*, a New York belle-letters magazine, reprinted in *Hamburgisher Correspondent*, 6 June 1875.

[2] *New York Times*, 9 May 1875.

[3] *New York Times*, 27 April 1875.

Captain Thomas, c.1875.

HARPER'S WEEKLY

CHAPTER 4

◆

Embarkation

The plaintive wail of a steam-train whistle and plumes of black smoke that belched upwards into the deepening blue of the evening sky, indicated the rapid approach of the Chicago, Rock Island & Pacific train from the west. As it loomed closer, knots of kinsfolk and friends at the crowded railroad depot were spurred to exchange hugs, kisses and handshakes with each other. Soon, with the bell that signalled the train's arrival clanging loudly, passengers from the city of Davenport, Iowa, collected up their baggage; and then, to heartfelt wishes for a safe journey and at the guard's 'All aboard', clambered up into the railroad cars.

Boarding the train that evening, Friday 23 April 1875, was the usual cross-section of Davenport society, much of which was of German birth or ancestry. Some of the travellers were aiming for destinations of a relatively local nature, but a sizeable contingent was bound for the Fatherland. Nineteen souls had tickets for a passage from New York to Hamburg on the steamship *Schiller*, purchased from Adolph Langfeldt, the Eagle Line's agent in Davenport.

Youngest of these and American from the very outset of life, were the two infant children of Carl F. Haase and his wife. Carl had been born in Hanover 29 years before, but emigrated with his parents to take up residence in Davenport in 1867, since when he had married and become a successful businessman. The family intended to spend the summer with relatives in Germany before returning that September.

Two more Davenport-born were the 19-year-old twins, William and Charles Frahm. Sturdily built and boisterous, warm-hearted youths, their gingerish-blonde hair and blue eyes evinced German parentage. Their father Matthias was one of the city's most well-known and respected citizens, the owner of a large brewery. He had arranged for the twins to receive some training in the brewery business in Germany. William was to study there for three years, while Charles was to return home next winter.

Most others were German born and intent upon revisiting the Fatherland. They included three of Davenport's most prosperous men; P.C. Roschmann, a retired businessman who had lived in the city for 12 years; P. A. Paulson, a jeweller and city resident for 20 years; and fellow jeweller Otto Kircher. Kircher had emigrated to America only in 1865, aged 23, but whilst working as a travelling salesman for a Chicago jewellers had met and formed a partnership with Fred Goos, with whom he had since taken over an established jewellery firm in Davenport. Now a wealthy family man, he was to spend the summer with his ageing parents and sisters in Karlsruhe, Baden. During his absence, his wife Tillie and their two babies were to stay with her parents at Blue Grass Town. Kircher had booked to share a second-class cabin on the *Schiller* with P.A. Paulson and the Frahm twins, and before leaving home added a $10 000 insurance policy to the life cover of $16 000 which he already held.

Two women had also booked second-cabin passages. One was a farmer's wife from nearby Liberty township, who with her young child was travelling to her old home in Germany for health reasons; the other was an elderly widow aiming to visit her daughter. The rest had booked steerage. These included three single men, one young and two elderly, who were intent on visiting relatives; and also an elderly couple who had no intentions of returning to Davenport. Having, from hard work, strict economy and the sale of their little house, accumulated a small nest-egg, they aimed to live out their remaining years where their childhood was spent.

John and Christine Joens were a younger married couple whose pockets also ran only to the price of steerage tickets. They had already travelled about 80 miles to reach the city and its railroad, for their home was in Benton County, Iowa, at the small town of Luzerne. The Joenses had arrived in America from Hollingstedt, Schleswig, in 1868, first settling in Davenport. Soon afterwards, they moved to Luzerne, a farming community of about 300 people, mostly Germans, comprising 40 buildings, a schoolhouse and a Lutheran church, all of which had evolved around the mid-prairie siting of a railroad depot by the Chicago & Northwestern Railway Company in 1867. Now aiming to see their parents in Schleswig, they had come first to Davenport to purchase tickets for the steamship from the Eagle Line's agency there.

As the train jerked and clanked, then slowly steamed away from the depot, hands waved from car windows briefly. But of all the parting tears shed by the well-wishing kinsfolk and friends left behind, none were so bitter as those of the 20-year-old eldest daughter and housekeeper of widower P.A. Paulson. She had opposed his journey to Germany ever since he had suddenly come up with the notion to take a vacation there and see his old home. Worse still, she had a dreadful premonition that the ship he was to sail on would suffer a disaster. Paulson had insured his life for $5000 before travelling.

If any such thoughts occurred to the travellers themselves, they kept their own counsel. Buoyed up with the anticipated joys rather than perils of sea travel, they were more in expectation of happy reunions in the land of their birth, or of meeting new kinsfolk in the parental homeland. But first there was the rail journey – over 1000 miles and almost two days of it. As the train left Davenport behind and rumbled across the Mississippi bridge towards Rock Island, its passengers settled down for their first night's sleep.

The Chicago, Rock Island & Pacific train, running on the trans-continental Union Pacific route first opened in 1869, steamed eastwards across 150 miles of open prairie to Chicago. There on the following afternoon, the Davenport passengers changed to the Pittsburgh, Fort Wayne and Chicago Railroad for a further 16-hour journey, which included their second night sleeping in railroad cars. After crossing the vast corn-fields of Indiana and Ohio to Pittsburgh, and a futher change to a Pennsylvania Railroad train, they arrived at their final rail destination, the huge depot at Jersey City, on Sunday evening.

There, a magnificent panorama awaited the travel weary, one familiar to those amongst them who had first viewed the scene on arriving from Germany as immigrants. Across the Hudson River, hemmed in with the tall masts, spars and rigging of sailing vessels and steamships lying there, could be seen Manhattan Island and its ever rising skyline, the commercial centre of New York City. To the north and south of the depot itself were the terminals of other railroad lines and miles of docks, each crowded with more shipping. Boats of all descriptions plied the river itself. Ferries criss-crossed between Manhattan, Brooklyn, Staten Island and the New Jersey shore. Huge white 'sidewheeler' river steamers with tall black smokestacks and a small pilot house perched atop their triple-decks, arrived from or set off for Albany and Troy in upstate New York. Black-hulled screw and paddle steamers ploughed out into the Upper Bay, bound for ports American and foreign, while others signalled their arrival from afar with whistles and hoots. Amid them all darted white-sailed schooners and sloops, and a myriad other boats and skiffs cruised up and down the river.

Closest to the Pennsylvania Railroad depot was the pier for Cunard steamers, where one of their latest liners, *Bothnia*, lay berthed beside a pier. *Schiller*, the vessel

Hudson River sidewheelers in New York harbour.

Below: *Eagle Line advert in* New York Times, *19 April 1875.*

for which Davenport passengers had tickets, lay a mile north, having arrived from Hamburg at the Eagle Line's Hoboken pier on 14 April. She was to sail on the afternoon of Tuesday 27 April. Then the 19 Davenport passengers would be joined by hundreds more from cities near and far; New York, Boston, Washington, Chicago, Detroit, Milwaukee, St Louis, Augusta and Philadelphia; as well as innumerable small towns from across the American states. People from all walks of American or German-American life, each with their different hopes and plans for the future, would be arriving by train, ship, the Hudson River steamers or ferry boats, by carriage or on foot; all with one overriding aim, that of sailing on the Eagle Line steamer *Schiller* from Hoboken to Plymouth, Cherbourg or Hamburg.

On the morning of 27 April 1875, the *Schiller,* berthed beside the Eagle Line pier at the foot of 1st Street Hoboken, looked impressive. Her long, black-painted hull, lined with strakes of iron plates and dotted with domed rivet heads, shimmered with the reflections cast up by the waters of the Hudson River. Above it, painted rails and lifeboats gleamed white, while amidships, the black of her dual smokestacks was contrasted half-way up by the white above red bands of the Eagle Line's colours. Towering above it all, the tall, light-brown iron masts reached skywards with white sails tight to the yards in 'harbour furl'.

Her Captain, George Thomas, would have viewed the scene with mixed feelings. He would have seen the *Schiller* from the Hudson River side as he crossed from New York on the ferry that morning. After the previous night's banquet honouring Captain Schwenson at Seignhörtner's Restaurant, Thomas stayed overnight at Daniel Baker's house in the city, for since befriending him on the *Holsatia* voyage he stopped off there whenever he was in New York. Now that this passage from New York was to be his last as master of the *Schiller*, the sight of the Eagle Line flag flapping idly in the breeze at the main-mast head, a black eagle in a white rectangle centred on a background of red, might well have brought a lump to his throat.

By early afternoon, most passengers were safely embarked, many feeling privileged and excited to be on board such a fine vessel with the prospect of a long ocean voyage ahead. One of them was somewhat less impressed, being familiar with the oceans and a captain in his own right. He had come up the gangplank with a cylindrical kitbag, as used widely by sailors, slung over his shoulder. It bore the name 'D.W. Percival, Barnstable' in one-inch high letters. The name Percival and the town of Barnstable had long been associated in the annals of Cape Cod's maritime history. This member of the renowned Percival family was 34-year-old Captain Daniel W., who had already experienced his full share of maritime adventure. Since the late 1860s he had been employed by Boston fruit importers Baker & Morill as captain of their barque *Sicilian*, usually plying the trade route between Boston and Messina, Italy. His last voyage, to Valencia, concluded a few weeks before, had allowed him some shore leave with his wife and child. Much valued by his employers for his strict attention to business, he was now travelling 'saloon' class to Hamburg, for he had been given command of one of the company's finest vessels, the square-rigged ship *Helen Morris*, soon to begin a three-year voyage from the German port.

Two other noticeable arrivals, seen safely aboard the *Schiller* by a crowd of boisterous male well-wishers and some tearful ladies gathered on the pier, were a young couple, looking flushed and self-conscious. They were down on the second-cabin list as 'Mr and Mrs Augustus Munte, New York'; and they were distinctly unfamiliar with any such title. Each sported on one finger a sparkling, brand-new ring engraved with their initials and date, 'A.W. A.M. April 27 1875'. Inside 23-year-old Augustus's pocket book was an equally pristine marriage certificate bearing the same date, while around his neck he wore a locket containing a picture of his young bride. They had been married only that morning.

Among the last to board was Frederick Wilhelm Zach, Consul of the German Empire at Havana, Cuba. Accompanied by his wife Johanna and their ten-year-old daughter Margarethe, they and the porters carrying their luggage pushed their way through the bustling crowds of the Eagle Line shed and pier, mounted the gangplank and sought out their stateroom. Zach had booked first cabin, or 'saloon', for his family's passage to Germany, the three being among the 59 persons whose pockets ran to the most luxurious and best appointed staterooms that the vessel had to offer. For this privilege he had paid a ticket price of '100 dollars gold' each at the offices of Nauth, Nachod & Kuhne, the Eagle Line's New York agents at 112 Broadway.

Providing a send-off for the family was the German Consul-General, H.A. Schumaker. During the previous evening he had been among the diplomats attending the celebrations at Seignhörtner's Restaurant, when Captain Schwensen of the Hamburg-Amerika Line was honoured for his 100 voyages. This was yet another official duty, but he also held Zach in high regard, not only as one of the most able of German diplomats but also as a personal friend. In spite of Zach's learned and somewhat prepossessing appearance, he had an amiable manner and was popular with people of all classes. Schumaker was happy to accompany the family to their stateroom and wish them 'God-speed'.

The Zachs were to journey first to Berlin on diplomatic business. Afterwards they aimed at enjoying a four-month holiday elsewhere in Europe. Zach had earned a holiday. At 50 years of age he had served his country with distinction for many years before attaining his position of Consul at Havana. First being posted overseas as an attaché at the Prussian Legation in Washington in 1865, he had then been transferred to the Consul-General's office New York, initially as Secretary, then as Vice-Consul to the North German Federation. From December 1871 Zach had served as Consul of the Imperial German Empire in New York until his posting to Havana in October 1873.

After wishing the Zachs 'God speed', Consul-General Schumaker returned to the bustling pier-side. There, he remarked to an associate that an unusually large amount of women were aboard the ship, both in the cabin classes and the crowd of steerage passengers who hung over the rails. His observation was well-founded. Of the 264* passengers, over 100 were females. About 60 of them were to be found in the first and

* Note: figures given vary about numbers of passengers – see Appendix B.

second cabins, where the accommodation was nearly full, it being the beginning of the new 'season' for travelling to Europe. In steerage, women accounted for almost a quarter of the 123 or more in total. There were also about 50 children on board ranging from six weeks to 15 years old; 11 in saloon, 14 in second cabin and around 25 in steerage.

Along with the passengers and their luggage, the previously loaded cargo made the *Schiller* quite full. Freight of all descriptions [see appendix C] was being forwarded from a variety of companies in the U.S. to Europe through the agency of Funch, Edye & Co. of New York. This general cargo weighed over 2000 tons. It included machinery of all sorts, the greatest proportion and the largest items being for agricultural purposes – 158 reapers, 68 mowers and 10 harvesters. Some of these were bound for places as far off as St Petersburg in Russia, and all of them were packaged in component parts. There were also clocks, knitting machines, sewing machines and cabinet organs in boxes; 900 bales of cotton for Amsterdam; 293 barrels of honey for London; and many barrels and boxes of other perishable goods such as wheat, beef, flour, starch, resin, bark extract, and cigars. Addressed to 'E.S. Ballin & Co., Paris' were six kegs, the contents of which were twenty-dollar pieces amounting to $300 000 worth of gold. The entire cargo, gold excepted, was valued at over $107 000. There were the mails too. Most of this was the Australian and New Zealand transcontinental mail, contained in 162 full bags and very much overdue through a series of mishaps and detentions. The remainder was made up of 91 bags of U.S. mails for Britain, Ireland, France and Germany – containing altogether around 36 000 letters.

The New York Postmaster, Mr James, knew Captain Thomas well from his duties with the transatlantic mails: he was also a friend of the Deputy Surveyor at the Port of New York's Custom House, George Klink. Klink's younger brother Dwight, still a youth, had travelled from Fruitport, Michigan, and was to join the *Schiller* for a passage to Europe. Through James's commendation, young Dwight, travelling saloon class, was taken into the care of the Captain for the journey.

Last of all the 264 passengers to arrive at the Eagle Line dock and board the *Schiller* was Marcus Powitzer, a young man aiming to return to his home town of Gniessen, near Posen, Germany. He had no ticket, such was the suddenness of his decision to go, but purchased a $24 steerage passage from the ship's purser and joined his fellow travellers for the ocean journey. Numbers of people missed the boat altogether through a variety of reasons. Most notable among these was New York's most

Schiller *at the Eagle Line pier, Hoboken, New Jersey.*

COURTESY PEABODY-ESSEX MUSEUM

successful German immigrant, ex-senator and Secretary of the Interior, Editor of *Harper's Weekly* and the *New York Post*, Carl Schurz. He was all set to travel on the *Schiller* with his family when he learned that a farewell banquet and serenade had been planned for him by the German residents of New York at Delmonico's Restaurant on 28 April. Cancelling their tickets, the family sailed two days later on the Hamburg-Amerika *Pommerania* – Captain Schwensen's vessel. Others who also cancelled and sailed later on the *Pommerania* included some people from Newark, New Jersey who found they could not make the *Schiller*'s sailing date. One of

Schiller's crew likewise missed the boat, but this was at the behest of the Recorder at Hoboken Police Court. The man had been arrested for drunkenness and jailed for five days. He was released on 28 April – by which time his ship was at sea.

One woman who later sailed on the *Pommerania*, actually arrived in good time and boarded *Schiller,* only to find her previously booked stateroom already occupied by a lady who 'stoutly refused to quit'. This staunch occupant was probably a hard-to-please saloon passenger from Staten Island, Mrs Clara Gregory, who though travelling to Europe to benefit her health, was nonetheless in a robust frame of mind. Having seen the first cabin stateroom assigned to her and her seven-year-old son Frank, she had voiced her dissatisfaction in no uncertain manner and threatened to leave the ship at once. An alternative stateroom was found which suited her, but was probably the one booked to this other woman. She, in the face of Mrs Gregory's obstinacy, abandoned her prior claim and left the ship to sail on the *Pommerania* on the 29th.

Just before three in the afternoon of 27 April, the *Schiller* and her complement were complete. With the Blue Peter flag signifying her readiness flapping at the foremast and the New York Bay pilot on the bridge with Captain Thomas, all was set to proceed out across the Atlantic. Passengers familiarised themselves with their staterooms and cabins, reviewed the arrangements and layout of the vessel, or awaited the ship's departure excitedly on deck. Her steam-whistle sounded shrilly across the Hudson, announcing her imminent sailing to the residents of New York.

CHAPTER 5

•◆•

Mrs Caverly's Premonition

At 3pm, the scheduled hour, dockers ashore withdrew the gangplank then cast off hawsers and mooring ropes tethering *Schiller* to the Eagle Line pier, while bronze-faced sailors drew them inboard. Captain Thomas and his officers, immaculate in their uniforms, stood imperiously on the ship's bridge and gave orders, engine room telegraph bells rang in the bowels of the vessel and the ship backed slowly out into the Hudson River. On the pier, an immense, animated crowd shouted and waved goodbyes with mirth and sorrow mixed, bidding 'God-speed' to departing friends and relatives. Above them, where the ship's black hull slid slowly by, passengers lining white-painted rails several deep called back and waved hands, handkerchiefs and hats in fervent reply. Gaudy flags and bunting fluttered gaily from her rigging as the huge vessel slowly slipped away; the drama and excitement of the occasion tempered only with the emotions of parting.

The ship backed further and further out until, beneath the counter of her rococo decorated stern, water suddenly churned white as the propeller changed rotation from astern to ahead. With her rudder hard over she slowly slewed around, leaving a widening arc of creamy froth on the dark waters of the Hudson. Mournful, ear-splitting blasts from *Schiller*'s steam-whistle signalled her departure as she headed out to midstream, trailing a long wraith of smoke behind. Outstretched hands and fluttering handkerchiefs, waving across the rapidly growing divide between a knot of people hanging over her sternrails and the pier end, retained communication for a while longer – until the ship was well downriver.

The jutting piers of Hoboken and steamships docked there were soon slipping astern. Then Jersey City was off the starboard rails with its railroad depots, stock yard and coal docks. At the wharf just beyond the Pennsylvania Railroad Depot, Cunard's

Map of New York harbour, 1875.

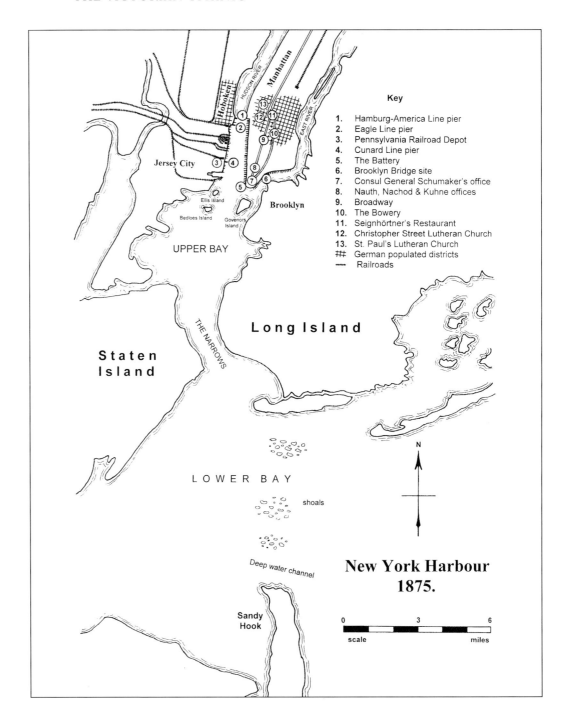

Key

1. Hamburg-America Line pier
2. Eagle Line pier
3. Pennsylvania Railroad Depot
4. Cunard Line pier
5. The Battery
6. Brooklyn Bridge site
7. Consul General Schumaker's office
8. Nauth, Nachod & Kuhne offices
9. Broadway
10. The Bowery
11. Seignhörtner's Restaurant
12. Christopher Street Lutheran Church
13. St. Paul's Lutheran Church
German populated districts
~~ Railroads

New York Harbour
1875.

latest liner, *Bothnia,* due to sail next day, lay in full view. Below Jersey City, off to port at the southernmost tip of Manhattan Island, was Castle Garden, with its immigration shed a reminder for many aboard of their first, bewildering hours in the New World. Rounding The Battery and its tree-lined gardens next brought the water-damming caissons and tremendously tall, Gothic-arched towers of the new bridge into view. When finished it was to connect Manhattan with Brooklyn, south of the East River, and be the longest suspension bridge in the world. Teams of men had toiled there for five years already, but it was a long way from completion.

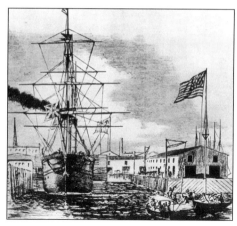

Cunard Line pier at New Jersey, c.1860s.

Past the ramparts of Fort Gibson on Ellis Island and the tiny Bedloes Island, both off to starboard, and then the larger Governors Island to port, the ship slowly made her way with sails furled and under steam power only, leaving her widening wake to lap at the island shores long after she had passed. The broad reaches of New York's Upper Bay followed, from where the city was subject to final, lingering looks by many passengers, appearing, as described in prose by a contemporary poet:

> *...rising out of the midst, tall topt, ship hemm'd, modern, American, yet strangely oriental, V-shaped Manhattan, with its compact mass, its spires, its cloud touching edifices group'd at the centre – the green of the trees, and all the white, brown and gray of the architecture, well blended...*[1]

Out in the bay, a few small craft that had accompanied *Schiller* from Hoboken with friends determined to cling to the very last, took their leave and turned back. Kisses were blown, hands waved and goodbyes called sadly across the dividing water, then the steam-whistle sounded a couple of blasts and the steamer was on her own.

The banks of Upper Bay were soon tapering to The Narrows, the mile-wide strait between Staten Island and Long Island. With this negotiated, the open waters of Lower New York Bay lay ahead. There, where hills receded in ever paler, more distant blue tones off the starboard bow, the horizon-to-horizon grey-green vastness of the Atlantic Ocean itself lay to port. For first the ship was steered southwards, directed by the pilot towards the long finger promontory of Sandy Hook, which beckoned the steamer towards the deep water channel that lay off its tip.

By then the harbour pilot was having misgivings. The *Schiller* was heavily laden with its cargo of over 2000 tons, the mails, and her complement of 384 passengers and crew. She was drawing 23ft of water and they had missed high tide by hours. There was a risk that the vessel would ground if she tried to pass over the bar at Sandy

Hook. After some discussion with Captain Thomas on the 'commander's bridge', the pilot refused to take the vessel further. Reluctantly, the Captain had her turned to port and at 6pm anchored off Long Island. There she would remain until the next day's tide.

Spending what should have been their first night on the ocean a mere stone's throw from Long Island shore was frustrating for passengers. But supper that evening was comfortable without the pitch and sway of the ship in full, deep-sea motion. The long racks laden with glasses and cruets suspended over the first-cabin dining tables hung still, not mirroring her mid-ocean roll to make the queasy feel worse still. Over this, their first meal aboard and an opportunity to get to know their travelling companions, people could concentrate on table manners and polite conversation without fear of a sudden lurch beneath them causing embarrassment.

The 59 first-cabin passengers who sat down to dine in the plush surroundings of the first-cabin saloon that evening were broadly representative of America's elite, with old-established wealth democratically rubbing shoulders with the newly arrived. 'High society' was mostly the province of a number of ladies who aimed to spend 'the season' in Europe for cultural reasons; languishing at fashionable spas and resorts, taking in the sights of Continental cities, or immersing themselves in art and antiquities to 'improve' their minds. Most men were highly successful businessmen, many having made their fortunes in just a few years since emigrating to America.

Probably the most well-connected among the former group was Miss Caroline M. Crane of Washington, a niece of Senator Edmonds of Vermont, at whose home she had just spent the winter months. A highly accomplished young lady of 20, she aimed to spend two years in Italy studying art. She was accompanied by two intimate friends, Bessie Greene and Susan Dimock, both from Boston. Miss Greene was 28 years old, cultured, familiar with foreign travel and a very popular figure in Boston society, where her homely, unpretentious nature and charity work had also earned her much admiration from the local poor. It was at the home of her uncle, the American Minister to Italy, that she and Miss Crane intended to stay while there. The third in this trio of friends, Susan Dimock MD, was a physician who practised at the New England Hospital for Women and Children and was closely involved in Mrs Elizabeth Garrett Anderson's College, where young ladies were educated in the medical profession. Aged 25 and considered 'an extremely pretty woman', she pursued her vocation single-mindedly, for unlike her two Italy-bound friends, Miss Dimock was to disembark at England, where she aimed at furthering her studies. Senator Edmunds had booked these three young ladies their passages on the *Schiller*.

Mrs Caverly, who occupied a saloon stateroom along with her 16-year-old daughter Amy, was a more mature lady with society connections. Recently widowed, her husband had been secretary to the U.S. legation in Peru. While he lived she had been a well-known figure in the genteel drawing rooms of both Washington and New York society, but since her bereavement had lived with her father, Judge Nathan Crosby of Lowell, Massachusetts. The Caverlys were travelling to Europe, mainly for daughter Amy's health, but also to accompany a close relative, Mrs Ridgeway. Before joining the ship, Mrs Caverly and Amy had stayed at Mrs Ridgeway's home at East 43rd street, in the exclusive Murray Hill district of New York.

Mrs Ridgeway had spent some years in St Louis, where among a large circle of socialites her reputation was that of 'a lady of wealth, culture and fine abilities'. But she had first been widowed and then her two daughters, each said to be very beautiful and accomplished, but of a delicate constitution, had died in Europe, one at Cannes and the other at Lugano. Mrs Ridgeway was now on a pilgrimage to those places where she and her daughters had spent their last days together. Tending her needs on the journey was her black maid, who, having once been her slave, remained faithful to her mistress long after emancipation. She was also accompanied by the widower and children of one of her deceased daughters. He was Charles Walter, a wealthy partner in the firm of Nichols, Walter & Nichols of Moore Street, Lower Manhattan, and owner of a manufacturing chemists at Greenpoint. The children, two little girls aged six and eight, were to attend a school in Germany while Walter accompanied his mother-in-law to the gravesides of his deceased wife and her sister.

Many male saloon passengers were travelling on business, several being regular commuters across the Atlantic. John Jacob Brunner, a wealthy partner in one of the oldest established commercial houses in New York, was one. He crossed the ocean frequently on behalf of his firm, Henry and J.J. Brunner, importers of dry goods, and on this occasion was bound for London, where he intended to make purchases for the firm. Carl Schmidt, a jeweller from Lower Manhattan's Maiden Lane, was also on what was essentially a business trip to Hamburg, but was taking his wife Catherine along with him. Such was the pressing nature of this business that he had disappointed his relatives by refusing to forego the Tuesday sailing of the *Schiller* to attend the wedding of his niece on the following day. Other businessmen travelled with friends. Marcus M. Stein, part-owner of a wholesale hat, cap and fur store in

Broadway, Milwaukee, was on a seasonal business trip to Europe instigated by his friend Jacob Lamfron, a merchant from Oconomowoc. Stein was more reluctant than usual to go, but having changed the arrangements several times they at last settled on a saloon-class stateroom in the *Schiller*.

Some businessmen had brought their families along with them. The largest family group in saloon was that of Michael Kornblum, a wealthy wholesale dealer in waste paper and rags with business premises in Howard Street, Manhattan. Kornblum, aged 26, was originally from Cracow in the Austro-Hungarian empire, but had been a popular resident in the Jewish quarter of Brooklyn for the past 13 years. Leaving his brother-in-law to tend his New York interests, he was journeying first to London, where he intended setting up another branch of the business. Afterwards, he was to take his wife, her maid and their three young children, Mollie, Isay and Louis, aged between five and two, on an extended tour of Europe. They planned to return in the fall, after which Kornblum was to spend two years managing his new branch in Britain. In Kornblum's luggage were 85 gold watches, £500 in coin and a considerable quantity of diamond jewellery.

Holidaying in Europe or visiting relatives were popular aims of families. The Stoeltings, Herman aged 38, his wife Ida and their 12-year-old son George, were one such family. They hailed from the silver-producing town of Georgetown, Colorado, where Herman took office as Territorial Assayer for the state in March 1874. Another, one of Milwaukee's best-known German families, popular in local musical and literary circles, was the Zinkeisens, Hermann, Celine and their charming 19-year-old daughter Annie. They were intent upon a holiday in 'the old country,' particularly at Hamburg where 53-year-old Hermann had relatives he had not seen in 20 years. His firm, Zinkeisen, Bartlett & Co., commission agents in grain, was left in the hands of his partners, while four young sons were being looked after by his wife's brother until they returned in the fall.

Also from Milwaukee and looking forward to holidays were two of the city's most prominent employers. Henry Friend was taking his wife Frances, mother to his 11 children, abroad for a silver wedding anniversary holiday. He was the principal partner of the merchant tailoring concern H. Friend & Brothers in Milwaukee's Broadway, which from its humble store beginnings in 1846, was now worth more than half a million dollars and employed 500 people. Probably the most wealthy man of commerce aboard was Joseph Schlitz, the Milwaukee brewer, banker and insurance mogul. He planned to visit his brothers in the town of Mayence (now Mainz) on the

Saloon-class passenger Henry Friend of Milwaukee.

Rhine, having left there at the age of 19 in 1850, equipped with the entrepreneurial skills of his wine-speculator father and a thorough training in book-keeping. Now, through good fortune and astute dealings, he owned a huge new brewery built on the corners of Third and Walnut Streets, whose product, Schlitz beer, was known across the states as 'The Beer that made Milwaukee Famous'. With the thoroughness and forethought with which he had pursued his multi-faceted business career, Schlitz had made a will before leaving Milwaukee, ensuring that The Schlitz Brewery Co. would continue under his name should he not return.

Saloon-class passenger Joseph Schlitz, a wealthy brewer from Milwaukee.
COURTESY STROH BREWERY CO.

Left: *The Schlitz Brewery, Milwaukee.*
COURTESY STROH BREWERY CO.

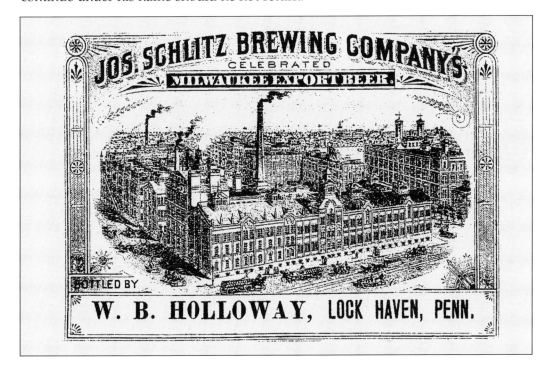

Several travelled in the hope that their health would improve on the journey or in Europe. Clara Just, the wife of Edward Just, a wealthy shirt manufacturer of Job, Just & Brothers in Broadway, New York, was a cheerful and attractive 29-year-old who hoped the long voyage to Hamburg would restore her spirits from a listlessness she had felt for some time. A 22-year-old nursemaid was assisting with her children, five-year-old Else and Edward, aged two. Infirmity had also struck Herman Bachmann, a man who had made his fortune from fur trading with Indians out west, now travelling east as an invalid. He had retired from business at the age of 35, ten years before,

The Schlitz Palm Garden, Milwaukee, c.1890.
COURTESY STROH BREWERY CO.

having amassed enough money to have lived comfortably since at his East 40th Street, New York, home. However, as he was incapacitated by severe sunstroke, his physician had advised him to take the sea voyage to Germany and return in the fall. His 'nurse' for the voyage was Mr M. Wasserman, a retired dry goods merchant from Maine who wintered each year in New York with Bachmann, his amiable friend.

Retirement in the Fatherland was the travelling aim of a few saloon passengers. The Weste family, Leo, Hermine and their daughter, from Philadelphia, had been residents of a high social standing in the city, where at Hudson's Alley, Leo Weste had long been proprietor of a popular restaurant. This he had recently sold, intending to retire to his native land where his father was once a noted military man, General Von Weste, of the Hanoverian army. Also planning to spend their declining years in Germany were Mr and Mrs N. Becker, aged 60 and 50 respectively. They had once owned a wholesale liquor dealership in Philadelphia, but more recently resided at West 56th Street, in a select area just off Fifth Avenue, New York. Having crossed the Atlantic together on eight previous occasions, this time was intended to be their last. Accompanying them was their servant for the last twelve years, Catherine Bonath. While the Beckers were in a saloon-class stateroom, she was in second cabin.

Most passengers soon found new friends to share time with during the voyage. First-cabin passengers Mrs Caverly and her daughter Amy made the acquaintance of

Henry Gellen, the master painter of the Eagle Line, who was supervising the work of two marine artists travelling aboard the *Schiller*. Their conversation during that first evening aboard ship probably turned to the Hudson River and its scenic beauty, particularly the steep gorge known as the Hudson Highlands. Theirs was to be a short-lived friendship though, for unlike other employees of the company on board, Gellen was due to leave next day with the pilot and return to Hoboken.

Afterwards, during the night, Mrs Caverly experienced some kind of nightmare premonition that had her and her daughter packing their trunks ready for carrying up to the deck first thing next morning. They were insistent upon leaving the *Schiller*, joining Gellen in the pilot boat, and making their return to New York. Gellen and Charles Walter, the widowed son-in-law of Mrs Ridgeway, who was accompanying the Caverlys, eventually dissuaded them from this notion. By late morning, when the *Schiller* weighed anchor and steamed towards Sandy Hook, mother and daughter were calmed enough to write letters to friends in New York for forwarding with the Eagle Line's master painter. Yet when the ship was finally clear of the bar at Sandy Hook and the pilot schooner came alongside for the pilot and Gellen to climb into, the two Caverlys, still in anguish, called down to him,

'We will never see the Highlands again.'

Their nervousness was infectious. During succeeding days Charles Walter grew increasingly certain that he would never reach England. Time and again he would ask the fourth mate if the ship was safe.

NOTES

[1] Walt Whitman: *Specimen Days in America*, Walter Scott, London, 1887.

CHAPTER 6

❖

Under Way

With the pilot's departure, the vessel was at last under Captain Thomas's full command. Setting an easterly course, with sails unfurled and set to take advantage of a light, but favourable wind, *Schiller* began to make real headway on the 3577 miles of Atlantic that lay between New York and Hamburg. But then, another delay occurred. A fishing net became entangled in the ship's propeller. Captain Thomas ordered the engine stopped and the vessel hove-to in order to clear

Schiller *at sea.*

it. This was done quickly but by the time they got under way once more the ship was almost a day behind her schedule.

The new Cunarder, *Bothnia*, had by then overtaken them, having left the Cunard wharf at the foot of Grand Street, Jersey City, at ten that morning. As *Schiller* got into her stride once more, with billowing sails and engine at full revolutions, she easily maintained the speed set by the other, much larger vessel. Passengers promenading on *Schiller*'s decks were to have ample opportunity to admire the lines of this most modern Cunarder, in service for just eight months. The sight, an orange-red, black-topped funnel over a long black hull, with the contrasting white of canvas billowing from her three masts, was to provide a focal point in the vastness of the ocean for the next five days.

Bothnia was not just new, she set new standards for Cunard, whose reputation had for many years been in decline. The company's innate conservatism had served them well in the past: they could boast of having never lost a passenger, nor a single letter, in more than 30 years. But by the early 1870s customers wanted luxury rather than the parsimonious, basic comforts offered on Cunard liners – candle lighting, no bathrooms and wooden bench seating in dining rooms being commonplace. Cunard's complacency was shaken in 1870 when White Star entered the transatlantic trade. Their *Oceanic*'s staterooms were double the Cunard size, with fan ventilation, steam heating, adjustable oil lamps and electric bells for summoning stewards. Her full-width saloon, situated amidships far from the vibration of the propeller, accommodated all first-class passengers at one mealtime sitting, with separate armchairs instead of benches.

Cunard had shrugged off a similar challenge from the short-lived American owned Collins Line in the 1850s, but responded to White Star with new, up-rated vessels. *Bothnia* offered her first-class passengers a full-width, amidships saloon, with all the most up-to-date luxuries. However, while over 1000 tons larger than *Oceanic,* her top speed was one knot slower. As White Star held the Blue Riband in both directions on the Atlantic there was little inducement for passengers seduced by the speed of the new line to make their return to Cunard.

With *Bothnia* an everpresent feature between them and the horizon, *Schiller*'s passengers adjusted to the routines of ship-board life. First-cabin, or 'saloon', passengers on board benefited from accommodation which was comparable to the best which the Cunard liner offered and far better than the Eagle Line's German competitors provided. It occupied almost the whole of an area 158ft long between the after funnel

Cunard Line's Bothnia.

and stern on the first deck. Wood-panelled staterooms there were equipped with the finest and most expensive fittings, furniture and fabrics. Closeted in well-upholstered luxury, those wealthy occupants, the Caverlys, the Kornblums, the Zinkeisens, the Zachs and others, could summon a steward at the press of a button, for each state-

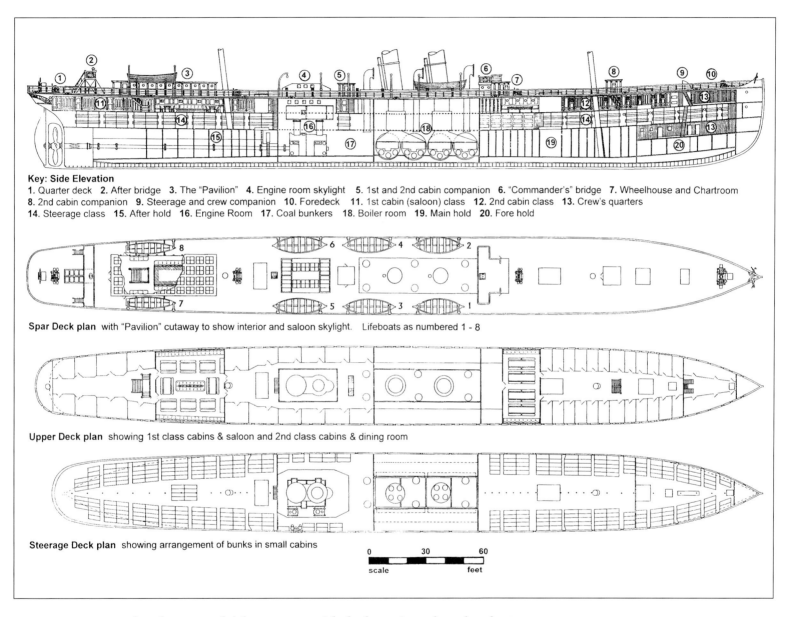

Key: Side Elevation
1. Quarter deck 2. After bridge 3. The "Pavilion" 4. Engine room skylight 5. 1st and 2nd cabin companion 6. "Commander's" bridge 7. Wheelhouse and Chartroom
8. 2nd cabin companion 9. Steerage and crew companion 10. Foredeck 11. 1st cabin (saloon) class 12. 2nd cabin class 13. Crew's quarters
14. Steerage class 15. After hold 16. Engine Room 17. Coal bunkers 18. Boiler room 19. Main hold 20. Fore hold

Spar Deck plan with "Pavilion" cutaway to show interior and saloon skylight.   Lifeboats as numbered 1 - 8

Upper Deck plan showing 1st class cabins & saloon and 2nd class cabins & dining room

Steerage Deck plan showing arrangement of bunks in small cabins

0   30   60
scale   feet

room was connected to the stewards' department with the latest in on-board gadgetry – an electric bell – just as in White Star liners.

Situated midway between first-cabin staterooms was the saloon. At 40ft square, it extended the full width of the ship. Along each side, beneath the rows of brass-

Schiller's starboard elevation and deck plans.

rimmed ports, were well-stuffed, button-studded, upholstered benches, while down the centre area was a long, back-to-back island of similarly opulent seating. Above this, a centre section of the ceiling formed a raised skylight, 14ft in height, which extended into a glass-roofed deckhouse above. Incoming daylight gave a bright and cheerful appearance to the saloon's rich decor of varied shades in warm coloured wood panelling and plush furnishing fabrics. It was large enough to seat all saloon passengers at one sitting during mealtimes, when the eight large dining tables there were each set with eight places – room enough for passengers and the ship's principal officers to dine together. From long sideboards at the fore end of the saloon, nearest the galley, the very best of German cuisine and a wide variety of beers and wines to suit the most cultured tastes were served four times a day by an army of stewards under the watchful eye of the chief steward of first cabin.

Typical Scenes in the first-class saloon of a transatlantic steamship during the mid-1870s.

Above: *Food.*

Right: *Dinner time.*

On the 'tween deck below them and extending the ship's entire length, *Schiller*'s steerage passengers lived out the journey in far more spartan surroundings. Here, there was no wood panelling, just painted iron bulkheads. Even so, they probably fared better than their contemporaries on Cunarders. As with most German lines, the immigrant trade was the mainstay of the Eagle Line's business, while Cunard had

Sunday service.

only deigned to transport this class of person after 1862 and then often on inferior 'B type' steamers. New as she was, *Bothnia*'s steerage accommodation still comprised the traditional long dormitories with tiers of narrow bunks ranged on either side of a central walkway, men on one side, women on the other and separate staterooms for families only. By comparison, *Schiller*'s steerage quarters seem 'superior,' as the Eagle Line claimed, for it was divided into small staterooms fitted with bunks for between six to 20 persons. There were also large dining rooms with tables; though as steerage space was always tight the tables may have been collapsible and 'triced' up to the ceiling when not in use, as was the arrangement on some vessels. Yet with the quarters well-lit by side windows, good ventilation throughout the ship and room for almost 800 passengers on their deck, this journey was not to be compared to those of sailing packet days.

Food for steerage passengers had also come a long way since then, when they were responsible for provisioning the whole of their voyage themselves. By the 1870s three meals a day were provided: coffee with bread or biscuit and butter, or with porridge and molasses for breakfast; soup followed by beef or pork and potatoes for dinner;

and at supper time, tea, bread and butter with an occasional treat of marmalade. Friday's dinner would be fish rather than meat and on Sundays there would be 'plum pudding' to follow. The shipping line would provide each steerage passenger with a large enamelled mug, a deep plate and a knife, fork and spoon: but while stewards would wait on tables for them, the washing up was always the passengers' responsibility; long queues for this duty after meals being a feature of steerage life.

Quite a few steerage passengers were intent upon visiting relatives and friends in Europe. Among them were several unaccompanied mothers and their children, where mostly because of cost, husbands had remained at home. One was Anna Meisner from Essex Street, Jersey City, a mother to seven children aged from six to 18. The five eldest had been left at home with her nightwatchman husband while she travelled with the two youngest, Sophie, aged ten, and Charles, aged six, to see her ageing parents at Himmelfurth, Hanover. Another, whose Garden Street, Hoboken, home stood only a few blocks from the Eagle Line dock, was Elise Neo. She was a teacher of music in a nearby private school, while her husband worked in New York as an advertising agent. Sharing her steerage cabin on the *Schiller* were their two boys, Henry, aged ten, and Walter, aged eight, and they were to visit her parents in Lubeck. There was also the young wife of a cutler from the New York State city of Troy, Sophie Holzhauer, who was accompanied by her two-year-old boy. She intended to see her parents in Glessen and hoped that the voyage would restore her health.

Two unaccompanied young mothers and their children were among 26 passengers intent upon disembarking from the *Schiller* at Plymouth. As close friends and also neighbours in the same Bleecker Street, New York, apartment block, they also planned to visit relatives. Frances Evans, aged 28, and known as 'Fanny' to her husband John, was originally from Leeds but anticipated showing off her four-year-old son John to his paternal grandparents in Bristol. Her friend Susan Duckfield was of the same age but had four children to parade in front of her husband George's parents in Bristol: Elizabeth Ann, Mary Matilda, Georgina and Edward France, aged between eight and two years old. The two women had lived in New York for several years, where their Bristol-born husbands both worked as shoemakers.

The majority of steerage passengers, individuals or families, were heading for Germany though. Oscar Cramer, a photographer with a studio in East 18th Street, New York, was taking his wife on a holiday there. Carl Jahns, a fringe and tassel maker, was returning to see his folks at Chemnitz, Saxony, leaving his wife and two children at home in New York's Leonard Street. Knowing Captain Thomas, Jahns would not travel in any other vessel than the *Schiller*. Philadelphia shoe dealer, Edward Mannhiemer, had also left two children behind at his South Second Street home, but was accompanied by his wife and older children, a boy of 15 and a girl of ten. Intending to see his parents near Hamburg, Mannheimer was yet another who hoped to cure his ill-health on the long voyage. Two families, the Katzenburgers of Troy, with three children, and the Burghards of Chicago with two, were returning to Germany for good. So too was one rather lonely steerage traveller, Louise Wercher from Baltimore, who had been widowed only two months before. With no income of her own she was returning home to her parents.

In more fortunate circumstances and superior accomodation were the second-cabin passengers, who on the *Schiller* were in cabins stated proudly to be:

> *…located on the same deck with the first-class passengers and the apartments are fitted with every attention to comfort and convenience.*[1]

They stretched from forward of the twin smokestacks to the forecastle, about 100ft in length. Although similarly arranged on either side of a large dining room, the surroundings would seem luxurious by steerage standards, but noticeably less plush than those in saloon class. On many ships, second cabin was largely distinguishable from steerage by virtue of cabin accommodation rather than dormitories and through occupying a more advantageous position within the ship. Other advantages over steerage conditions would be the provision of crockery rather than enamel plates at mealtimes; reserved places at table; pudding twice a week instead of once; the washing up done for them; and the use of the terms 'ladies and gentlemen' instead of 'men and women' when referred to by stewards.

The dining room for *Schiller*'s second-cabin passengers was only half the length of the saloon but likewise covered the ship's full width. With similarly upholstered bench seating down either side and wood panelling, it would have been comfortable enough, even luxurious. Space at mealtimes, with 75 people seated at the four large, 14ft-long refectory tables there, may have been rather lacking in elbow room but was conducive to a less formal and more friendly atmosphere than in the first cabin saloon.

The passengers who congregated there to dine had largely similar aims to other passengers aboard, with often the family visit being uppermost in their minds. But a rather poignant story lay behind the long journey of a young mother from Milwaukee. Originally from Austria, Marie Miltner was a daughter of the Austrian nobility. But when she fell in love with an army officer, Colonel Carl Miltner, and then married him against her parents' wishes, they had summarily cast out and disinherited their lovelorn daughter. Carl then resigned his commission and the couple emigrated to America, where he managed to obtain work as a clerk in the Milwaukee offices of the Mutual Hail Insurance Company. The young couple were poor and Marie and her baby would not have been travelling back to Austria at all but for an elderly aunt, a countess, who had written begging her favourite niece to come and see her, as she was infirm and might not live much longer. She had enclosed $500 for Marie's fare.

Among several mother-and-child couples were Maria Schuhr and Bertha, the wife and little daughter of a barber from East 23rd Street, New York, and Ernestine Furst, the attractive 33-year-old wife of a dealer in hats and caps of South 5th Avenue. She was journeying with her three-year-old daughter to see her mother in Berlin and intended to remain there until the fall.

Louise Holzmaister was all alone but was a recent bride, having been wed on the previous 3 December last at St Paul's Lutheran Church, on the corner of 6th Avenue and 15th Street, New York. Her Austrian-born husband, Lewis, had lived next door to Louise's parents' home in East 4th Street before their marriage. Now he was an importer of kid gloves, with rising prospects and business premises in Broadway, while the couple's new home was at East 14th Street, where Louise was earning a reputation for the warmth of her hospitality. Having sadly left home and husband for a while to visit some German relatives, Louise could at least look forward to celebrating her 24th birthday shortly after arrival.

Homesickness motivated Lina Kirchmayer of Baltimore. She had long yearned to return to Germany and see her parents once more in her beautiful native town of Boppard on the Rhine. Charles, her husband, a jeweller of South Republican Street, advised his 28-year-old wife to travel by a North German Lloyd steamer from Baltimore to Bremen. But as Lina, or 'Minna' as he called her, wanted to pay a visit to friends in New York along the way, she booked a second-cabin passage on the Eagle Line ship instead.

Second cabin also had its share of those with ailments. Louis and Elise Selig, having recently sold out their dry goods store in Hoboken – where Louis had been 'unfortunate' in his business dealings – were bound for Hamburg, from where they

Marriage certificate of Louise Holzmaister.
NEW YORK CITY ARCHIVES

hoped to return when Louis's health had improved. Infirmity was partly the travel aim of one of the wealthier couples on board, Herman and Augusta Deckritz of Court Street, Brooklyn, both in their mid-sixties. Herman was a prominent architect with Mundell & Deckritz at the corner of Myrtle Ave. and Fulton Street – the partners who had built Brooklyn's Courthouse. In his 20 years in America he had amassed a fortune of over $100 000. As he was suffering badly from rheumatism, the couple decided to visit relatives in Dresden and hoped that the long sea voyage would aid his recovery. They took with them U.S. bonds to the value of $10 000, but in spite of their riches, they travelled second-cabin class.

As in saloon, business was the main aim of many male passengers. George G. Leonhardt, a 34-year-old employee of a jewellery firm at Augusta, Georgia, was taking a large amount of valuables abroad. But his 30-year-old wife Mary and eight-year-old daughter Jennie accompanied him, as he intended to mix business with family pleasures and visit Mary's father in Stuttgart. Ferdinand Kreuter, a rather tall man, an optician with a shop and residence at East Houston Street, New York, was a frequent voyager on business matters. He thought that close confinement in his trade was undermining his constitution and another sea journey would restore it. At first, his step-brother was to accompany him on the *Schiller*, but he later decided against it and sold his ticket. Kreuter then vacillated on whether to change ships to the *Pommerania*, but ultimately kept to his original plan. Left behind with his wife were six children.

Several other men travelled alone aiming to see friends and relatives in Europe. A Swiss, Frederick Uhlmann, a bookbinder and bookseller of Broad Street in Columbus, Ohio, having been fifteen years in America, decided to visit his parents in Berne but left his wife and four children behind. J. William Metzger, a 22-year-old clerk at the German-American Bank in Chicago, had been in America only four years but was intent upon a three-month visit to relatives in Frankfurt. Richard Feederle, who had served as a captain in the Union Army in the civil war and owned considerable real estate in his home town of Akron, Ohio, was travelling to stay with friends at Schwartzwald, leaving his wife and a married daughter at home. Another ex-military man, Dr F.J. Kern of Shenadoah, Pennsylvania, was a veteran of two wars, having fought as a private in the Mexican war of 1848 and as a surgeon in the latter, civil conflict. He was anticipating much pleasure in revisiting his old university haunts at Berlin.

Between meals, passengers of all classes occupied themselves in a number of ways. The first three days of reasonably fine weather allowed ample opportunity for passengers to promenade on deck. First-cabin passengers emerged on to the quarter deck through the doors of the long, glass-roofed deckhouse known as the 'pavilion', from where two wide staircases lead down to the vestibule aft of the saloon. Promenading allowed the wealthy to parade their finery: men in swallow-tail and frock coats wearing the 'de rigueur' hats – derbys, 'stove-pipes' or stetson; the ladies, heavily corseted and bustled, flaunting the latest style 'apron-front' dresses complemented by pill-box and flower-posy hats invariably worn tilted forwards and tied under the chin.

Second cabin shared the midships companion stairs with first cabin and were also allocated the forward companion way. To some extent they shared the social aims of first cabin in their promenading but within a lower rank, enjoying a casual stroll, standing idly to watch the distant Cunarder, *Bothnia*, or observing the social graces in formal exchanges with others of their standing. The less well-bred and poorer-

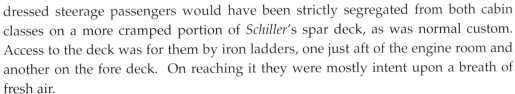

Passing time aboard a transatlantic steamship during the mid-1870s.

Above left: *Fashionably dressed passengers at the rail.*

Above: *Sleeping.*

dressed steerage passengers would have been strictly segregated from both cabin classes on a more cramped portion of *Schiller*'s spar deck, as was normal custom. Access to the deck was for them by iron ladders, one just aft of the engine room and another on the fore deck. On reaching it they were mostly intent upon a breath of fresh air.

Steerage passenger Franz Schnellenberg, aiming to visit his native village near Glauchau, Saxony, used his time on deck to examine the ship thoroughly. As a seasoned Atlantic voyager, he noted with satisfaction the machinery and equipment aboard and the manner in which the ship took the roughest of seas. Less promising he thought was the apparatus for lowering the six large lifeboats; their davits seemed too corroded to turn and the ropes so thickly coated with paint that they could not possibly pass through the pulleys. Thick paint also covered the trigger of the signal cannon, and despite Schnellenberg's efforts to prise it loose, it remained stuck. He was expecting the lifeboats to be lowered and the signal cannon to be fired in a test while at sea, as he had witnessed on previous voyages, yet this did not occur.

Most others occupied their time with more frivolous concerns. Deck games were popular entertainment and 'Shuffleboard' – a sort of outdoor version of shove

Passing time aboard a transatlantic steamship during the mid-1870s.

Playing shuffleboard.

ha'penny – was a great favourite. Groups of people of both sexes would gather enthusiastically to play, wielding long-handled, fork-ended sticks to push a large ring across a numbered grid marked out upon the deck. The many children aboard, with sailor suits much in fashion for both boys and girls, amused themselves in time-honoured ways with ball games, skipping and the like. Men of a gambling disposition would be seen gathering at noon each day near the chartroom, when the ship's position and her 'run' of the previous 24 hours were posted up for all to see. The winner of the day's pot would have provided the closest estimate to the distance covered by the vessel during that period – averaging about 300

Above left: *Posting the ship's 'run'.*

Above: *Betting on the daily run of the ship.*

Left: *A card game.*

miles per day. Evening entertainment was provided by passengers themselves. At night, first-cabin people thronged the saloon dressed in their best finery. There they would engage in conversation, read books from the ship's library, or play cards, board games and dominoes. Often, the air about its brightly lit skylight was vibrant with music: a soirée or a concert, with songs and recitals or dancing to some suitable accompaniment on the saloon piano, would have been arranged by the more culti-vated socialites amongst them. Sometimes, the strident tones of fiddle and concertina might waft upwards from below, where it could be heard satisfying the more home-spun tastes of those quartered there. German lines in general were noted for music and their ship's bands, formed from musicians who were usually engaged to double as second-cabin stewards, would play selections of German favourites each morning on deck, weather permitting, for all aboard to enjoy.

Time too was spent in consolidating new friendships. People of a like social stand-ing and disposition were drawn to one another or looked askance at others, as ashore. Some had a more gregarious appeal. Well-known and liked by all on board were the roly-poly twins, Charles and William Frahm, sons of the Davenport brewer. They each had a capacity for merriment as huge as their appetites for food, which they ate with a rapidity which astonished their fellow diners in second cabin. Among the saloon set, where the honour of dining at the same table as Captain Thomas was eagerly sought, it was the other ship's captain aboard who was quite often the life and soul of any social occasion. Captain Daniel W. Percival, the Cape Cod mariner bound for a new command at Hamburg, proved a great favourite there with his cheery dis-position and tales of adventure on the high seas.

Among Percival's more notable forebears were John 'Mad Jack' Percival, who had circumnavigated the world in his ship *Old Ironsides* during 1844–46, and his grandfa-ther, Captain Thomas Percival, whose schooner *Patriot* had turned turtle then righted itself during a gale in 1812 – both he and a surviving seaman then spending a week on the battered hull before being rescued. During the civil war, when Confederate privateers were waylaying and sinking vessels from Union ports, it was Daniel W.'s turn for adventure. He then served on Captain Franklin Percival's ship, the *Charles Hill*, one of 20 North Atlantic ships that fell victim to the C.S.S *Alabama*, a 1050 tons steam sloop armed with eight cannons and commanded by the South's debonair and most successful captain, Raphael Semmes. The *Alabama* stopped the London-to-Montevideo-bound *Charles Hill* on 25 March 1863 and destroyed her by fire. Percival, along with the captain and crew of the *Charles Hill,* was taken captive aboard the

Conversation in the saloon.

Confederate raider to join crews from other Yankee victims; being released only when she arrived at Bahia, Brazil in May that year. The *Alabama* later raised her total of prizes to 64 in the South Atlantic and Indian oceans, but was eventually sunk by the U.S.S. *Kearsarge* in a fierce battle off Cherbourg in June 1864.

Another of Percival's tales was about buying a wild goldfinch in Messina, Italy, during the winter of 1869–70. He kept it in a cage aboard his barque, the *Sicilian*. Next spring, when she was between Philadelphia and Boston, it escaped and flew off to perch on the spars of the Five Fathom Lightship. The *Sicilian* continued her voyage for another 36 hours and 120 miles, until they were off Long Island. There, when among about 30 other vessels, a small shore bird appeared and was seen to be making straight for the *Sicilian*. It finally landed on one of the barque's spars and then entered the goldfinch's cage. Percival and his crew were surprised to find their lost goldfinch had returned to them.

Soon, a time would come when Percival's maritime experience and good humour would prove invaluable to a few of his fellow passengers.

NOTES

[1]   *New York Times*, 8 October 1873.

The Schiller, *as depicted in* Illustrated London News, *15 May 1875. From a photograph taken by T. Coates of Acton, London, when serving as an engineer on* Goethe.

CHAPTER 7

•◆•

Across the Atlantic

As passengers idled the days away, 120 crew members toiled on their behalf. Chief among officers involved in passenger related duties was the ship's purser, E. Schmettan, a former Hamburg merchant, aged about 40. C. Putfarken, tall, blonde and moustached, was suitably distinguished in his role as chief steward of first cabin, while Augustus Felkstow did duty as chief steward of second cabin. The crew themselves, like *Schiller*'s officers, were mostly German, although there were a few American and other nationals among them. Not all were male; there were several women stewards aboard, among them Maria Felkstow, wife of Augustus, the chief steward of second cabin.

Stewards and stewardesses were most visible below decks, being particularly numerous at mealtimes when conveying laden dishes from the galley to the awaiting tables. Some were on hand throughout the day, called by electric bell to serve the requirements of saloon passengers, or doing their daily duties such as making up beds and attending to other comforts. Mostly invisible, but equally crucial to the physical well-being of passengers, was the corps of cooks, butchers and bakers labouring within the confines of the galley, bakery and ice-room, preparing everything from the basic ingredients that made up a steerage meal to the culinary complexities of table d'hôte for saloon passengers.

Seen cleaning paintwork, polishing brass, scrubbing decks, tidying ropes and tackle, or trimming the sails to the wind when all was well, would be the on-duty watch of sailors commanded by one or the other of the ship's first and second mates. Any significant change in the weather, and the shrill of a boatswain's whistle would have them manning the halyards or swarming up the shrouds and edging out along footropes strung beneath the yards to set or reef sails according to the strength of the wind.

The crew were assisted by several men who lacked the funds to travel as passengers, even in steerage. Herman Baumgarten and Richard Nautch were young Germans who had arrived in New York only six weeks before from Breslau in search of employment. Having found none and being penniless, they had gone to Hoboken and asked Captain Thomas if they could work their passage back to Germany on the *Schiller*. He allowed them to sign on as deck-hands; at which Baumgarten looked forward to surprising his wife and two children when he arrived home. Eleven other men in the same straits were similarly employed.

Another working his passage was an employee of another shipping line. When the Holland-America steamship, *W.A. Scholten,* had arrived in New York on 21 April, it was after a protracted battle against heavy ice which had resulted in her forward compartments being broken in and flooded. Her surgeon, Dr W.A. Sanders, was a young man from Rotterdam who had graduated at Utrecht shortly before he joined Holland-America in June 1872. While his own ship was detained for repairs, and wishing to occupy his time usefully, he had volunteered to act in his professional capacity to replace the *Schiller*'s own surgeon, Dr Boll, who had telegraphed from Philadelphia to say he was ill and could not make the sailing. In the event, Dr Boll had finally come aboard to sail, but many passengers thought Dr Sanders, was the ship's official surgeon.

Two non-crew employees of the Eagle Line aboard *Schiller* were both marine artists. Godfred Altmann, aged 27 and from Mannheim, was undertaking the voyage to study sea-scapes and make paintings of the Eagle Line's ships. A Viennese artist, Mr Osquorn, who was normally engaged in this work at the Hamburg offices of the Eagle Line, was similarly employed for the voyage. Osquorn had taken the opportunity of his week's stay in America to take a steamer trip up the Hudson River and to visit Niagara Falls. It was the work of these two men which Henry Gellen, the master painter of the Eagle line, had supervised between boarding *Schiller* at Hoboken and leaving with the pilot schooner.

Schiller's officers, inclusive of the captain, numbered 13 in all. The four mates were all very experienced men; each held a master's certificate, a condition of employment as an officer in Eagle Line ships. Theirs were gained in Germany, where, unlike the British system requiring a seaman to study in his own time and then qualify by experience and through sitting exams for mate's and master's certificates, several years sea experience was followed by a long college course with the master's exam taken at its conclusion.

First mate was Heinrich Hillers, a Hamburg man who had at one time been master of a sailing ship on the North Atlantic run. Aged about 45, he had been at sea for 24 years and had gained his master's certificate at Hamburg in 1862. He had been in the service of the Eagle Line for about a year and was, like Captain Thomas, about to complete his seventh voyage for the company. Four of these had been served under Captain Wilson in *Schiller*'s sister ship, *Goethe*.

The second mate, Erwin Polemann, was a tall, good-looking fellow, of about 30. His home town was Hanover. Like Hillers, he also had previous experience commanding a sailing vessel – a barque sailing to the China coast out of Hamburg. His master's certificate was dated 1867 and before he joined the Eagle Line, in January 1874, he had been with the Hamburg-Amerika Line.

Of the other two mates, Richard Heintze the fourth mate was from Mecklenburg and on his first voyage with *Schiller*. He had spent the previous six years with ships of the Hamburg-Amerika Line, mostly on their West Indies routes. Heintze was junior officer in Hillers' watch, while Polemann had G. Freese, the third mate, as his junior. Immediately under them was chief boatswain Simon Jensen, on his fifth voyage with *Schiller*.

Less visible to passengers were those whose job entailed attending the ship's primary power source. While the work of sailors above was dominated by the many and varied moods of the heavens, the 'black gang' toiled below in surroundings more akin to hell. Where steep iron steps descended into the bowels of the vessel, this small army sweated and slogged to satisfy the ship's vast appetite for steam coal in conditions of the utmost grime and swelter. *Schiller* had four scotch boilers of the double-ended type, each with six furnaces facing outwards into narrow stoke-holds. In a relentless procession, coal-trimmers trundled barrow loads from the Stygian blackness of coal-bunkers to these stokeholds, where in the harsh glare of open furnace doors firemen and stokers fed the red heat and cleared flame-deadening clinker with long-handled 'slicers.' On the skill of these men would depend most the ship's speed and her punctual arrival at port.

Further aft, the ship's monstrous marine engine[1] operated in an atmosphere of oily fumes and stultifying air, while the hiss of escaping steam, the repeated 'click' of valve gear and the reverberation of the long propeller shaft, sounded perpetually in the iron hull. It was claimed that:

The machinery was very powerful, and worked so smoothly as to hardly impart any vibration to the ship, and the motion of the screw was hardly felt at all.[2]

Chief engineer Leonard Fahrig and three subordinate engineers kept a watchful eye on steam and water gauges there, while overalled greasers pumped lubricants into journals and bearings, hot from incessant, hour-upon-hour, day-after-day motion as the ship ran on across the ocean. Fahrig also supervised the maintenance of 13 smaller, independently operating steam engines that powered winches and windlasses, a 'starting and stopping engine'[3] and a steering engine situated beneath the midships 'commander's bridge', which gave immediate control of the vessel with little effort.

Fahrig was a 30-year-old German from Hamburg, where he had a wife and two children. His previous experience included serving on Hamburg-Amerika steamers sailing between Hamburg and Valparaiso or Zanzibar. His engineering skills were highly valued by the line he now served. About six months beforehand, the company's agent at Hoboken had desired to put a 'Hirsch screw' into the *Schiller*. This was a four-bladed, sickle-shaped screw patented by Herman Hirsch in the 1860s and fashionable after 1870, when they were fitted to a number of vessels with the aim of increasing speed by about one knot. At Hoboken, no engineer was competent enough to carry out this task, nor did they have the tools and equipment required. When the problems were made known to Fahrig, he manufactured the necessary tools and fitted the screw himself without fuss. The fitting of a Hirsch screw had proved most invaluable. The company's directors reported:

> *Especially satisfactory is the patent Hirsch screw, which causes much less vibration in the ship.*[4]

With the weather fine for the first three days after leaving Sandy Hook, the *Schiller* made good running. A moderate south-westerly breeze was blowing and Captain Thomas took advantage of it by ordering a full spread of canvas aloft. The new month bought a change in the weather though; the sky became overcast and grey, and drizzle drove promenaders from the deck. Cabin passengers who wished to take the air or keep watch on the ocean could do so in the sanctity of the 53-by-20ft, glass-roofed deckhouse situated over the saloon skylight and popularly known as the 'pavilion'.

Sunday 2 May was particularly rough, with heavy rainstorms and high seas – 'a wild sea', as one passenger called it. The *Bothnia*, bound for Queenstown and Liverpool, soon vanished from sight in the poor visibility. A great deal of crockery

Stormy weather in the Atlantic.

Dining in the saloon.

and glass broken in the saloon, where the wooden racks above the tables swung violently. Stewards fitted 'fiddles' to tables in an attempt to contain plates and cups against the pitch and roll of the ship among the troughs and crests of the Atlantic breakers. But on that day and the next, few passengers had the stomach to go to the saloon or other dining rooms for their meals. Almost all of them were seasick. Doctors Boll and Sanders were much in demand.

Although passengers complained, it was the sort of weather that Captain Thomas and his crew were well used to. The last five of their outward-bound passages had been awful. *Schiller*'s third crossing, in August 1874, had been one of strong westerly winds and fog for most of the way; in October heavy westerly gales and high seas beset her fourth outward passage for a similar duration; and the same weather was repeated for the final crossing that year from late November to 9 December. So far, 1875 had provided them with no improvement. Having left Hamburg on 21 January to arrive at New York 14 days later, Thomas had reported:

> *Experienced heavy gales and strong weather throughout, with very rough and turbulent sea. The S. (Schiller) was detained outside (New York) six hours by fog.*[5]

Tending the needs of sick passengers.

The outward passage for the current voyage, arriving in New York on 14 April, had been little different either, as Thomas reported:

> *...experienced strong westerly winds and high seas the whole passage. April 10th, 42 lat., 50 long., passed enormous iceberg at a distance of ten miles...*[6]

It was all very different from the climatic conditions which George Thomas had experienced during so many of his sea-going years.

A weak, hazy sun showed through the cloud cover for a while on 4 May, the first sign of it that month. Climbing to its zenith it allowed the ship's navigating officer to take an observation which would determine their position. In fine weather the sextant was used at noon to measure the angle of the sun relative to the earth's surface, enabling calculations to be made which would accurately fix the ship's latitude. Longitude was assessed with chronometers, the time of day experienced on board from the overhead sun being compared to Greenwich Mean Time. That noonday reckoning on the 4th was the last in which proper celestial observations were taken to fix the vessel's precise position on the chart. From then onwards the weather was to stay dull and overcast, or 'covered' as it was termed on board.

Schiller's first and second mates, Heinrich Hillers and Erwin Polemann, assisted Captain Thomas in his noonday calculations to ascertain the ship's position during the next three days. As there was no sun visible, only thick cloud from horizon to horizon, it was necessary to resort to 'dead reckoning'. With longitude figured in the usual manner by the ship's chronometers, the course on which the vessel had sailed since the previous day's noon position had to be plotted on the chart using compasses and parallel rule. Knowledge of the ship's speed was essential to their calculations and this would have been obtained at two bells (1am) and again at six bells (11am) through heaving the log.

On *Schiller* there were two such logs; one a patent device with a rotor-driven counter; the other a 'common log' – the traditional wooden 'log-ship' which was heaved over the stern. It was the 'log-ship' which was invariably used. When heaved, an attached line calibrated with knots passed through the hands of the mate from a reel held by another seaman as a specified time elapsed on a sand 'log-glass' and the ship moved forward away from the floating log. The number of knots counted gave the vessel's speed. For the three days up to 7 May, with a south-westerly wind blowing, all sails set and the engine at full speed, the *Schiller* maintained a speed of 14 knots.

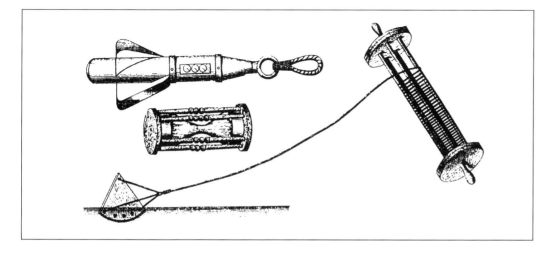

Rotor-driven log, log-glass and log-line with log-ship.

Checking the ship's speed by heaving the log – note the sailor holding the 'log-glass'.

By dead reckoning it was possible to get a reasonably accurate fix on the ship's position – longitude by the chronometers and latitude from the course and their speed along it over the previous 24 hours. But with the sky so consistently cloudy it meant there was no chance to check calculations by 'shooting the sun' with the sextant. Hillers and Captain Thomas worked up the reckoning on 7 May from a position gained by their dead reckoning of the previous day – this too based on their dead reckoning of the 5th. Having run 345 miles in the previous 24 hours, they concluded that *Schiller* was positioned at 49° 50' North latitude, 10° 23' West longitude (approximately 200 miles due west of Land's End). From this estimation they continued on the course steered throughout the day before, East, 30° South (or south-east by east) .

To help keep the vessel on course there were four compasses; two on the 'commander's bridge' and two on the after bridge. Being constructed of iron meant that the ship's hull would exercise some magnetic influence on the compasses, causing them to deviate slightly from magnetic north. Compensation for this was by adjustable magnets let into the deck; but as this magnetic influence varied according to the direction the ship was travelling in, there were 'deviation cards' kept in the chartroom to show the extent in different meridians. Of the four compasses, one on the after bridge was the 'standard compass' – the one most accurate from which all course directions were given.

Apart from 'local deviation' to be taken into account when setting the ship's course, there was also the 'variation' between magnetic and true, geographical north. At the longitude in which *Schiller* sailed at noon on 7 May this variation was figured at 31° West – magnetic north being that distance west of true north from their position in the Atlantic. By subtracting this and making other adjustments for deviation, their true-course as opposed to the course steered by the ship's compass could be ascertained.

However, in approaching the mouth of the English Channel there was another factor to be accounted for. A strong current emanating from the Bay of Biscay and running north-westwards across Ushant (Ile de Ouessant) to Scilly, known as Rennel's current, would make the vessel drift northwards. Its strength varied considerably according to wind direction. Considering all these factors, Captain Thomas and Heinrich Hillers concluded that the ship's true-course was E 3° S, as distinct from the course steered by the compass of E 30° S. By continuing on it they should pass the Bishop Rock lighthouse by seven miles to the south.

Ever since the bad weather had set in on 2 May Captain Thomas had not slept in his cabin, but had remained either on the bridge or in the chartroom, sleeping there and dining there also on several occasions. When Hillers's watch ended at noon that Friday, his opposite number Erwin Polemann came on duty, joining the Captain in the chartroom at about 1pm. Captain Thomas took a compass and a pair of dividers and measured the distance to Bishop Rock from the noon position. He told Polemann that it was about 150 miles away. At their present speed of 14 knots they should run into its visibility circle and see its light around nine, he added.

The weather remained leaden and overcast well into the afternoon, with increasing haze and frequent rainy squalls. At around 6pm, however, the sun showed briefly through the drifting masses of cloud. It shone for just long enough to enable

Polemann, then beginning his 6–8pm 'dog watch', to take three observations of azimuth to check the variation of the standard compass. This he discovered was 27° West – as he thought, agreeing with the variation they were already working to. With *Schiller* still being steered East 30° South, he concluded that with the variation and allowances for deviation and the drift of the current, their true-course was a little to the north of due east.

On completing his watch at 8pm, Polemann went down to where the Captain was having supper and informed him of his findings. Then both men went to the bridge. By this time the weather had become quite foggy. Visibility at 4pm, when Polemann's previous watch ended, was between seven and eight miles. Now it was down to five miles. The fog was thickening fast, but Captain Thomas seemed to think that it would not hinder them too much.

'I will make Scilly,' he told his second officer, 'I always do.'

Making the Isles of Scilly was important to the Captain; as important as it would have been to any other master of a transatlantic steamship bound for the English Channel and one of England's southern ports. British naval directions advised that ships heading up Channel should make for the islands first in order to align themselves correctly. There was another reason though: once within range of the islands, steamer captains would signal to the Lloyd's shipping agent on the main isle of St Mary's that they were passing by. In daylight, Schiller's RDQP code name was displayed by signal flags. At night-time each line had its own code of signals: the Eagle Line's were, first a blue light, then a rocket and finally a fire-ball. The agent would then acknowledge receipt of their signal by signalling in return before telegraphing ahead to the ship's next port of call, informing them of its imminent arrival. All Eagle Line vessels signalled again as they passed the Lizard.

First mate Hillers replaced Polemann at eight, taking the watch from then until midnight. As he joined the Captain on the bridge he was told that they were 25 miles from Bishop Rock and on course to pass by it seven miles to the south. The fog was becoming thicker by the minute though. Junior officer in Hillers's watch was Richard Heintze, the fourth mate; and from where he stood, on the after bridge, he could not see all of the ship's length. Soon, the gradual blanketing out of some of the ship's superstructure was sufficiently worrying to Captain Thomas for him to give the order for the steam fog-whistle to be sounded at half-minute intervals. Yet she was still making 14 knots, steaming along on full power and with all of her sails set. The *Schiller* had a reputation for arriving in port punctually – and Captain Thomas intended to keep it.

Such speed was not unusual: few transatlantic liners slowed for fog when out in the ocean, relying instead on their fog-whistles to warn others of their approach. Yet there had been many collisions in fog at sea. The worst had occurred in September 1854, when the Collins Line *Arctic*, a wooden-built paddle steamer, collided with a small, iron steamship in dense fog 60 miles south-east of Cape Race. At first, the *Arctic*'s master believed the other vessel was in trouble and launched a lifeboat to search for her and give help. But it was the *Arctic* which was holed, sinking within four hours. Only 45 people survived out of around 380 on board. Among the dead were shipping line owner Edward Knight Collins's wife, his only son and a daughter. Captain Thomas had himself witnessed a very near miss in similar circumstances, when the *Holsatia* on which he was travelling almost collided with the *City of Limerick* in April 1873.

The sea was running high and the wind blowing heavily from the south-west. It had blown consistently from the same direction throughout the *Schiller*'s passage, enabling the Captain to utilise the maximum amount of sail at his disposal and try to make up for the day lost at the outset. The ship was almost back on its schedule to dock at Plymouth on 7 May, for she should arrive in the early hours of the 8th. Soon though, with the realisation of the fog's widespread density, the dangers of surging ahead in limited visibility impressed itself upon Captain Thomas. It was time to forego a little of his reputation for punctuality. At 8.30 the order was given for all sails to be taken in. Sailors in Hillers's watch under the direction of chief boatswain Simon Jensen clambered up the shrouds and out along the foot-ropes beneath the yards to begin the job of hauling in, clewing up and furling the sails with rope gaskets.

Two other men from Hillers's watch were posted as forward lookouts at 9pm. This was done from common practice rather than as a particular precaution due to the foggy conditions, for at this time darkness was fast approaching. Able seaman Friedrich 'Fritz' Beckhaus was one, positioned at the port side of the fore deck. From there he could not see the full length of the ship stretching out behind him, nor even the bridge clearly. By then the two staysails had been taken in, but as furling all the sails would take some time yet and the fog was becoming more dense, Captain Thomas gave the order for the ship's engine to be slowed to half-speed. After this was duly rung on the engine room telegraph, fourth mate Heintze heaved the log. The vessel's speed had come down to ten knots. He could just make out the ship's smoke-stacks from the after bridge – barely half the length of the vessel ahead.

Down in the depths of *Schiller*'s iron hull, where the feeble glow of oil lamps made little impression on the cavernous gloom of the engine room, Silas Hexter, a German passenger from Highland, Illinois, bound for Kurhessen, was watching the ship's engine in motion. He heard the engine room bell ring for half-speed and saw the engineers take action that slowed the hiss of the pistons and the rotation of the crankshaft. Then he went up on to the spar deck to see if land was visible yet, for he had earlier been told by some officers that they should be able see it around 9pm.

Quite a few people were already there, most of them men taking the evening air or intent on a stroll and a smoke. Among a group of off-duty stewards idly amusing themselves before turning in for the night was Wilhelm Blohm, a mere youth in age, who heard the Captain telegraph down to the engineer for half-speed at 9pm. The knowledge that the *Schiller* should be within sight of the beam from the Bishop Rock lighthouse had brought several passengers on deck; some of them thinking they might see a pilot boat to guide the ship. Steerage passenger Marcus Powitzer came up from below at this time and was quite shocked by the density of the fog obscuring on-board objects. Henry Sterne, a Jewish commission agent for Jonas Sonneborne of Pearl Street, New York, who was on a periodic business trip to Berlin, came up on deck from the saloon around 9pm fully expecting to see the light. Making his way forward to the fore deck he looked out over the port side rails, peering myopically northward into the white, nebulous mass which now engulfed the steamship. He hoped to see at least a faint glimmer to show where the lighthouse stood.

NOTES

[1] Engine: Compound 2-cylinder, inverted vertical, direct acting (cylinders and connecting rods directly above the crankshaft) with high-pressure cylinder of 60ins bore and low-pressure cylinder of 104ins bore, each with a piston stroke of 54ins. It was of 550 nominal horsepower but the effective horsepower attributed to it – the actual work done by the engine in propelling the ship – was 3000 horsepower. From the engine 125ft of steel shaft drove a four-bladed screw 19ft in diameter and with a pitch of 20ft – one revolution theoretically advancing the ship by that distance.

[2] *New York Times.*, 9 May 1875.

[3] This was probably a small starting and reversing engine which drove the valve link motion.

[4] *New York Tribune,* 10 May 1875.

[5] *New York Times,* 4 February 1875.

[6] *New York Times,* 3 April 1875.

CHAPTER 8

•◆•

The Retarrier Ledges

Captain Thomas and first mate Heinrich Hillers watched anxiously from the bridge as the night-darkened fog swirled and closed in around them. Peering back along the ship's hull, past the tall smokestacks and the lights of the pavilion, they could just make out the sternrails. People walking or standing in groups on deck appeared ethereal – pale shadows of their former selves. Ahead, beyond the foremast and prow, there was nothing to be seen except the greyness which encircled them and enveloped them in its chill, illimitable vastness. Sound too was deadened and muffled: the throb of the engine, the wind in the shrouds, the slap of the waves on the hull and even the passengers' voices were unusually muted. Only the shrill tones of the steam fog-whistle, sounding at half-minute intervals, cut through the all-embracing greyness.

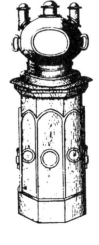

Binnacle and compass.

Hillers had experienced 'thick' weather before during his years as master of an Atlantic sailing ship, but never as thick and foggy as this night. Beside him, the Captain had good cause to recollect remarks he had made to Daniel Baker on the *Holsatia* – about his concern and feelings of helplessness when in fog. Discussing the situation, Hillers proposed that they change course. It would be safer to pass the night further out in the English Channel, where there was no danger of running the ship ashore, he suggested. Thomas said they were still 20 or 25 miles from land, but agreed, and at 9.30 rang the engine room telegraph for quarter speed. At the same time he sent orders to the helmsman to change course from E 30° S to south-south-west. He then watched the needle and card in the lighted binnacle until the manoeuvre was completed. With the variation for magnetic north allowed for, they were then on a true-course just to the east of southerly and making around six to seven knots.

Steam-driven steering engine.

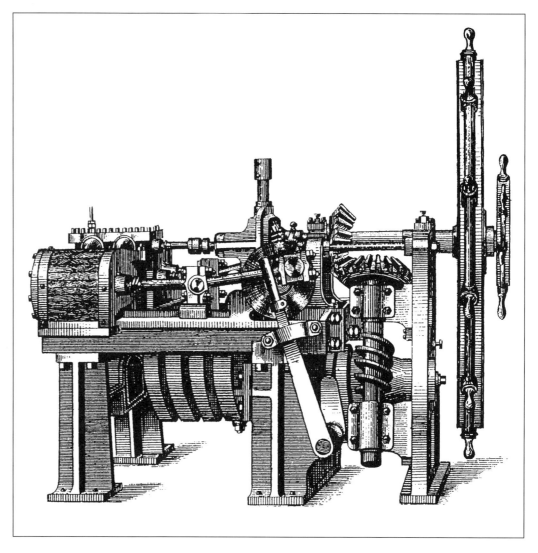

Schiller's sails were not yet entirely furled. Chief boatswain Simon Jensen and the watch were still high on the yards of the mainmast, working hard to draw in and furl the last remaining sails. The new course brought the strengthening wind across the starboard bow rather than from astern, making their job more difficult as recalcitrant canvas flapped 'aback' instead of bellying forward. But the ship slowed into the wind. It was slowed still further at 9.40, when Captain Thomas rang down to the engine room for dead slow.

Franz Schnellenberg had been on deck all day. Like others there he was eager to see land after being at sea for so long, but he was too tired to wait any longer. Requesting a friend to come and wake him when it was sighted, he walked past the wheelhouse, noting its clock hands pointed to 9.45, then went forward to the steerage companion and downstairs to his bunk. Young steward Wilhelm Blohm left the deck about the same time and having heard the Captain's ring on the engine-room telegraph just before leaving, descended by the same stairs to the crew's quarters and his bed. Most of the off-duty watch were already in theirs. Able seaman Max Goldberger lay asleep in his bunk wearing a nightshirt. The officer of Goldberger's watch, Erwin Polemann, was fully dressed and slumbering soundly on the sofa in his cabin. Some of the ship's day workers, like sailmaker Wilhelm Hinsch, had long since turned in for the night.

Although quite a large number of male passengers were still on deck, waiting to see land or the Scilly light, the majority were below. The saloon was crowded and full of conviviality; with the first-class socialites talking, drinking and playing games, while someone at the piano further enlivened their evening. Similar amusements were taking place in other areas of accommodation too. In their second-cabin stateroom, the Frahm twins, Charles and William, were engaged in a game of draughts. Nearby, Birmingham-bound Edward Ball, aged 65, was busy writing the day's events into his journal. He began the next day's entry too, anticipating the ship's arrival at Plymouth, but leaving a blank where the time could be filled in later. He was to leave the ship there and travel up to Birmingham, the city that had been his home until he left for the United States over 25 years beforehand. One of his two sons was a school-teacher at Birmingham and Edward intended a surprise visit. He was a widower: his wife had died on the return passage after a previous visit to their son, when only one day's sailing from New York.

Most women and children were in bed. Those who were also to leave the ship early next morning at Plymouth, like steerage passengers Susan Duckfield, Frances Evans and their five children, had retired a while before to their bunks. Some men had likewise chosen to have an early night. Joseph Legenore from Kentucky, was to disembark at Cherbourg later the following day, but he had climbed into his narrow steerage bunk at 9pm and was soon sound asleep. Others were busy preparing themselves for a night's rest. Just before 10pm, New York tailor, Johannes Rink, bound for Biedenkopf in Germany, undressed and was about to draw back the blanket of his bunk. In another of the steerage staterooms, husband and wife John and Christine Joens from Luzerne, Iowa, were putting on their nightclothes.

At about the same time Erwin Polemann woke up. Having lain on his cabin sofa since coming off watch at 8pm, he was aroused from sleep by the noise of the ship's fog whistle. He realised at once from the repetition of the steam-powered, shrill tone and the laboured ship's motion that the fog must have thickened considerably and they were proceeding ahead at dead slow. Turning over to resume his sleep, he suddenly felt the ship bump hard – so hard that he almost fell off his sofa.

A sound, rumbling through the hull of the vessel and accompanied by a bumping sensation, was the first indication that something had occurred. Few on board had the remotest idea of the cause. People's experiences of the moment differed so much that while some were immediately fearful, others remained calm and unconcerned. Silas Hexter, standing on deck by the engine room skylight, felt a sudden impact accompanied by a noise and then a shuddering sensation which he thought was the ship running on to sand. Below decks in the forecastle, boy steward Wilhelm Blohm had been in bed but a few minutes when he was almost thrown from his bunk by the impact. Two off-duty sailors fast asleep there, Max Goldberger and the ship's sail-maker Wilhelm Hinsch, awakened suddenly, realised at once that a collision of some sort had occurred, and rushed up on deck – Goldberger still in his nightshirt. In steerage, Joseph Legenore was awoken from his deep sleep by a noise and sensation which he first attributed to the ship's anchor being dropped as it docked, and Franz Schnellenberg, about to undress for bed, thought exactly the same. Johannes Rink thought the sound resembled the discharge of field guns. By contrast, steerage steward Frederick Wermke, busy attending his duties, noticed only a slight shock and was in no way alarmed by it.

Franz Schnellenberg's steerage cabin was one of the farthest forward in the *Schiller*. Hurrying upstairs immediately, filled with fear at the rattling noise and jarring sensation, he felt several hard bumps and then one large one which stopped the ship completely. He guessed she must have passed over several hundred feet of rocks before running against a very large one on the port side.

People on deck were as confused as those below. The initial shock, rumbling noise and bumping sensation was all there was at first – and nothing to see which had caused it. Forward lookout Fritz Beckhaus peered over the port rails into the all enveloping fog, but could not see what was hindering the vessel. He heard the Captain call out,

'Are we in collision with another ship?'

Beckhaus walked back along the deck to the bridge, sure of one thing at least.

'Its not a ship, Sir!' he called up to him.

In the meantime Captain Thomas had rung the engine room for the engine to be stopped.

Stockbroker Henry Sterne, still on the fore deck where he had stood for the last hour, hoping to see the Bishop Rock light somewhere to the north, could hear breakers on the starboard side. But he could not see anything either. The sound

Map of Schiller'*s course on 7 May 1875 and the Isles of Scilly.*

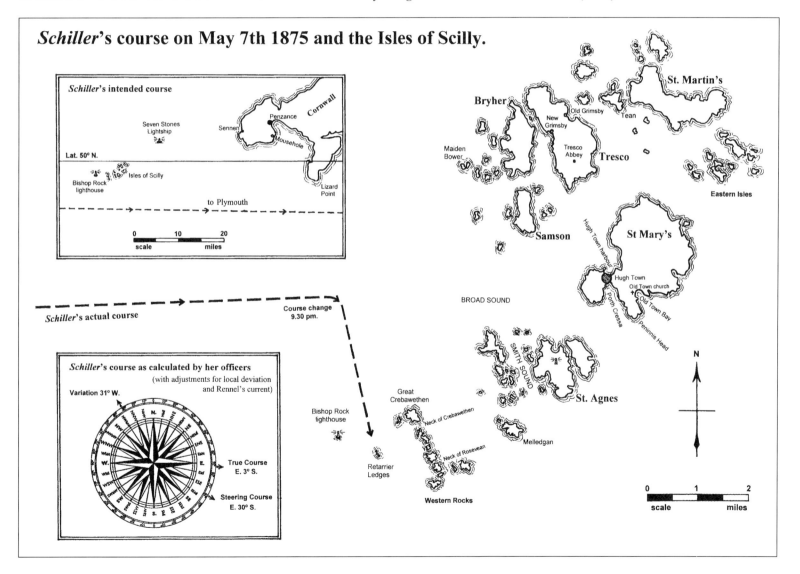

Schiller's course on May 7th 1875 and the Isles of Scilly.

was of the wind-driven waves smacking against the now stationary hull of the ship; for unbeknown as yet, the *Schiller* had struck at the port bow and was fast on rocks which barely if at all broke the surface of the water. These, the Retarrier Ledges, are about two thirds of a mile south-east of the Bishop Rock lighthouse. In waters generally 20 to 30 fathoms deep, this range of vicious, jagged rocks rise up steeply from the sea-bed to peak above the waves only at low or one-third flood tide.

Instead of passing the Isles of Scilly seven miles south of the lighthouse as plotted on their chart, they had sailed to a point several miles to the north of Bishop Rock, changed course to a southerly heading with the intention of making for mid-Channel, then passed the lighthouse unwittingly when it stood less than a mile off to starboard. Worse, they had done so without ever having sighted the fresnel-intensified beam of its light, or heard a single peal of the six per minute rung on the lighthouse's fog bell, or even knowing where they were at all. The *Schiller* had struck the terrible Retarrier Ledges – and was stuck there. The ship and all on board her were in the most deadly peril – but they did not know that either – yet.

The initial shock seemed slight to some; but soon the *Schiller*'s hull bumped again much harder. Knowing now that they were fast on rocks by the bumping and from ominous grinding sounds from beneath the ship's hull, Captain Thomas gave the order for the steam-whistle to be blown continuously as a distress call. He also ordered soundings of the hull to be made to find out if it had been breached. To Hillers he gave orders to clear the lifeboats, which meant first cutting them free from the boat-chocks in which they stood on deck, before swinging them out on the davits. Most of the first mate's watch were still on the mainmast at the time of the ship strik-ing, with chief boatswain Jensen and others clewing up the last sail, the main topsail. They came down straightaway to assist Hillers with the lifeboats, leaving the sail unfurled and hanging loose from the yard.

Jumping up from his cabin sofa at the impact of the ship striking, Erwin Polemann had rushed up the companionway, only to meet Hillers coming down to inform him of the catastrophe.

'We are shipwrecked!' exclaimed the first mate to his second.
Both men then rushed back on deck, Hillers to the lifeboats and Polemann to the bridge for orders from the Captain. As he mounted the steps leading up, the ship's storekeeper came to him from forward to report that the ship's compartments there were filling rapidly with water.

The Retarrier Ledges and Bishop Rock light-house with the Western Rocks in the foreground.
ILLUSTRATED LONDON NEWS

When Polemann arrived on the bridge, Thomas was just about to telegraph 'full speed astern' to the engine room in the hope that this would pull the vessel back off the rocks. Polemann told the Captain what the storekeeper had reported to him and warned him not to try reversing for fear of a greater inundation inside once they were clear and more open to the sea.

'I don't know what else to do!' replied the Captain.

He telegraphed for this to be done, but the reversed engine had no effect. While the great screw churned away, turning the waters to foam beneath the ship's stern, *Schiller* remained wedged on the submerged rocks, which like giant barbs held fast in the broken iron plates of her hull.

Although a few passengers were sufficiently alarmed to shout or scream at the initial shock of impact, most remained calm. It had not seemed violent enough to indicate any serious problem. Even the shrill, piercing sound of the ship's steam-whistle, wailing its distress call, had many believing it was a warning of approaching danger – not that they were already in it. But having heard a few shouts and screams, passengers and crew below decks hurriedly left their amusements or their beds, and rushed upwards, pouring out through the companionways on to the spar deck to find out for themselves what the fuss was all about. The Frahm twins hastily abandoned their dominoes and second-cabin stateroom for the companionway to the deck. Joseph Legenore, aware now that the ship was not docking, managed to dress quickly enough to be on deck when the Captain gave orders for the engine to be reversed. Others, especially women who first had to rouse children from sleep before shep-herding them, drowsy and bleary-eyed, up on deck, arrived later. Most, having had so little time for themselves in the rush, were still wearing nightclothes.

Confirmation of what had happened took some time in reaching the throng which swarmed up through the companion-way doors and spilled out on to the fog-thick night air, to stand bewildered and scared in their wide variety of clothing. Henry Sterne, walking aft from the forecastle to the saloon, met William T. Smith, a fellow saloon passenger, who as managing director of a New York hosiery importers, was on one of his twice-yearly business trips to Europe. When Smith asked him what was the matter, Sterne told him calmly, as if it were nothing too problematic,

'The ship is on rocks.'

Word about the dire situation which the vessel was really in reached everyone soon after though. Someone close to the bridge had heard the storekeeper tell Polemann about the water coming in to the fore part of the ship, and the cry that the ship had struck rocks and was holed quickly gathered momentum, creating growing conster-nation and panic. The real fate of the *Schiller* was made more apparent by the sight of the ship's officers and crew rushing to attend to their lifeboat duties.

In safety terms the *Schiller* was adequately equipped at a time when legal require-ments were minimal. There were six large clinker-built, double-ended wooden lifeboats, each 28ft long with a beam of 8ft, situated on either side of the funnels.

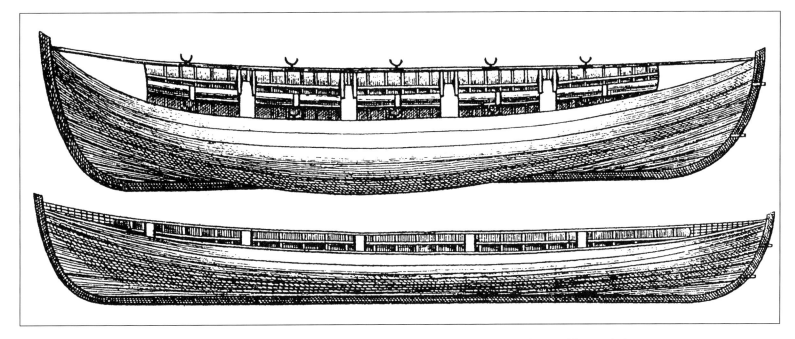

Lifeboat and gig.

These were packed with cork for additional buoyancy. Two smaller gigs of normal clinker-built construction, over 24ft long and with a 6ft beam, were kept on the quarter deck, making up the total number of lifeboats to eight. All lifeboats were kept in boat-chocks mounted on the decks, but in use would be swung out on 'goose -neck' davits fitted with block-and-tackle apparatus. The lifeboats conformed with British Board of Trade requirements and their total carrying capacity was about 400 people. Additional safety equipment included 12 circular lifebuoys attached to the ship's taffrail, and cork life-jackets beneath each bunk with more still in lockers – about 800 all told.

With the ship's engine still at full speed astern, but ineffective, Polemann was sent down to the engine room to ascertain whether water was getting in there. Chief engineer Leonard Fahrig assured him it had not yet reached the engine, but soon after Polemann had raced back to the bridge, a fireman ran up to tell him and the Captain that the stokehole was full of water. Shortly afterwards, the fires were inundated and extinguished. Captain Thomas then ordered the engine to be stopped. The engineers and stokers remained below, shutting down and blowing off steam from the boilers to prevent them from exploding as the cold Atlantic waters rose up around them.

Within minutes the *Schiller* bumped several times more on the rocks beneath her, each bump grinding and cracking open the iron plates of her hull still more. Then she slowly slewed around, pivoting on the port side of her bow and gradually swinging her prow further and further westwards. At the same time she listed over to starboard. It was now obvious to all that the vessel was a total wreck. Women screamed loudly and repeatedly, children began to cry and shriek, men with their faces drained of colour rushed about in search of their loved ones, bawling and shouting frantically. Everyone's worst fears had become reality; the ship was wrecked on rocks in thick fog and the blackness of night, with a strong wind blowing and a heavy sea running. Almost all had no idea even of where they were.

Ship's officers knew that with the vessel holed and stuck on rocks, the rising tide would eventually reach and cover the deck completely. It was imperative to get people off into the lifeboats. But with the deck crowded with passengers in a high state of panic, the sailors were having immense difficulty getting to the boats, let alone releasing them from their chocks for launching. As Hillers's men worked to cut them free of their lashings they were surrounded on all sides by people imploring them for advice or help, impeding their efforts. Sailmaker Wilhelm Hinsch tried to swing his axe at the restraining ropes but was prevented from doing so by the press of people around him. Captain Thomas shouted repeatedly, ordering all passengers to go below and wait until the crew had the lifeboats ready for them, but his voice, though aided by a speaking trumpet, was drowned by the blowing of the wind, the crash of waves breaking against the ship and the roar of steam being let off from the ship's boilers. Few heard him, and many who did were too frightened to move from the deck.

Some did remain calm despite the panic around them. Henry Sterne joined forces with his friend William T. Smith and widower Charles Walter, descending to the saloon with the aim of pacifying ladies and children gathering there. They were all fearful but in general, stayed calm. Second-cabin passenger Silas Hexter had the same intention when he ran down to his own class of accommodation. There the situation was chaotic, with women and children running in and out of cabins in dread and despair. He wanted to help but was soon unnerved. A woman was clinging tightly to Morris Harrison, a businessman from Hawkinsville, Georgia, exclaiming,

'Oh we are lost!'

Harrison was doing his best to pacify her,

'No, it's all right!' he told her.

But as he spoke Hexter saw that the man's face was as white as a sheet; and at that he lost his nerve completely and ran back up on deck.

Returning to his berth for a coat, Franz Schnellenberg noticed with horror that the steerage was filling with water. He grabbed his coat, and reached the stairway to return up on deck once more, then recollected there were life-jackets in a cupboard close by. It could not be opened because a thick coating of paint had closed the gaps between its doors. Some friends helped him break it open and the life-jackets were distributed among them. But in fastening the belt of the life-jacket, Schnellenberg realised his coat would make swimming difficult, so he removed it, went and took two blankets from his bunk and draping them around his shoulders returned to the deck above. His friends laughed at him: they felt secure at that time.

The Schiller *soon after striking the Retarrier Ledges – listing to starboard and firing distress rockets.*

On deck, Captain Thomas had given orders for the lifeboats to be launched as quickly as possible; life-jackets to be issued to all passengers; and for distress rockets, flares and signal guns to be fired. Although the vessel had turned around to face westward and was listing to starboard, she was fast on the rocks and in no immediate danger of sinking. Both he and his officers tried hard to convince passengers that 'the accident was without consequence' and that the ship would be safe until morning when everyone would be taken ashore. Yet the real danger was that the heavy north-westerly swell of the rising tide would slowly engulf them, until the decks were awash.

Each of *Schiller*'s eight lifeboats was numbered. The six large, cork-lined boats on either side of the smokestacks and further aft were ranged in even numbers to port and odd to starboard. The other two boats were the gigs, numbered 7 and 8, both well aft on the quarter deck. Number 7 gig was already slung out to starboard from its davits as it always was – ready to save life at a moment's notice. All boats had the number of crew members intended to man them painted on their sides, and an officer to take charge was specially assigned to each. Hillers's lifeboat was number 1; Polemann's number 2; third mate Freese's number 3, and so on through their ranks. But despite these arrangements and the provision of a list of lifeboat stations for passengers kept posted on the chartroom, the launchings were to be attended with escalating chaos.

CHAPTER 9

•◆•

To the Lifeboats

Polemann went first to the quarter deck to launch the two gigs. The starboard sloping deck was thickly crowded with passengers, many tearful and panicking, or shouting and screaming, with others numb with fear and apprehension. He had to force his way through them, ignoring their pleas and brushing aside the hands clutching desperately at his sleeve to gain attention or reassurance. Reaching number 7 gig, ready in its starboard davits, he found chief boatswain Simon Jensen at his assigned station, awaiting the order to lower away. Polemann commanded three sailors there to get in the boat with Jensen; sailmaker Wilhelm Hinsch, forward lookout Fritz Beckhaus, and one other. He ordered Jensen to remain alongside the ship, intending them to be ready to take passengers on board as soon as possible. The gig with the four men inside was then successfully lowered into the sea, where it stood off, out of danger of being dashed against the ship's side. But subsequent attempted launchings were to prove difficult, disastrous – and ultimately, impossible.

Captain Thomas, first mate Hillers and other sailors still struggled to cut the ropes lashing the other lifeboats to their crutches against the pressure of passengers around them. The situation with the lifeboats was made worse still when the first waves broke over the fore deck at about 10.30pm. Hysteria gripped people still more, prompting men, most of them steerage passengers, to tear away at the tarpaulin covers and clamber in while the boats were still on deck. Fighting broke out as they struggled to gain a place in them.

Other men, more fatalistic, took to drinking heavily soon after the ship struck. A number of the ship's firemen gathered up all the spirits they could find and proceeded to get hopelessly drunk. Several male passengers joined them. Hillers noticed an 'American captain' (possibly Richard Feederle of Akron, Ohio) drinking brandy alone in his cabin, so much of it that he eventually fell down insensible on the floor.

In the meantime Captain Thomas's direction that life-jackets be issued to all was more or less successfully carried out. There were life-jackets stowed under every bunk, but in the panic so many people had forgotten them or would not return for them they had to be supplied from other large stocks held on board. Henry Sterne had left the ladies of the saloon for a while and managed to obtain one of the circular lifebuoys attached to the taffrail for himself. On his return to the saloon he joined Hermann Zinkeisen, a fellow stockbroker from Milwaukee, and C. Putfarken the chief steward of first cabin, in obtaining life-jackets from a hatchway in the passage to the staterooms. These were distributed among the women and children gathered in the saloon – the last one going to Mrs Becker of New York.

Heinrich Hillers helped one very distressed woman without a life-jacket. The lady was in absolute terror and surrounded by weeping children. Her husband, a very stout man, had one for himself and refused the officer's suggestion that he give it to his wife. So concerned was this man for his personal safety, that he utterly ignored his own family and offered the first officer 'a fortune' if he would save him. Hillers scorned the man but managed to obtain a life-jacket for his distressed wife.

Less successful in obtaining one was Silas Hexter. When he had run on to the spar deck from the second-class cabins, unnerved by the alarm among the women and children there, he went in search of a life-jacket for himself. He raced down to the saloon to get one but was told by Sterne and the others that they were all gone. Returning then to the spar deck, he tried desperately to get into the number 5 lifeboat, still in its chocks and filled with men. They drove him out at first but he succeeded at his second attempt. Then he was approached by a man who asked,

'Please help me in too, you know who I am, my name is Williams.'
Hexter helped the man in but realising that the boat would never be raised with the weight of people inside, got out and ran back down to the saloon again to try to get himself a life-jacket.

Hexter was not alone in his confusion and alarm. Women shrieked and sobbed, clinging hysterically to their menfolk, while children wailed incessantly. Other more selfish and desperate men fought each other for places in the boats. Few had obeyed the Captain's order to go below and leave the decks free for his crew to attend to their duties with the lifeboats and signalling, and the many that had not were wearing his patience thin. Everywhere that Captain Thomas went he was thronged by passengers, most of them women who clung to him and clutched at him, imploring him for help, weeping and wailing, crying out for some small crumb of comfort from the one man whose authority was above all others. Many times he had to use force to free himself from their clutches and move on.

Throughout this he remained outwardly calm and collected, even trying to maintain his usual cheerfulness in the dire situation which had befallen them all in a vain attempt to reassure the frightened passengers. Again and again he urged them to go to the saloon or their own cabins. There, lights were still burning, all was dry and they would be safe from the sea which more and more broke over the angled decks, swilling across to make them slippery and treacherous and saturating everyone there with chilling Atlantic spray. For a while he even went down to the saloon, begging those who followed him down to stay there. In his frustration, and wanting so much to restore some kind of order to the calamitous situation on deck where neither he nor his crew could do their best to save life, he lied deliberately.

'The tide is going down,' he told the passengers congregating there, 'You will be perfectly safe!'
The ladies especially respected him and believed his every word. They stayed there. But if women had tried the Captain's patience to breaking point, it was the men who would force him to use the most desperate measures.

Hexter arrived back in the saloon in his frantic search for a life-jacket soon after. He recognised one man and his family there, Michael Kornblum, the wealthy wastepaper and rags dealer from New York, with his wife and three small children. He heard an officer explaining to them that this was the safest place on the ship and that they must not leave it,

'Stay there, it's the best thing you can do,' he told them.
The Kornblums all wore life-jackets and were standing quiet and still when Hexter went back up on deck again, having not yet obtained one for himself. He then ran aft to where Polemann and other sailors had just launched the starboard gig and were about to raise the port gig to its davits.

In the gig were several male passengers, sitting there while the sailors heaved on the tackle ropes to raise it. One of them was Marcus Powitzer from Posen, Germany, who Hexter knew well as a friend. Powitzer was wearing a life-jacket and when asked by Hexter where he got it from, explained that it was from under his pillow. At this Hexter raced back to the first-cabin companionway, intending to go down and make his way forward to second cabin for a life-jacket. As he reached the number 5 lifeboat he suddenly changed his mind and attempted to climb in to it once more. But when his hands were on the gunwale a gruff voice speaking in German told him,

'If you don't let go I will cut your hands off!'

Hexter took the threat seriously and let go. Then he returned to the port gig.

This, the number 8 gig, was proving much more difficult to launch for Polemann and his men, among whom was fourth mate Richard Heintze and able seaman Max Goldberger – straight from his bunk and wearing just his nightshirt. To port, the ship lay broadside-on to the wind-driven sea, which crashed against the hull and rode up over the rails with tremendous force. As they struggled against the constantly over-whelming waters and the weight of passengers already in the boat, another struggle ensued inside it.

Steerage steward Fredericke Wermke had not been particularly perturbed at what he thought was a slight shock when the ship struck. But arriving on deck a little later, he soon realised the true danger of the situation. He then went straight down to his berth, removed his uniform except trousers and shirt, and taking two knives ran back up on deck. Soon afterwards, he made his way to the quarter deck and got into the number 8 gig. Following him into it were a number of male pas-sengers. A scuffle between crew and passengers followed, in which most of the passengers were ejected from the gig, then it was finally swung out to begin its descent.

Commanding the gig was the ship's second carpenter, with five sailors including Max Goldberger and steward Wermke from the crew. Somehow overlooked when ejecting passengers were Marcus Powitzer and his friend Silas Hexter, who had given up his search for a life-jacket for a place in the gig. Yet the difficulties with the launch were not over. As it descended the ship's side, waves struck at it again and again, banging the wooden boat hard up against the iron plates of the *Schiller*. Then a rope jammed in a pulley and had to be cut free. The gig fell only a short way but the moment it touched the sea a huge wave inundated it completely and drove it under the steamship's stern.

At this the second carpenter leapt out, hoping to jump across to the ship's side and save himself, but he was swept away and lost to sight in a moment. Powitzer and Goldberger were also thrown from the boat. Powitzer was quickly dragged back in by others still there, but Goldberger found himself being drawn under the ship's counter with the gig drifting well away from him, as he thought, capsized. He swam desperately and managed to grasp the ship's screw, hauling himself upon it and from there clambering up over the sternrails on to the deck once more. Then he went to the forecastle to get some dry clothes.

Onlookers on deck thought, like Goldberger, that the gig had capsized and its occupants lost. But it was afloat, though quite full of water. Wermke, Powitzer, Hexter and the other four sailors, sitting up to their chests in water, bailed with everything they had; hands, hats and boots were all put to work in scooping the water out. They managed to get back in towards the *Schiller* and called for a baler. Polemann heard them and putting a compass in a bucket threw it into the sea beside them. Try as they might to reach, it just floated away from them.

For some time they bailed furiously, but seeing the other gig some way off through the swirling fog they called out, appealing to them for a baler. Jensen and the sailors in the number 7 gig, rowed away, shouting back that they had no such thing on board. It seemed to those in gig 8 that the others feared being asked to take on more men, for they shouted,

'We are full already.'

In spite of their efforts the water in the gig continued to rise. The reason, it was found, was there was no plug in the boat. A makeshift plug of clothing was stuffed into the hole and they made for the *Schiller* again to lay alongside as close as they dare. Steward Wermke had taken charge of the tiller, and he advised that they would be most sheltered there; but with fog and darkness all around they could only just make out the lights of her cabins.

Having failed to get a bucket to the port gig, Polemann then went to the starboard side of the ship and called to the sailors in the number 7 gig to come in closer as they were too far out. He wanted them to come alongside to take on passengers. The reply from Jensen through the fog was that their boat was half-full of water and they could not risk it – most likely what was meant by shouting they were 'full already' to the other gig. Their gig too was without its plug, or it had come out when being lowered, and the crew were bailing with anything suitable and had stuffed the hole with clothing. Polemann shouted back that if they came alongside he would lower a baler to them, and at that they rowed in and tied up beside the *Schiller*.

Once there, a bucket and a compass were lowered down to Jensen. Taking advantage of the rope and the opportunity it offered, a first-cabin steward, Theodore Hoffmann, quickly took hold and slid down it into the gig. Above them on deck, Polemann was desperately trying to persuade some women standing at the rails to do the same; he would lower them safely he offered. But it was to no avail, in spite of his entreaties the ladies would not be lowered by rope – they must have steps they insisted. All this took time and when Polemann finally gave up the attempt and looked below, the gig was gone.

Jensen had cut the rope and fallen astern once more, claiming later that it was not safe to remain alongside any longer. Captain Thomas witnessed the gig rowing off into the fog and shouted out to them,

'Who is in that boat?'

He ordered them to come back and take some passengers on board with them. But Jensen and his crew stayed well out of sight.

One of Schiller's *two gigs, No 7, off her starboard quarter.*

Having seen to the launching of the two gigs, Polemann's next task was to assist Dr Boll, the ship's surgeon and chief engineer Leonard Fahrig in distributing life-jackets to all who were without one. They gave out about 40, but even this minor task was not without difficulties. Most passengers seemed unable to grasp the idea that the cork jackets needed to be fitted well up under the armpits and fastened tightly. They wanted them fixed around their stomach. Polemann warned that the life-jacket would then slip lower and result in them drowning. He had particular trouble with two men who objected to being told that if the belt was below the waistline it would up-end them and force their heads under water.

During the first hour after the *Schiller* struck, other officers and sailors were busy on the fore deck preparing the signalling equipment which would hopefully draw attention to the plight from other vessels nearby or people on the nearest coast. Men under the supervision of third mate Freese began firing rockets, roman candles and fireballs into the sky from the starboard side of the bridge and burning blue lights upon deck from around 10.30pm onwards. Others under first carpenter Erhling brought the ship's signal guns out and began preparing them for a cannonade which should have sounded for miles around.

Standing near to the signal guns were Franz Schellenberg and his friends from steerage. He watched the sailors load and fit the priming cap to one of the guns, knowing that the string-pulled trigger which should detonate it was stuck with paint. One of his friends, Wilhelm Kock from Rockport, Illinois, had once served in the artillery, and seeing the difficulty rushed to the bridge for a rocket. This he lit and playing its flame over the signal gun's trigger, burnt off the paint until it was released.

The next lifeboat to be launched was number 5, second from the stern on the starboard side. This was a proper, cork-lined lifeboat with a capacity for 60 or more people. It had been freed from its chocks but remained on deck, thickly crowded with men, one of whom was Cornish miner, Richard Williams, the man assisted into it earlier by Silas Hexter. A number of sailors working with Hillers and Heintze had already tried without success to order or coerce these men out so that it could be raised and swung out-board by the davits. Now that it was about to be launched, more men rushed in, fighting for a place there.

'The women and children had no chance,' said Henry Sterne later, who witnessed this despicable scramble.

Then, pushing his way through the crowds surrounding the boat, came Captain Thomas. Shortly afterwards Polemann arrived, having just completed distributing life-jackets. Although his assigned lifeboat was number 2, Polemann was ordered by the Captain to get in and take charge of the number 5 boat. It was no use, the boat was so thickly crowded he could not even get over the gunwale. Captain Thomas then urged him to drag them out by force but that too proved impossible. At length, the Captain drew his revolver and brandishing it above his head shouted,

'All landsmen, come out of that boat!'

Some refused point blank, others sat sullen and silent, but all remained there. The Captain squeezed the trigger of his pistol, firing three or four shots over their heads. At this show of determination several men scrambled hastily out of the boat, among them Richard Williams. Others remained, some now cowering beneath the boat's thwarts to hide from the Captain's wrath. This was not what the Captain wanted: he seems to have intended to clear this boat for women and children, but was prevented from doing so by these utterly selfish, self-preserving males. He tried then to cajole the men inside,

'If you will be quiet and come out, I will get you all safely ashore!'

But it had little effect.

The actions of these men would not have surprised the Captain too much. What was happening on the *Schiller* was no isolated case. The notion of 'women and children first' in times of shipwreck was as much ignored as it was honoured. With lifeboat drill an unheard-of discipline, it was often the strongest and fittest who survived best in the chaos and general panic which ensued following a wreck. The chance that lifeboats would be commandeered by men, even the crew itself, in utter disregard of women and children aboard, was high. So when his pistol failed to shift them from the lifeboat Captain Thomas gave up. Knowing that time was against him, he probably aimed then to get it launched quickly and move on to another boat in which women and children would be accommodated.

With a few having left it, the boat was light enough to be raised and this was done quickly by Hillers's sailors heaving on the block and tackle ropes. But as it hung suspended from the top of the davits, several large waves in succession broke right over the ship and the lifeboat. Some inside it were so scared they jumped back down on deck, but still 30 or more remained. Captain Thomas signalled Polemann to take charge and gave the order to lower away. As sailors operating the pulley ropes started the boat on its descent, he called out to his second officer,

'Goodbye old fellow, remember me to my friends.'

Christine Joens and her husband John had re-dressed hurriedly, having just undressed ready for bed when the *Schiller* went on to the rocks. Now they were on deck and had made their way through the crush of people to the ship's starboard rails, where the number 5 lifeboat was about to be lowered. John saw an opportunity. As the lifeboat began its descent he lifted Christine in his arms and threw her into it. Then he jumped down to join her. But they were not saved yet.

Immediately afterwards a large wave struck the lifeboat, raising its stern so high that the after tackle became unhooked from its davit, allowing the boat to drop suddenly at that end. At the same moment the fore tackle fouled a man's leg, dragging him up to the top of the davit from which the bow was suspended. The lifeboat then hung vertically, stern downwards. Most of those inside fell out, to struggle for life among the turbulent waves. Others still in the boat clung desperately to save themselves from the same fate. A quick-thinking sailor cut the boat free so that it toppled down into the heaving sea, but there it was capsized.

Several of those in the sea beside it, including the Joenses, managed after a while to right the lifeboat, which although upright was utterly swamped, its gunwales only inches above the water. They dragged themselves and each other inside. Many more, less strong or fortunate, drowned in the heavy swell or drifted away. Several were drowned inside the boat itself where they had stowed themselves beneath its thwarts to avoid the Captain's fury. Polemann had drifted away but swam until he was exhausted and managed to regain the boat, where he was dragged back in by those inside. Captain Thomas shouted encouragement to him but he had swallowed too much water to reply. At the same moment, a man near the Captain climbed up on the ship's rails and taking a chance leapt into the sea beside the lifeboat and hauled himself aboard. It was Richard Williams, the Cornish miner.

From the 30 or more originally in the lifeboat, there were just 12 survivors. Along with Polemann were seven crew, one of them being the youthful steward, Wilhelm Blohm. The only passengers were John and Christine Joens, Richard Williams and Charles Jantzen, a steerage passenger from New York who had a wife with him somewhere on board the ship. They were all standing waist deep in water with no baler, no oars, no compass; and they were drifting off into the swirling fog and pitch dark of the night in a water-filled boat which rode the waves in a way that seemed to threaten to founder at any moment. Behind them the *Schiller*'s mast and funnels were silhouetted in a blaze of flares and rockets fired off against the fog-grey night, while cabin lights glowed brightly in line along its hull. Captain Thomas had given the order for the signal guns to be fired as the lifeboat left the ship and the first of seven to ten charges was touched off with a loud report as Polemann and his waterlogged boat drifted off into the darkness. Compared to those still on board the mother ship, with still a chance that someone would see or hear their distress signals, the prospects for the 12 in the boat seemed by far the worse.

In the hour it had taken to launch three lifeboats, Hillers and Heintze had managed to get seven of *Schiller*'s complement of eight free of their crutches and swung out from their davits ready to be lowered into the sea. These were now all under the strict supervision of officers and sailors, keeping watch to prevent a repetition of the fiasco with number 5 and ensure that passengers were only allowed in when they were ready for launching. But the sea would no longer allow it. None of the port-side boats could possibly be lowered where waves were continually sweeping up and over the rails, while the tremendously heavy swell to starboard made it unlikely that any lifeboat could live in it. The Captain decreed,

'Boats must not be lowered until the order is given at a good chance,'

– meaning when the seas had subsided enough for long enough to favour success. The occasion never arose.

The tide was inexorably rising. It was low tide when the *Schiller* struck upon the rocks, but the water's steady encroachment inside the hull was approaching the first- and second-class passenger decks. Knowing well that inundation was inevitable, ex-Philadelphia restaurateur Leo Weste tried repeatedly to get his wife Hermine and their daughter to recognise the fact and leave their first-class stateroom for the spar deck. But they would not budge; their reply to his entreaties was,

'The Captain says we are safe here and must not move.'

Weste argued that the Captain had only said as much to keep down the panic among the women, but to no avail. They, like other ladies huddled together miserably with their children in the seclusion of gloom-filled cabins or the doomed opulence of the once cheerful saloon, retained full confidence in their Captain. They clung to the small ray of hope he had provided for them in this, their darkest hour.

Then there was hope – or so it appeared to those on the ship. At about 20 minutes to midnight, a finger of light pointed a path through the drifting fog and illuminated their darkness with long, searching rays. As the grey blanket lifted awhile, the winking lamp and tall, dark tower of Bishop Rock lighthouse became visible about two-thirds of a mile off the starboard bow. Now that they realised where they were – the Isles of Scilly, and in full view of the lighthouse keepers – rescue no longer seemed so remote a possibility. Some passengers expected the keepers to rescue them personally in a boat kept at the lighthouse; others thought they would surely telegraph news of their predicament to the nearest land, from where a lifeboat would soon come. Even if they had to await morning for salvation, they felt that the ship would surely survive intact through the night. The *Schiller* was a new ship and built of iron. In spite of the rocks grinding beneath its hull and the constant battering from the ever-rising, worsening sea above, they would all be saved.

The wreck of the Schiller *– as depicted by a* Harper's Weekly *artist.*

CHAPTER 10

•◆•

The Long Night

When able seaman Max Goldberger returned to the *Schiller*'s deck from the forecastle, having changed from his soaking wet nightshirt to dry clothing, he noticed immediately that the sea was beginning to sweep the decks from end to end. The strengthening wind was driving waves up and over the port side which then swilled down the sloping decks to drain off through the starboard scuppers. On that side of the vessel the heaving swell of an advancing tide rode in successive sweeps along its rivet-studded iron plates, occasionally lapping at the long row of first- and second-cabin portholes. Making conditions for the people on board worse still was the constant downpour of cold, fine drizzle.

It was not long after, about 11.30pm, that the first of the many gathered on deck, cold, wet and scared beyond measure, were plucked from their handholds on the ship by the growing force of the waves and swept off into the boiling surf. Their pitiful screams and cries as they were carried over the side were often scarcely heard above the tumult of crashing breakers, and in the pitch darkness they were lost to sight in an instant. The firemen and male passengers who had joined in a drunken debauch with the ship's store of spirits, had ended by throwing themselves down on deck in a stupor. They made little or no sound as they in turn were carried off by the waves.

With the sea becoming more tumultuous and angry, all hopes of launching the remaining lifeboats disappeared. Sailors watching over them dispersed one by one to seek their own means of survival, leaving passengers to climb in if they dare. New York tailor Johannes Rink and two other men made several attempts to get into lifeboat number 1, being driven back time and again by the roughness of the sea before they finally succeeded. On the ship's port side, three others including Frenchman Joseph Legenore clambered into number 6, braving the dangers of repeated, overwhelmingly large breakers there. From that boat Legenore bore witness to scenes of utter confusion and desperation. In the minutes before midnight and for some time afterwards people searched vainly for some part or place on the ship which would afford them shelter from the worst of the waves. They huddled together in groups, women screaming and wailing, children sobbing, and the hardiest of men cringing under the perpetual onslaught from icy Atlantic waters. Some moved slowly around the decks in their search for protection from the seas which broached over the vessel. At times Legenore's boat was full of people believing that it was the best place to be in; then they would move to somewhere else which appeared to offer greater security, leaving the Frenchman and his two companions to themselves – until another group joined them. Every now and then individuals or even whole groups of people would be dragged screaming over the side by some huge, merciless wave and lost to sight in the darkness.

Legenore had not been there long when the lifeboat just forward of his was lifted out of its davits on a wave which dashed it against one of the ship's funnels. As the rising tide made the *Schiller* list more dramatically, the incline to starboard was creating a great deal of stress upon the lofty smokestacks, and the sudden shock from a heavy lifeboat driven against the after one was too much. The 35ft-tall ironwork broke away at its base and plummeted down towards number 3 lifeboat, in which third mate Freese and several sailors remained on standby for launching. A number of passengers, Captain Thomas and Heintze the fourth mate, were standing nearby. The falling smokestack struck the boat, smashing it to smithereens and killing Freese, his sailors and some passengers all at once. The Captain and Heintze had narrow escapes.

A few waves later it was the turn of Legenore's lifeboat to be dashed inboard from its davits, landing on deck with force and filling with water at the same time. His two companions were so frightened they jumped out leaving the Frenchman alone to face further onslaughts from the sea. When the next came the boat was carried almost over the ship's side, throwing him out. He clambered back in only to then find it being driven hard against the mainmast and himself tossed out once more on to the deck. By then the lifeboat was full of holes where it had struck against projecting irons and other deck equipment, but still he returned to it and awaited what fate would bring next.

Johannes Rink, in lifeboat number 1, the furthest forward on the ship's starboard side, was having a similarly rough time. Soon after he and two other men managed to board it, one end of the boat was unhooked from its davit causing it to drop down into the sea, this probably caused by the crash of the funnel on to its neighbouring boat. The two others fell and were immediately washed away. Rink also found himself in the water but was able to keep his handhold on the boat. For a long time, possibly hours, he clutched grimly at the up-ended lifeboat as it plunged and rose with the swell, banging and bumping against the iron side of the ship. But as the vessel's list worsened and the tide rose, his lifeboat gradually began to float on a more even keel. At length, the end still tethered to the davit above was smashed in by the constant battering against the ship's side and broke away, leaving the remainder with Rink clinging to it floating free.

With all means of escape by their own lifeboats gone, the *Schiller*'s sorry occupants could only hope for rescue from the shore. But the Bishop Rock light which had blinked across the waves at them for almost an hour raised only false hopes in their hearts. When its glimmer vanished as the fog descended once more at 12.30, there was only hour upon hour of waiting in the mounting horror of a black, storm-lashed night ahead of them. It was becoming increasingly difficult to remain on the sea-swept, slippery decks, yet there were only a few places of refuge with a chance of surviving left to them.

Franz Schnellenberg and his steerage friends found sanctuary of sorts in a small room by the wheelhouse, where pails and ropes were kept. Many cabin passengers returned to their staterooms, remaining huddled there alone or with family and friends, often in prayer. In the saloon, ladies sat pale and motionless, resigned to their fate; the mothers among them comforting red-eyed and tearful children as best they could. The rising tide soon drove them upwards. Most abandoned their staterooms or the saloon as soon as the sumptuous carpets were awash, hastily treading the waterfall cascade of the steps in the vestibule to the shelter of the pavilion, or mounting other companionways to the deck and making their way via handholds to other deckhouses. Wheelhouse, chart-house and pavilion were soon crammed tight and the doors slammed shut to keep out the sea. Almost all of the ship's complement of over 50 children were divided between these three deckhouses. Inside them, they clung to each other and their mothers, all of them crying out aloud to anyone who passed by on deck to save them.

The majority of the women and children, Hermine Weste and her daughter among them, gathered together in the pavilion. All were packed together, as many as 100 people in a 53-by-20ft glazed iron construction situated over the central sky-light of the saloon. Many were dressed only in nightclothes or with a coat thrown hastily over them after their initial rude awakening from sleep. Oil lamps burning there illuminated the frightened, huddled mass, their faces pallid and ghastly in the glow as the waves beat mercilessly against their four-walled sanctuary, shaking it visibly.

After the fall of the smokestack on number 3 lifeboat, Captain Thomas and Richard Heintze made their way to the bridge. Being raised above the deck by ten feet or so there was less chance of being swept overboard by the successive waves. Other crew members joined them there, including able seamen Max Goldberger and Hans Beck, Dr Boll the ship's surgeon, fourth engineer J. Kundel and chief engineer Leonard Fahrig. Soon, considerable numbers were gathered there, clinging to the rails around it and packed together tightly. Franz Schnellenberg deserted his cubby hole by the wheelhouse for a place on the bridge. Dwight Klink, the young man entrusted to the Captain's care, was also there, as were others eager to keep within range of George Thomas's calm assurances and show of bravery. The whole of the party centred on Mrs Ridgeway – her son-in-law Charles Walter and his two little girls, her black maid, her friend and relative Mrs Caverly and daughter Amy – all congregated on the bridge with the Captain.

Some passengers and crew chose to try their luck further aloft in the rigging and yards of the masts. First mate Heinrich Hillers climbed half-way up the foremast at around 12.30, joining Norwegian steward Hans Peterson among the many crewmen there already. Eventually, 30 to 40 people were there, including five women, clinging tight or lashing themselves to ropes, chains and shrouds. Another group of 34 were in the mainmast rigging, trying equally to place themselves above the breakers crashing and rolling unremittingly over the decks below.

Several of the passengers on the mainmast only ventured aloft at the instigation of one man. Captain Daniel W. Percival, the master mariner from Cape Cod bound for a new command at Hamburg, had urged them to take to the rigging, and cajoled them into climbing further and further aloft to save themselves. Leo Weste still felt bitter that his wife and daughter had not trusted his word over Captain Thomas's, and were now taking refuge in the pavilion, but he was the first to follow Percival. Up the rat-lines crossing the lower shrouds they climbed, then on to the small platform of the 'main top', where the lower-mast gave way to the topmast and where the top chains from which the main yard was raised and lowered stretched above them.

Next to follow were Henry Sterne and Carl Kuhn, another saloon passenger from New York, heading for St Gall, Switzerland. Urged on upwards by Percival, Sterne climbed right to the upper topsail yard and went out some way on its starboard side while Kuhn took position higher still on the topgallant-mast. Others who joined them included able seaman Henry Wallis. Many people lashed themselves into position with ropes and lines – Henry Sterne tied himself to the yard but was careful to use a slip knot.

The last firing of *Schiller*'s signal guns was at around 1.30am. Over a period of two hours, between seven and ten charges had been set off, each one in a bag said to have been two handbreadths in size and capable of making a very loud report. Eventually the powder became so damp it would no longer ignite and the guns were abandoned. All was not quiet though. Out in the troughs and peaks of the Atlantic swell the seven men in number 8 gig could distinctly hear the *Schiller*'s iron plates cracking as the rocks below her ground into them. Silas Hexter thought it sounded like thunder. The cracking from *Schiller*'s hull was accompanied by almost continuous screams from women and children which tore at the hearts of the men in the gig. The pistol shots heard earlier had left them wondering what had happened. Keeping as close to the ship as they dare, always keeping the prow of the gig towards its lights, they were partly intending to rescue people from the sea around her and partly hoping that should a ship come from the shore they would be picked up.

Number 7 gig had long since left the vicinity of the mother ship, after its commander Simon Jensen had ignored the Captain's call to return for passengers. He hoped to find land somewhere, and the five crew rowed steadily through the mountainous seas, taking good care to steer clear of any breakers where they suspected rocks might be lurking. After an hour or more the beam from the lighthouse cut a swathe through the fog over their heads. They rowed on towards its source, hoping to get help.

The fog lifted as they drew nearer to the lighthouse, enabling them to see the number 5 lifeboat drifting helplessly about a half-mile away. Polemann and the 11 others standing waist deep in the almost submerged boat saw Jensen's gig at the same moment and called out to them for assistance. Their ordeal had lasted for three hours and they were utterly exhausted. Despite their predicament, Christine Joens, the sole female among them, was in noticeably good spirits, although she had hurt her side badly when thrown into the boat by her husband.

Jensen's crew changed tack straight away, but when they reached the lifeboat Polemann expressed doubts about embarking his boatload into their gig, as it was so much awash from having lost its plug when being launched. At first, only four men and Mrs Joens were transferred to it. Jensen's men then passed three oars to Polemann and the other six men remaining in the lifeboat so they could row it. This proved impossible with it being so water-logged. Assured by Jensen that the gig could hold 25 people, Polemann and his six men then also clambered across and settled into the narrow craft.

They tried at first to tow the lifeboat behind the gig, but being so heavy with the water inside, the task proved too difficult and was eventually abandoned. Polemann proposed that they go back to the ship, get back on board and await the dawn, when he was sure that rescue would come. This was attempted for some time, but the gig always went well astern of *Schiller* due to the tide. There were people struggling in the sea around the wreck, but they were unable to get close enough to offer assistance. Then an attempt was made to reach the lighthouse, getting within range enough to hear its fog bell very faintly. But finding they had not the strength to continue rowing against the strong pull of the tide, they finally shipped oars and laid-to until morning.

As the tide rose the sea became more monstrous. With the set of the tide to the south-west and the strengthening wind blowing in the opposing direction, it was whipped to a frenzy of foam and spume, rolling pitilessly over the stricken ship in endless, crashing succession. People whose chilled-to-the-marrow hands relaxed in their tenuous grip on the ship's superstructure were ruthlessly plucked away with every overwhelming wave. The two remaining lifeboats, numbers 2 and 6 on the port side, badly battered and knocked around on the deck, were finally swept away into the raging sea. In number 6 was Joseph Legenore; bruised and half-conscious by his long tenure inside it, he only became aware that he was in the sea and away from the ship much later.

Steerage passenger Franz Schnellenberg had followed the example set by Heinrich Hillers, abandoning the bridge to wade through the waves and climb the foremast. It was a timely move, for as he reached a rope ladder to cling tightly to, a huge sea inundated the bridge and swept many of those huddled there away. For a while he stayed on the ladder, unable to climb further up because of others crowded above him. At length he reached out to a swinging rope and was able to pull himself up on to the 'crow's nest' (probably the topmast cross-trees). Below him the scene was horrific:

> *…four women with their children held tight to a bench and with supernatural strength fought against the deluge, their piercing cries reached me each time a wave took one of them away. This fight against death lasted about one half-hour, when a sympathetic wave took the last one away.*[1]

Penetrating screams came from forward, where a man lay with his leg trapped beneath the anchor chain. He was tossed violently back and forth by the waves, but no one dare go to help for fear of being carried overboard. His screams later turned to sobbing and then finally, silence.

Captain Percival was doing his best to keep up the spirits of his shivering, water-drenched companions on the mainmast. His maritime experience instilled confidence and his good humour cheered them in their most dire and desperate moments. He carried on a long conversation with Henry Sterne and had kept up his encouragement of the others for over almost two hours when, without warning, one of the chains above him gave way and crashed down, striking him a blow to the head. It killed him instantly, dashing his brains out and scattering them over those below. Leo Weste was next to Percival in the main-top, where the body remained lodged. He was suffering so severely from the cold and wet that he overcame his repulsion and used the dead man to shield him from the constantly overwhelming spray. Sterne seemed not to have noticed the sudden death of Captain Percival lower down, and when he received no answers to his attempts at conversation, assumed he had succumbed to the cold.

But for Weste and others on both masts with wives and children in the pavilion, a worse horror was soon to follow. At about 2.30am a gigantic roller crashed over the vessel. It pounded into the pavilion with terrifying force, smashing its glass panes to smithereens, and sweeping up the entire iron structure in its tremendous, headlong rush. Women and children who huddled inside, wretched and petrified but believing themselves to be in the safest place on the ship, were in an instant torn from each other and tumbled overboard to an icy death in the deep, dark waters. As they went their screams sounded loud and pitiful above the tumult of the sea. Henry Sterne recollected much later:

> Such a shriek was raised as I trust I shall never hear the like of again… A long, loud cry for help, then the piercing cry of a child, and then nothing was heard but the waves as they beat over the ship.[2]

To those who witnessed the destruction of the pavilion and the terrible and abrupt end of all those sheltering inside, the shock was hard to bear. Leo Weste was just one man who had lost his wife and daughter in those few seconds of utter mayhem. Other men on the masts or elsewhere on board shared his agony at the loss of loved-ones; wives and mothers, sons and daughters snatched away from them by the maw of the pitiless ocean.

Further forward on the ship, Captain Thomas was mustering all of his indomitable spirit to cheer and encourage the passengers and crew around him to stick together. Whatever his true feelings in the terrible situation he bore the brunt of responsibility for he put on a brave face to all and was never less than positive. To people on deck still, who asked him what they should do, he called out,

'Come with me to the bridge!'

– as if somehow he held the key to survival. Passengers especially looked to him above all others for the means of salvation, and he acted out the role of saviour as best he could. But no one was safe anywhere on board.

As the seas became more formidable in their destructive power and began to break over the bridge itself, the numbers clinging there were inexorably whittled away. The weak, the weary and the unwary were one by one caught up and swept off into the raging surf. A few sailors abandoned the increasingly untenable position for a safer place; Heintze leaving to join Hillers and the others on the foremast in the early hours of the morning, while Goldberger and Beck went to the mainmast. Others less strong or resourceful in seafaring ways left as victims of the endless, onrushing waves: Dwight Klink, Charles Walter and his little girls, Mrs Ridgeway and her black servant, Mrs Caverly and Amy; all being washed away in turn. Whatever Mrs Caverly's nightmare of that first night aboard ship had been, it was overtaken by an infinitely worse reality.

At 3am only three men remained on the bridge; Captain Thomas, a quartermaster and an elderly sailor who clutched with grim determination to the railings. They were on the weather side where it was highest above the water but lashed constantly by the sea. Every time a wave broke over them they disappeared from sight as if washed away, only to re-emerge as it rolled on. Their clothes were gradually torn to pieces by the force of the waves. Captain Thomas dragged his trousers off with his feet as they were in shreds.

The quartermaster was first to go. A wave took him unawares, wrenching his grip free to drag him away. He swam desperately against its force and managed to reach the bridge again, almost to regain his foothold. But then another wave caught him and carried him well out to sea. Soon afterwards, someone called out to the Captain from the deck below, asking for assistance. He went down to help but as soon as he reached the deck a large sea rushed across it, tearing off his coat as he tried to save himself and then taking him too over the side. He was holding tightly to the foretopsail brace and managed to cling on for a while, but it swung wildly in the wind and the sea dashed him up against the side of the ship. Weakened and stunned after three successive heavy blows, he let go and was swept away. Then, only the old sailor remained on the bridge. He held firm for a while but finally joined the others

Even at this late hour there were some people below decks, where the rising tide must have been well advanced. At 3am, Hexter and the others in gig 8 could still hear screaming coming from the ship's cabins, the lights of which glimmered through the fog. Apparently, there was nobody on deck by that time. Not long afterwards all the lights except that on the ship's masthead went out, but screams were still to be heard for up to another hour. Hexter said later:

The last screaming that I heard, and which I shall never forget, was the voice of a little child, who was, we believed, in the first cabin. [3]

Yet the deck was not entirely devoid of people at three. The Frahm twins were there until 3.30, when the sea finally wrenched them over the side together. Once in the heaving sea, they were soon split up. Charles managed to swim to a floating plank and cling to it for some while. Then a door came his way upon which he was able to pull himself out of the chilling seawater. Even the position of those who had climbed up the masts was becoming more perilous. Apart from the biting wind, continuous rain and salt spray from which each suffered terribly, the arrival of high tide at around 5am brought the sea level up by 25ft from where it was when *Schiller* first struck the rocks. Only the tops of the port-side davits were not submerged, and the swell came up to the mainsail yards. On occasions a large roller would break over the masthead itself, overwhelming people and tearing at them as they clung tenaciously to wires, shrouds and spars.

Beneath them, the vessel's hull strained terribly with each movement of the waves, and loud, ominous cracking sounds came from where it ground against the rocks. Passenger trunks and luggage, mail bags and cargo, floated out and away from the ship through large breeches in its iron plates. The ship settled even more to the starboard side, listing about 15 degrees, until the ends of its lower yards began to dip into the sea. Her stern was beginning to break away.

NOTES

[1] Franz Otto Schnellenburg, *The Shipwreck of the 'Schiller' on May 7, 1875 Near the Scilly Islands off England*. Personal account.

[2] *Manchester Guardian*, 10 May 1875

[3] *The Times*, 11 May 1875

The stricken Schiller *breaks up on the Retarrier Ledges – an impression by artist Clive Carter.*
CLIVE CARTER AND RICHARD LARN

CHAPTER 11

•◆•

Rescue

Rapid and *Shade of Evening* were luggers engaged in lobster fishing that worked out of the small port of Sennen, near Land's End. On 7 May they had been fishing off the Isles of Scilly and they and their crews, ten men in all, were spending the night lying off St Agnes. When Jacob Deason, the superannuated pilot who lived there, decided to dress and put to sea on a rescue mission, it was these men and their luggers he turned to. Two hours had passed since he had heard the reports he surmised were from a vessel in distress near Bishop Rock, and he decided they should wait no longer for conditions to improve.

Deason was a man in his seventies. As a youth he had been captured by a French privateer while fishing off the islands and taken to South America, from where he had returned eventually after jumping ship. His companions were equally tough: all men brought up in a close-knit seafaring community and experienced in the rough waters west of Cornwall; four brothers and a father and son being among them. But as they rowed out from the island at three in the morning, into the darkness, the thick fog and high seas, each one knew that their powers of seamanship would be tried severely. They searched the Western Rocks for two hours, but were unable to sight any vessel. In such perilous conditions they dared not venture further, so they returned to St Agnes, convinced that no shipwreck had taken place. The cannon shots heard must have been from a passing steamer, they reported, on arriving back at the island.

At 3.30am, half an hour after the Sennen luggers had set off, Stephen Hicks, the ex-ship's carpenter turned pilot, got a first glimpse of daybreak. At that, he lay his pipe down, got off his sofa, and went to call his brother Obadiah. Obadiah and his wife Mary were joint owners of a 30ft-long gig, the *O & M* (Obadiah and Mary) which was used frequently to relieve the lighthouse keepers on Bishop Rock. Having also heard

A St Agnes gig lying alongside the lifeboat later stationed on the island.

the signal guns, Obadiah was ready to put her to sea. She left St Agnes at 4am with a crew of six, three of whom were just lads. Pulling hard into the wind on their long ash oars, they headed the gig into the blanket of fog and out to cross three miles of terrifyingly rough water to the Western Rocks. At about the same time but unknown to them, two other six-oared gigs, the *Thomas* and the *Bee*, left St Agnes on the same mission. The narrow, Cornish elm gig was an eminently seaworthy craft, having been in times past much favoured by Scilly smugglers, who thought little of rowing and sailing the 250 miles across to Roscoff in Brittany for contraband. Yet this, much shorter outing, was no less risky a venture.

George Gould's watch at Bishop Rock ended at 4am and senior keeper James Daniel took over once more. The fog was then very thick but began to clear in patches at around 5.45. The wrecked ship became visible again. Through his telescope Daniel could see that only the masts stood out of the water and many of her sails hung loose, which he supposed were from the gaskets having given way. On one mast he counted 26 people. There was a woman in the starboard rigging in a sitting position between two men, probably lashed there, he thought.

Minutes passed and then Daniel saw two gigs rowing around the neck of Great Crebawethen, the most northerly of the Western Rocks, situated about two-thirds of a mile from the wrecked vessel. They were from St Agnes. He recognised the white hull with a black stripe along it as being the Hicks family's gig which relieved the lighthouse-keepers; the other was a yellow boat. The two gigs stopped and the men in them appeared to be consulting each other and pulling bits and pieces out of the water. Afterwards, they seemed to turn away from the wreck; but the fog descended once more, so thick that Daniel was unable to see them further

The *O & M* and her crew had spent more than two hours rowing out to the Western Rocks and groping their way in and out of the rugged, reef strewn islets through the fog. On reaching Great Crebawethen they were ready to turn back, having seen or heard nothing. Even the sea birds on the islets were quiet, and this led them to suppose that there was nothing out of the ordinary around to disturb them. With the fog lifting a little they then saw the yellow gig (either the *Thomas* or the *Bee*) for the first time. Its occupants had not seen anything either. Both gigs were about to turn back for St Agnes when Obadiah Hicks, steering his gig, saw the masts and sails of a ship to the westwards. She seemed to be riding at anchor. The Hickses waved the yellow gig to follow them and started towards the ship, rowing through the Neck of Crebawethen and into the heaving Atlantic beyond. But then the fog closed in and they were unable to see it any longer, though they continued rowing in its direction.

Further east, the islanders of St Mary's had no such intimations of a shipping disaster. At six that morning the nightwatchman at John Banfield's signal station was relieved in the usual fashion by the day-man and commenced to walk home. Meeting a coastguard and exchanging views, he learned from him that a gun had definitely been heard during the night. The nightwatchman's doubts about the nature of the noise which had rattled the watchtower window during the night were dispelled by this information, though he could not believe it was the *Schiller* signalling her passing. Even so, he went straight to Banfield's house and told him about hearing a signal gun at 1am. Banfield went immediately to the St Mary's telegraph office, awoke the telegrapher, and sent the message to the Eagle Line's agent at Plymouth:

> *Watchman heard one gun just before one o' clock this morning: may possibly have been Schiller. Weather then and still thick.*[1]

By telegraphing, Banfield was mindful of the previous overlooking of an Eagle Line steamer's signals: he was determined that *Schiller* should not arrive at Plymouth unannounced.

Just before dawn the fog cleared for a while, enabling those on the *Schiller*'s masts to see the lighthouse once more. They shouted and waved for help, but most were weak and exhausted from their continual soaking by rain, the overwhelming seas and the effects of the fresh, biting wind. With one foot on the cross-trees and the other on the sloping foremast, Franz Schnellenberg needed all his concentration to remain there. When the sea came over him he often lost his foothold and found himself clinging to a rope 'like a flag floating in air'. Others were plucked away one by one. Nearby, lashed together in the shrouds were Augustus Felkstow, the chief steward of second cabin, and his stewardess wife Maria. Exhausted, they eventually disappeared together into the sea.

Leo Weste was so numb that he could no longer retain his hold on the mainmast top, where the body of Captain Percival still sheltered him. His grip faltered until he fell away from the ship, into the heaving sea below. Once there he was fortunately able to locate some floating wreckage to cling to. Shortly afterwards, the mast which had given him and many others the hope of survival, sheered off at its base, where the sea had beaten and weakened it for hours on end, and plunged over the side.

The heavy iron mast with its full weight of wet sails, wire shrouds and rigging hit the sea, along with a terribly cry of anguish from those upon it, and went to the bottom almost immediately. As he fell with it Henry Sterne let go of the lifebuoy he had carried since cutting it from the taffrail long beforehand, and went down with the mast to the seabed. There he managed to release the slip knot he was tied with and rise quickly to the surface – others more securely bound drowned. On the surface he soon located his lifebuoy and with that around one shoulder and his other arm over a floating spar, was able to keep afloat among debris from the ship. An American trunk soon came his way on which he was able to lever himself up with the spar. He then lay upon it as it floated, gripping tight to its handles as it rose and fell among the waves.

Able seaman Max Goldberger fell into the sea with Sterne. Once there, he gathered up pieces of board from among the floating wreckage by the ship, and lashing them all together with a ratline, managed to improvise a raft. On to this he assisted four others; Carl Kuhn, able seaman Henry Wallis and two stokers. These five, together with Sterne and Weste, were the only ones to survive from the 34 people who had been on the mainmast when it fell. One other, sailor Hans Beck, managed to get to the deck and make his way to the foremast.

Having lost sight of the ship when the fog rolled in shortly after they had first sighted it, the Hickses and their companions in the two St Agnes gigs were most surprised to see when she re-emerged into view that far from being at anchor, she was a wreck. Moreover, she had lost a mast since they had first spied her. Pulling harder still at their long oars they soon found themselves among floating wreckage from the vessel. Then they heard the shouts of men swimming amongst it.

Sterne, Goldberger and the others had been in the sea for about 40 minutes. Two had been washed on and off rocks and most were in a state of exhaustion when the St Agnes gigs drew near to them. First to be taken up was Leo Weste, dragged into the *O & M* in a state of insensibility. The Hickses also picked up Henry Sterne; he had shouted to them for help after sighting their boat from the crest of a wave when he was in great danger of being washed against some rocks. Goldberger and Carl Kuhn made up the full complement of survivors in the *O & M*, while Wallis and the other stoker were taken up by the yellow gig.

Once they were on board there was little more that the crew of the gigs could do. The *Schiller* with its foremast crowded with people was a further quarter of a mile to the west and although they made several brave attempts, it was quite unapproachable because of the rough sea and wreckage around it. Their position was dangerous enough as it was: the Hicks gig had 11 men in it, one of them baling all the time, and they had lost their rudder amongst the floating wreckage. All they could do for the best was turn and make for St Mary's as quickly as possible to summon the lifeboat. They changed direction, with the piteous cries for help from those still on the wreck borne to them on the wind, tearing at their ears. Once they reached the Neck of Rosevean, a narrow gap in the Western Rocks, and the comparatively smoother waters beyond it, they set sail and scudded to St Mary's on the wind.

In the meantime, Jacob Deason and the men of the two Sennen fishing luggers were dissatisfied with the result of their earlier, unsuccessful mercy mission. At 5am they put to sea for a second time. Once again they searched fruitlessly for two hours or more until, arriving at Great Crebawethen, the fog had lifted sufficiently for them to see the wrecked vessel with its one surviving mast thick with people. The two luggers were rowed out beyond the rocks towards them, into seas which were becoming more dangerous by the minute. With the set of the tide running against the wind, water was breaking over their gunwales continually and in each of them a man was baling out the whole time. To lessen the risk to themselves the two luggers ran as close as they dare to each other, so that if one should founder the other would rescue its crew.

It was just before 8am when the two St Agnes boats led by the Hicks gig arrived at Hugh Town Harbour, St Mary's. Once the fate of the wrecked steamer was known there, the lifeboat *Henry Dundas*, established only during the previous year under the terms of a legacy, was swiftly manned and got ready, directed by her coxswain, Alfred Hicks. To save some of the time it would take for the 12 men manning the lifeboat's oars to reach the scene of the wreck, Captain Gibson of the 150-ton *Lady of the Isles*, the West Cornwall Railway Company's little screw steamer, then offered to tow them. She left harbour with the lifeboat and the two St Agnes gigs behind her as well. But events on board the *Schiller* were not going to await her arrival.

At the time that *Lady of the Isles* and its little fleet was steaming out into Broad Sound, around 8am, there were 29 men remaining from their overnight ordeal on *Schiller*'s foremast. None of the five women there earlier had survived. Sailor Hans Beck had climbed on to the mast only after the mainmast was lost, but most had been there all

West Cornwall Railway Co's Scilly-Penzance packet steamer Lady of the Isles.

night. With the sea having now risen well up the mast so that the lower yards were almost under water, there were few places left to find refuge. Twenty men, including Beck and Hillers were clinging to the foretopsail-yard, Schnellenberg was lodged in the cross-trees, while the remainder were further up in the chains and rigging. Having already witnessed the rescue of men from the mainmast by the St Agnes boats, they were expectant of other boats arriving shortly and all eyes searched hopefully for signs of activity on St Agnes, just visible to the north-east as the fog drifted and slowly dispersed.

A whistle and the puffing noise of a steamer was heard in the distance and the men's spirits raised in hope. But it was then that a strong gust of wind filled the loose

Packet steamer leaving Hugh Town pier.

sails. The mast gave out an ominous crack below and began slowly to twist and tilt over. At this the men clambered higher and higher up, 'like so many rats' – as Hillers later described. It gathered momentum quickly with their weight uppermost, accelerating into a terrifying dive, tearing loose shrouds and rigging wires which flailed and whipped through the air about the petrified men on its yards, who were dropping off and diving into the tumbling waters below. The tremendous splash as it hit the sea signalled the end for most of them.

Hillers swam, supported by the life-jacket he had obtained from below his bunk before climbing the mast. After some time he came up to a body wearing a circular lifebuoy. He recognised the man as the ship's quartermaster and clung tenaciously to this lifebuoy and its dead occupant. Fourth mate Heintze, wearing another lifebuoy, swam nearby. Three more from the *Schiller*'s crew, Peterson, Beck and a sailor, who had thus far survived the fall of the foremast, also swam or drifted in the vicinity.

Steerage passenger Franz Schnellenberg found that his life-jacket kept him afloat, but the waves often closed over his head forcing him to hold his breath. He too eventually reached a floating body and supported himself with it for some time, until one of the sailors, clinging to a window frame, drifted nearby. This the sailor refused to share, saying it was too small for both, but at that moment a long board drifted close by on which Schnellenberg was able to raise himself. He lay upon it for a long time, allowing the waves to wash over his tired limbs, until the attention of sea birds gave him cause for alarm. Screeching loudly, they swooped so close to him he could feel the wind from their wings. He was afraid, and shouted to drive them away, but they kept returning. Then his limbs grew increasingly numb and his hands would no longer grip the board. Fatigued, he finally slipped into unconsciousness.

They were in the water for about an hour before the Sennen fishing luggers arrived. The luggers had not progressed far from Crebawethen when *Schiller*'s sole remaining mast fell. Approaching near to the wreck, the men rowing them heard a call and saw seven men floating ahead. They pulled towards them and took them on board. Hillers and the dead quartermaster were taken up by Jacob Deason and the crew of the *Rapid*: Heintze was picked up by the *Shade of Evening*. The other four men were found places in either boat. As there was no one else alive in the vicinity to be saved, the crews then turned and pulled away towards St Mary's, using the Neck of Rosevean to shorten the journey as did the two Hicks gigs before them. One of the rescued men was in a bad way and on their arrival at Hugh Town died, in spite of extended efforts to revive him by a surgeon and other helpers. When he came to, Franz Schnellenberg found himself being carried along a street by two men. He was safe at Hugh Town, where he was to receive the best of care.

By mid-morning, the known survivors of the disaster numbered 12, all of them brought in by the two gigs and two luggers from St Agnes. There was no living person at the scene of the wreck to welcome the arrival of the *Lady of the Isles* and its flotilla in tow behind. In fact, had they not known the precise position of the wreck

View of Hugh Town harbour, 1875.
GRAPHIC MAGAZINE

Hugh Street, Hugh Town, St Mary's.

it would have been difficult to spot her. All that was left of the once elegant steamship above the waves was wreckage; cargo, lumber, mailbags and luggage spread over a wide area. They had passed several bodies on the way out to the scene and returned to St Mary's with just 29 mailbags.

NOTES
[1] *The Times*, 4 June.

CHAPTER 12

...•...

Final Tally

It was around the time that the mainmast fell, at around daybreak, that the *Schiller*'s own gigs left the vicinity of their mother ship and went in search of land. Polemann, Jensen and the others in number 7 were drifting near the lighthouse when, as the fog drifted and lifted awhile, they saw the wreck silhouetted against the glow of approaching day. It was some distance off but they could see that one funnel was gone. Both masts were then still there, crowded with people. When they glimpsed the grey outline of St Agnes appearing on the horizon, they rowed towards it. Number 8 had remained throughout the long night as close as her men dare to the *Schiller*, rowing slowly around her. The men in the gig were bitterly disappointed, thinking that by this time a passing steamer should have come and rescued them. When the mainmast went over the side, and on it the ship's sole light, they could no longer see the vessel, only hear the sea washing over it. At that, they too set off to find land.

Number 7 gig, with Jensen's crew plus Polemann and those rescued from lifeboat number 5, first tried to reach St Agnes when it was seen briefly through the fog at around 6am. For a time though, they had been forced to shelter in the lee of some rocks out of the intensity of the wind, and the island was lost in the fog when they tried to resume the journey. With the compass on board out of order they had no means of maintaining a course, and in avoiding the many rocks and rocky islets soon lost all sense of direction.

Eventually, having rowed around for hours in the fog, they saw land and a small harbour where a ship was riding at anchor. On their approach a boat put out from the shore and towed them in. The time was around 8.30 and they were at last safe in the village of New Grimsby on the west coast of the isle of Tresco. Some, including

Left: *New Grimsby harbour, Tresco, with the Isle of Bryher beyond.*

Above: *New Grimsby village, Tresco.*

Christine Joens, were by then in a very poor state; two men had lost consciousness altogether.

The other gig left the vicinity of the *Schiller* a little later. The men inside had no compass at all and had not seen any sign of land to guide them in choosing a direction to row. After an hour passed by a cry was heard. Silas Hexter turned from rowing and saw first a naked body floating and beyond it two men alive in the water. He and his companions shouted 'All right!' to let the men know they were seen. The first man to be dragged into the gig was utterly exhausted and barely conscious. He was later found to be steerage passenger, Charles Henry Percy, of London. The other man was in better shape, for it was he who had called out them. He was floating on a door and was rather heavily built, so heavy that the crew had great difficulty in lifting him from it into the gig. Once there his first words were to ask after his twin brother William – his name was Charles Frahm.

With ten men now in the gig they rowed for another hour without any clue to their direction. Then the noise of a steamer was heard through the fog. They headed off in the direction of its whistle but failed to find it. Later on, as the fog cleared a little, they saw some sailing vessels, but in spite of hailing them they were not seen and the ships sailed away. Then there was something black in the distance. It was a cloud some said, others argued that it was land. Drawing closer, the realisation that it actually was land gave them hope for the first time that they would survive.

Pulling at their oars with a new spirit, they passed along a rocky coastline to starboard until a house came into view. But before making that final run in to the shore, where deliverance awaited them, the oars were shipped for a few moments of prayer. Then they rowed in and dragged the gig on to the sandy beach. Realising that the house was part of a small village, they separated and went to different houses, where a friendly welcome, dry clothing and food restored them after their ten-hour ordeal. It was around nine in the morning when they arrived at Gimbal Porth, the north entrance to Old Grimsby harbour on the east side of the isle of Tresco. Without knowing it they had been carried miles northwards, right around the northern end of the islands of Bryher and Tresco.

Three more men still floated out at sea. Frenchman Joseph Legenore, whose much holed lifeboat was washed off *Schiller*'s deck in the early hours, drifted alone throughout the darkness and on well beyond dawn. Passing at one time within sight of the ship's gigs, he had been driven by the wind, and later drawn by the subsiding tide, to the north-west. Holding tenaciously to his floating but mostly submerged craft, he too was submerged with it at times and had to hold his breath awhile. Then, when the tide turned, he was brought back, coming close to St Mary's even at one point. The crew of a cutter from Bryher eventually picked him up.

The cutter, also named *Rapid* like one of the St Agnes luggers, had just set out from Bryher that Saturday morning when its crew saw something waving at them through the fog. Heading towards it they came first upon a man in a life-jacket floating along with one arm through the rope loop of a boat's fender. He was picked up in a very weak condition. The cutter then went on to the source of the waving, which proved to be a man in a submerged ship's lifeboat. Joseph Legenore's hours of misery were at last concluded as he also was taken aboard the cutter. The other survivor turned out to be Louis Reiderer, a second-cabin passenger bound for Ellwangen in Wurtemburg. Reiderer's wife and little girl had been accompanying him on board the *Schiller*. The two men were taken to St Mary's, arriving at about 10am.

Last to be saved was Johannes Rink, the young New York tailor. Having departed the *Schiller* grasping tightly to a large, broken piece of a ship's lifeboat, he had remained afloat for nine hours in tremendously high seas in and around the jagged rocks of the islands' coastline. Much earlier in the night he had once been spotted by the men in the number 8 gig, cresting the top of a wave before disappearing from sight in a trough. But from then on he was lost to the dark and fog. By 11am next morning, cold, stiff, soaking wet and barely conscious, he was floating along in Smith's Sound, a channel between St Agnes and the islets of Hellwethers and Annet to the west. Uriah Legg of St Agnes found him there, and taking him into his boat carried him to the island, where his condition was restored before he was transferred to join the other survivors at St Mary's.

Until noon, the known survivors at St Mary's were those rescued from the ship's masts and the two men taken up by the Bryher cutter. News that other survivors had reached Tresco was brought across to St Mary's by Algernon Dorrien-Smith, Lord Proprietor of the Isles of Scilly and resident of Tresco Abbey, who arrived at Hugh Town by boat around midday. He brought with him the *Schiller*'s second mate, Erwin Polemann. Polemann, not yet knowing that others had survived and were already on St Mary's, intended to make a deposition at the German Consulate and requisition help. On arrival he met Hillers and Heintze and from them learned of the rest of the night's events on board the doomed ship. They had already made depositions before the Receiver of Wreck, along with saloon passenger Henry Sterne.

All survivors were united sometime later that day on St Mary's, where they were boarded at the two inns which Hugh Town boasted. New clothing was provided for them by John Banfield, the Lloyd's agent, who was also the islands' German Consul. Dorrien-Smith was equally attentive to their needs and sent food across from his home on Tresco.

The Old Quay, Hugh Town harbour.

Hugh Town harbour and houses, c.1910. The central tower is an air pressure indicator, erected mid-nineteenth century, that served as a barometer for sea-goers.

It was strongly hoped that more survivors would be found. Large numbers of boats searched the area of the wreck and all round the islands all day long. But the numbers to which Johannes Rink was the last addition, when brought over from St Agnes that Saturday afternoon, were final. Out of a total complement of 384 passengers and crew on board the *Schiller* when she left New York, a mere 43 were safe and sound at Hugh Town. Only 15 of these were passengers; Henry Sterne, Leo Weste and Carl Kuhn from first cabin; Silas Hexter, Charles Frahm and Louis Reiderer from second cabin; Marcus Powitzer, Charles Henry Percy, Richard Williams, Carl Jantzen, Franz Schnellenberg, Joseph Legenore, Johannes Rink and John and Christine Joens from steerage. Mrs Joens was the sole woman saved. The surviving crew numbered 28: Hillers, Polemann and Heintze the only officers, with eight sailors, eight stewards,

The two Schiller *gigs nos 7 and 8 (one centre, one extreme right) on Hugh Town beach.*

three stokers, two boatswains, one boilermaker, one sailmaker, one coal-trimmer and a storekeeper among the rest.

Naturally enough, the survivors were immensely grateful to those who had saved them. Henry Sterne was amazed at the sheer youthfulness of two crew members in the Hicks family's gig which saved him. The 'two little boys', he said afterwards:

Worked and pulled with a bravery which could not be excelled. Such plucky young fellows I never saw before.[1]

Also saved in the *O & M* was Leo Weste. Having survived a night of unimaginable horrors himself and witnessed the terrible end of his wife and daughter in the pavilion, he was so moved by his indebtedness to the men from St Agnes, that on their arrival at St Mary's he emptied his pockets to provide them with an immediate reward of £60. Then, much to Obadiah Hicks's surprise, he embraced him and kissed him on both cheeks.

NOTES

[1] *Manchester Guardian*, 10 May 1875.

CHAPTER 13

•◆•

The Slimy Recesses of the Ocean

'Knauth, Nachod & Kuhne, general agents', of number 112 Broadway, were the Eagle Line's New York agents. On the morning of Saturday 8 May, the principal partner Mr Knauth opened the offices at 9am and with two clerks in attendance commenced business as usual. Not long afterwards, a telegram arrived on his desk. It came from the Associated Press office in the city and relayed the words of a cable they had received earlier from London:

> *Intelligence of a shocking disaster has just reached this city. The Eagle Line steamship Schiller, Captain Thomas… has been wrecked off the Scilly Isles. It is believed that 200 persons have perished.*[1]

The source of all news concerning the *Schiller* was a privately owned telegraph cable laid between the isle of St Mary's and Penzance in 1869. This cable, as was somewhat scornfully recorded a few days later in a Bristol newspaper:

> *…contained but a single wire, and is the property of a private company who restrict its use by retaining the old-fashioned charge of half-a-crown for 20 words, press messages not excepted.*[2]

Its limitations, in an era when only one message at a time at a speed of 30 words per minute could be transmitted, were to prove woefully inadequate during the next few days of intense use by journalists, relatives of the dead and other agents.

As *Lady of the Isles* had set out for the Retarrier Ledges with the St Mary's lifeboat and St Agnes gigs in tow, the first report of *Schiller*'s loss was tapped out along this

One of the first reports of the Schiller's *wreck from St Mary's, transmitted by telegraph at about mid-Saturday morning. The weekly* Cornish Telegraph *newspaper published it in their next edition – on Wednesday 12 May.*

CORNISH STUDIES LIBRARY, REDRUTH

wire to the Penzance telegraph office and from there relayed to Plymouth and London. Barely two hours had passed since Lloyd's agent John Banfield had awoken the St Mary's telegrapher to report to the Eagle Line's Plymouth offices that the *Schiller* had passed by during the night, when he was sending another, very different report. His new message read:

> The Schiller, Hamburg Steam Ship Company's steamer, which left New York on 27 April, was totally lost on the Retarrier Ledges, near the Bishop's Rock, last night, at ten o' clock. It is feared there has been a great loss of life… She is said to have had 266 passengers, of whom 26 were to land at Plymouth…[3]

Transmitting this message precipitated a deluge of incoming messages and people clamouring to send outward messages at the little shop in Hugh Town which doubled as the telegraph office. Their supply of official telegraph forms were used up within the hour and scraps of paper of all colour and description were pressed into use to write further messages upon. Many were in German and difficult to decipher. To make conditions more difficult still, the line itself was faulty and incoming messages on the 'relay' emitted such feeble clicks that the telegrapher, Alexander Gibson, could only hear them by lying across the bench with his ear pressed to the vibrating part of the Morse sounder. Other members of his family assisted by writing the incoming words as he dictated them, or through separating the lines of text being transmitted with black paper. But as he was the sole trained telegrapher he had to man both sounder and key all day and then at night by the light of a paraffin lamp, with wet cloths applied frequently to keep him awake. With no one to relieve him, this situation was to last for nearly two weeks; until he collapsed entirely and slept for 30 hours.

The messages were relayed to and from St Mary's by the main Post Office at Penzance, at which, as in St Mary's, the pile awaiting despatch grew ever higher. Postmaster there, Mr J.G. Uren, was soon forced to set his clerks working in two-hour shifts to deal with the constant calls. On occasions he had to refuse to accept any more until their backlog was cleared.

From London, Lloyd's and Reuters news agencies soon despatched news of the disaster further afield. Their initial reports gave no mention of survivors, for the news that five crew and two passengers were saved – the men brought to St Mary's by the St Agnes gigs in the first instance – was only sent to Lloyd's at 11.15am. The names of all 12 men saved from the ship's masts was received from St Mary's at 11.27. By noon, London newspapers had hastily printed second editions containing particulars of the disaster and newsboys' cries of 'Extra!' were sounding above the noise of the city traffic.

It was about noon when Algernon Dorrien Smith, Lord Proprietor of the Isles of Scilly, arrived by boat at St Mary's from Tresco, conveying tidings of the 27 more survivors from the ship's lifeboats who had landed there between 8 and 9 that morning. His duties on the islands had begun only the previous year, when with his new bride Edith he took up residence at Tresco Abbey. That morning, they had been precipitated into a disaster of a magnitude unknown anywhere else on Britain's coastline, one which would test the 26-year-old Dorrien-Smith's organisational powers to the utmost. Taking the first news of these survivors across to St Mary's showed one of the difficulties – there was no telegraph link between the two islands, or any of the other islands. New York, 3000 miles across the ocean, knew of the *Schiller*'s loss before people on St Mary's were aware that other survivors had landed on an island just two miles away and over three hours beforehand.

Reports of the tragedy had arrived early that morning, their time, on the eastern seaboard of the United States via the transatlantic cable. Yet the messages received by Associated Press in New York, five hours behind Greenwich Mean Time, were often hours old when transmitted from London. The first indication that there were any survivors at all was included in a despatch tapped out at 12.30am in London – over an hour after the 12 saved from the ship's masts was known of there.

New York newspapers carried a brief report in their second editions that morning, informing the city's one million or so inhabitants of a disaster which would touch upon the lives of many in their midst. In the streets to the east of Broadway and north of the Bowery, almost wholly German populated, the excitement and concern was intense. Almost every person there knew someone or had a relative on board the *Schiller*. The ordinary business of the day was soon abandoned.

In Hoboken, with its predominantly German populace and the Eagle Line's pier jutting from its own 1st Street into the Hudson River, the loss was as keenly felt as any civic disaster. Second-edition local newspapers, that morning recorded:

Extra! Terrible Marine Disaster. The Schiller of the Hoboken Line, Lost. Over two-hundred persons drowned.[4]

SECOND EDITION

EXTRA!

Terrible Marine Disaster.

The Schiller, of the Hoboken Line, Lost.

OVER TWO HUNDRED PERSONS DROWNED.

LONDON, May 8th.—Information just received here reports another terrible marine disaster.

The German steamer Schiller, from New York for Hamburg, went ashore on Retarrier ledges last night and is reported totally lost.

The vessel had a large number of passengers on board and a great loss of life is anticipated.

No particulars of the disaster have yet been received.

Later--Names of Some of the Saved.

LONDON May 8.—The disaster to the steamship Schiller occurred during a dense fog and resulted in a great loss of life. The vessel struck on the rocks off Peste.(?)

Among the passengers known to have been saved are Ludwig Reideret, Henry Stearn, Carl Kuhn and Frank Schillenberg Several of the crew were also rescued.

The rest of the passengers and crew are believed to have perished.

Later Still—Captain Thomas Drowned

LONDON, May 8th.—The loss of life by the disaster to the steamship Schiller will, it is believed, reach two hundred persons, passengers and crew.

Captain Thomas was drowned.

The vessel was wrecked on the Scilly Islands.

Headline news in the Jersey City Argus, *8 May 1875.*

JERSEY CITY FREE PUBLIC LIBRARY

Soon afterwards, the Eagle Line dock was besieged by people, imploring the officers there for more news.

Reporters from local newspapers hurriedly scanned passenger lists, searched directories for their home addresses and rushed there to interview relatives. In Garden Street, Hoboken, schoolteacher Elise Neo's husband opened his door red-eyed from weeping, yet he stalwartly answered their queries about his wife and two young sons. In upstate New York, *Troy Times* reporters found Sophie Holzhaur's husband completely unaware of his loss at his little cutlery shop in North 2nd Street. When the news was broken to him he seemed confused. For some reason he gained an impression that the *Schiller* had been in trouble and was due back in New York that very day, bringing his wife and child home to him. When the truth finally dawned he was overwhelmed with grief.

At the Eagle Line's Broadway agency, Knauth had telegraphed Thomas Jones Stevens, the Eagle Line's agent at Plymouth, for official confirmation and further details as soon as the Associated Press telegram had arrived. But by then, having received Banfield's second telegram at 8am, Stevens had wired company headquarters in Hamburg and promptly left Plymouth on the train to Penzance, from where he hoped to board a steamer for the Isles of Scilly. Until lunchtime the only reports to arrive at the Broadway offices came from Associated Press. The second of these recorded that although there were some survivors landed by St Agnes boats, 200 lives were lost; the third, half an hour later, stated that five crew and two passengers were saved; it was a further 1½ hours before a list of names of the men saved from the ship's masts was cabled through.

Meanwhile, anxious friends and relatives of *Schiller*'s passengers began to descend upon the offices. Knauth and his two clerks did all they could to make the reports readily available, copying each telegram out several times over and spreading them along the counter for the people crowding in to read. But definite news of individual passengers was not easily ascertained. By lunchtime all they had to offer the frantic and despairing crowding before their counter was a list of names, mostly crew, but including some garbled passenger names, together with a later report that 26 people had landed on Tresco.

The first communication from the Eagle Line arrived at the Broadway office at 1.20pm. It was from Knauth's partner Kuhne, who happened to be in Hamburg on business at the time. His telegram added nothing to what was known already and served to confuse matters further by stating that only four passengers were saved.

When he forwarded their names a little later – Sterne, Kuhn, Reiderer and Schnellenberg, omitting Weste who had been named in a garbled way earlier – the so few numbers caused devastation among the gathering there before the counter.

'Oh lieber Gott!' exclaimed one elderly man, in tears, 'Was there no woman saved?'

With the office on the first floor of large business premises, where shipping clerks bustled about with bills of lading, most of the inquirers, though devastated, were somewhat subdued in their grief. One man visibly in deep distress was Charles Schuhr, a barber from East 23rd street, whose wife Maria and little daughter Bertha were among the cabin passengers. He cried out,

'But Bertha, my Bertha, is she too lost? My own little Bertha gone? Oh my God! my God! Why did they go?'

He then left the office weeping bitterly and explaining to bystanders,

'My wife and child are lost.'

A teenage boy strode up and down the office wringing his hands and crying aloud but otherwise unable to communicate his feelings to anyone: his brother-in-law Michael Kornblum, the wealthy waste paper and rags merchant, had been on the *Schiller* along with his married sister, her three children and the family servant. Friends of Oscar Cramer and his wife, the photographer of East 18th Street, left in deep distress, as did those of John Jacob Brunner, the city merchant from Leonard Street. A member of the Stock Exchange Board called repeatedly to enquire about Mrs Caverly and her daughter Amy, but each time he left more and more distraught.

At 3pm two working men, both shoemakers, came into the Eagle Line office and enquired about the latest despatches concerning the *Schiller*. They had heard of the wreck of the ship only at noon that day. Both men were dumbstruck when presented with the list of survivors, unwilling to believe the little that was before them and unable to accept its terrible conclusions. When comprehension struck home, shoemaker George Duckfield realised he had lost his wife Susan and their four children, Mary Matilda, Elizabeth Ann, Georgina and Edward France – all aged between eight and two years of age. His friend and neighbour in the same Bleecker Street apartment block, John Evans, was now equally alone, for his wife Frances – 'Fanny' as he always called her – and his four-year-old son John were also among the lost. Neither of the grief-stricken men could understand why just one of their little ones had not been among the saved.

Hopes were raised around 3pm when Kuhne telegraphed once more from Hamburg: his message reading, 'Keep good hearts, more saved.' This was closely

The Isles of Scilly packet steamer Queen of the Bay *retrieving mailbags on her passage to St Mary's.*

followed by a cable from the Plymouth agent Stevens, then in Penzance. He had missed the steamer *Queen of the Bay*, which had left for St Mary's by the time he had arrived at the Cornish port, but he was able to give the New York offices what would eventually prove to be the final tally of survivors:

First, second and fourth officers, with forty passengers and crew known to be saved.[5]

Their names would follow as soon as he had them, he promised.

The office was by this time packed out with family and friends of the *Schiller's* passengers, all anxious for the merest scrap of news which offered hope that their loved ones had survived and now praying that he, she or they might be among the 40 saved from the wreck. Yet when the list finally came through from Stevens at around 4.30, it contained only 20 or so names, most of which were crew members and many again garbled during transmission. One of the problems Stevens faced was expressed in an earlier transmission to Associated Press which gave nine of the saved passengers in a fairly accurate form and explained that four others could not yet be named, 'as they are in a state of insensibility'. This latest cable had been sent at around nine in the evening from Penzance and as there seemed little chance of anything further coming through that day, Knauth closed the office. Stevens had promised to send a complete list next morning and Knauth told the awaiting crowd that he would reopen then, even though it would be Sunday. They dispersed, sad and confused that their hopes for family or friends were still unresolved.

On Sunday New York newspapers carried the full story on their front pages and inside sheets. The *New York Herald* printed its report in both English and German. Page one of the *New York Times* had two lists: one of a few inches headed 'List of the Saved' and another of a column and a half in length under the title 'List of the Probably Lost'. These lists were fairly conclusive, having been drawn up from late evening and overnight despatches to Associated Press by cable from London. Yet when Knauth opened up the Broadway offices at 9am, there was a large crowd awaiting him, seeking verification of the disastrous news. Throughout the rest of the day more people entered in the hope that further survivors had been found, only to leave disconsolate as no additions to the published list were made. Much to Knauth's annoyance, no cable arrived from Stevens to correct or amend the previous night's unsatisfactory list or to provide any explanation of why the disaster had occurred.

It was John Banfield on St Mary's who finally telegraphed a complete list of surviving passengers through to the Eagle Line office. In his role as German Consul on the Scillies, he also sent details of the wreck and lists of passengers and crew saved to H.A. Schumaker, the German Consul-General in New York. Schumaker's office at Bowling Green had also been inundated with callers on the Saturday afternoon, many of them coming straight there from the Eagle Line office, as if hoping for better news from him. He was in no mood to cope, the loss of his friend and fellow Consul, Frederick Wilhelm Zach, had left him feeling very low.

Among numerous callers enquiring after news at the Broadway office that Sunday were friends of the Zinkeisen family and of brewer Joseph Schlitz of Milwaukee; the Leonhardt family of Augusta, Georgia; Richard Feederle of Akron, Ohio; and Mr and Mrs Carl Schmidt of New York; all of them cabin passengers on *Schiller*. Several callers sought news of Michael Kornblum and family of New York, and accepting that they were most likely dead, telegraphed Stevens urging him to do all he could to retrieve the bodies and arrange to have them returned for internment in America. Steerage passenger Anna Meisner's eldest son was less prepared for the bad news that their Jersey City home would in future be motherless and bereft of two of the seven children. When told there was 'no hope', the grief of the tall, fresh-faced youth was heart-rending to onlookers.

Two husbands had their worst fears verified that Sunday morning. Herman Furst, a hat and cap dealer of South 5th Avenue, was told that his wife Ernestine and his little girl were among the lost. He stood for a few minutes as if incredulous, then sat with his head bowed dejectedly, after which he arose and walked out of the office looking vacantly ahead. Lewis V. Holzmaister, an importer of kid gloves, of Broadway, took the news that his recent bride Louise was among the dead equally hard. He kept returning to the office, hoping that further reports would somehow provide better news.

Where New York's newspapers had been fairly accurate with their lists, others elsewhere in America were not, either with numbers or names of survivors. One very hopeful man entered the Broadway offices clutching a telegram he had received from a friend in Baltimore which read:

This morning's news has 50 passengers saved. Among them is the name of Lina Kirchmayer. We live in hope. Charles Kirchmayer.[6]

MILWAUKEE, MONDAY

THE SCHILLER.

A Steamship Wrecked on the Rocks Off the English Coast.

Three Hundred and Seventy-nine Persons on Board— Forty-three Saved.

Complete List of Passengers and Officers---Names of the Survivors.

Six Well-known Citizens of Milwaukee Among the Lost.

The Scene of the Disaster---Recovery of Bodies---The Vessel and Her Cargo

The Milwaukee Daily Sentinel *announces local losses, 10 May 1875.*
MILWAUKEE HISTORICAL SOCIETY

It was a hope that was unfounded; Lina Kirchmayer, so homesick for the town of her birth, Boppard, on the banks of the Rhine, had not survived. The man left in a shocked state.

Rumours abounded. In Milwaukee there was an early story that the wealthy brewer Joseph Schlitz had reached Queenstown in Southern Ireland. But when on Sunday the final list of 15 passengers saved came over the line at the telegraph office, not one among them was from Milwaukee. Ex-Austrian Army Colonel Carl Miltner was there waiting when the wire came that inadvertently told of his bereavement. It was certain that Marie, the girl who had given up the pleasures of wealth and privilege for love and a new, but poorer life in America with him, was dead along with their baby. He fell to his knees and sobbed.

With accurate information hard to come by outside of New York, telegrams flooded in to the Eagle Line offices from cities and states far away enquiring about passengers. From Boston came one from the fruit shipping line Baker & Morrill, asking, 'Is the name of Percival among the list of saved on Schiller?' Another, from Goos & Kircher, jewellers of Davenport, Iowa, read, 'Is Otto Kircher saved? Answer at once.' Knauth and his clerks were reluctant to answer queries from private citizens, or even from their fellow Eagle Line agents in other cities, until they were in command of the full facts, however.

For some newspapers well beyond New York and its environs, the lack of facts did not get in the way of providing a story on the wreck. In the midwest city of Davenport the fate of the *Schiller* occupied a lengthy but largely imaginative piece in Saturday evening's newspaper under the title 'An Ocean Horror'. It told how that once the vessel had struck, there was so little time or opportunity to save lives that:

The precious human cargo were hurled into eternity without a moment's warning… in one fell moment they are snatched from the world…

With lurid sentimentality it went on to lament the local dead:

…lost ones who will never again be seen, who this moment are doubtless lying stark and stiff in the slimy recesses of the ocean.[7]

Nineteen passengers from the Iowa city and surrounding district had been on board the *Schiller,* and those they had left behind were soon besieging the telegraph office, the newspaper offices and the Eagle Line's local agent for information on survivors. Adolph Langfeldt, the Eagle Line agent, cabled London and New York immediately, but the response was inconclusive, while the private telegrams received by others made conflicting claims. He arranged to have the telegraph office opened on Sunday, hoping that despatches then would prove to be more informative.

Sunday brought confirmation of sorts about survivors via the reports of Associated Press, but nothing definite from the Eagle Line's New York agents, who were having trouble of their own in obtaining reliable news. Nevertheless, on the strength of what was known, Fred Goos, partner to Otto Kircher in wholesale jewellery, drove out to Blue Grass township where Otto's wife Tillie was spending time during his absence with her two babies and her parents. The news of her husband's death left her prostrate with grief. By contrast, August Haase tried hard to keep all reports of the *Schiller*'s fate from his wife until such time as he had something definite regarding their son Carl, his wife and their two young children. But the old lady happened upon a copy of Saturday's *Davenport Democrat*, and with the lurid details there before her eyes, fainted clean away.

Monday's news was conclusive – in its fashion. A private telegram to Fred Goos from the Eagle Line agents at New York confirmed his well-founded fears for his business partner by answering his wired request of Saturday, 'Otto Kircher is not on the list of the saved.' Another from the same office to Langfeldt, the Davenport agent, stated, 'John Joens and wife, and C. Frahm saved.' Nothing else was transmitted to them that day and in the absence of further reports it had to be assumed that of the 19 happy, expectant souls who had stood at the railroad depot on the 23rd of the previous month, 16 were dead. The fact that, unlike many other towns and cities in America, three of their own were to return, was of little consolation to the parents, children and friends of those who would not. The eldest daughter and housekeeper of widower, P.A. Paulson, had seen her terrible premonition become reality.

But it was to the living that the Davenport telegraph was then put to use. At 4.15 Langfeldt got a reply to his transatlantic cable enquiring about the health and current whereabouts of the Davenport survivors, Charles Frahm and John and Christine Joens, the married couple from Luzerne. From the Eagle Line's Plymouth offices came the reply, 'Tolerably well; proceeding to Hamburg via London.' Matthias Frahm then sent a draft for $100 to his surviving son through Langfeldt, who also requested that all the help possible should be given to any more Davenport people who might survive. That hope was not yet extinct.

WE MOURN OUR LOSS.

Further Particulars from the Scene of the Schiller Disaster bring no Tidings to Relatives Here.

Only Fifteen out of 320 Passengers known to be Saved.

And only One out of all that went from Davenport Saved.

A List of the Saved and a List of the Lost from this City.

There are many tear-stained faces to-day in this city. There are many homes mourning over loved and lost ones. There are many sad, heavy and broken hearts that cannot be comforted or healed, for all that was dear to them has, without word or warning, in a moment of time, gone down to watery graves. An awful calamity has been visited upon homes in our midst; a deep, funereal gloom hangs over our city; darkness pervades many a family circle; the death angel has walked over the waters, gathered a rich and bounteous harvest, severing the life-chords of many—young and old—and fathers and mothers mourn sons and daughters, wives will look in vain for husbands, and husbands yearn for the love and affection of wives, whom the dark waters have closed over—until the resurrection day. Who can tell of the sorrow and anguish which reigns in these homes; who can pen paint the misery and despair of the widows and orphans; what balm will relieve the broken hearts throughout Davenport to-day! Our soul sickens, and our hand falters as we think of them, while our heart is too heavy to write methodically details of the horrors of that feast of death, which has brought weeping, wailing, mourning to so many homes in our very midst.

The Davenport Democrat's *florid sentimentality, Monday 10 May.*

SCOTT COUNTY, IOWA, GENEALOGICAL SOCIETY

Hope still lingered on into Monday at New York, where numerous callers at the offices of Nauth, Nachod & Kuhne in Broadway enquired about additional persons rescued. It seemed inconceivable to them that more would not be discovered. Others telegraphed, requesting the same from states and cities widespread across America. But the latest information available only reiterated the position late on Saturday. A cable from Kuhne at Hamburg early that morning read:

> *Only fifteen passengers saved from Schiller. Names telegraphed you yesterday. We do everything to recover and identify bodies.*[8]

This was enough to crush all hope from the hearts of the enquirers. Many gave vent to their feelings, wailing loudly; some men crouched in corners weeping and refusing all attempts at consolation by the office staff.

One who called in person that Monday was a Mrs Nautch. She asked if two young men who had lodged at her home in Hester Street, Herman Baumgarten and Richard Nautch, had been saved. They had been working their passage back to Germany on the *Schiller* and their names had not figured on any published list, 'saved' or 'lost'. She was told they must be lost.

On a less charitable mission and a friend in name only was the small but dapper Deputy Sheriff E.M. Friend, who came into the office enquiring about the fate of Louis Selig of Meadow Street, Hoboken. In his possession was a warrant for Selig's arrest, dated 16 September 1874, for having left some 'unsettled business' at a fancy-goods store he had owned in Jersey City. Friend had made several attempts at collaring Selig but he always eluded him. If Louis Selig had intended to evade his creditors and put himself beyond the reach of the law by taking a passage on the *Schiller*, he had succeeded in no uncertain manner.

Having learned with certainty that their friend or relative was not among the survivors, or miraculously found days later, the next anxiety for callers at Broadway was what to do in the event of their corpses being recovered. Many of the more wealthy favoured embalming and return to America, as had the friends of Michael Kornblum. That also was the wish of Deputy Surveyor of New York Port, George Klink, should the remains of his younger brother be found. Relatives of the Caverlys, Mrs Ridgeway and Charles Walter and his children thought likewise, as did those of Staten Island's Clara Gregory and her young son Frank; they telegraphed acquaintances in Europe to arrange the matter.

The barber from East 23rd Street, Charles Schuhr, called again at the Eagle Line office from which he had departed in tears on the Saturday to tell Knauth and his clerks that if the bodies of his wife Maria and daughter Bertha were recovered they should be buried in marked graves. He intended to sail that Thursday on the Hamburg-Amerika steamer *Cimbria* to find them and bring them back to New York personally. Others less well off resigned themselves to the fact that if their loved ones' remains were found at all, they would be laid to rest in a foreign and inaccessible part.

Optimism remained intact for just a little longer in some American quarters, though without foundation. While most Monday-morning newspapers carried reports of bodies being recovered and identified at St Mary's, the *Boston Evening Transcript* kept alive the city's hopes for their well-known and respected lady physician Susan Dimock MD and her best friend Bessie Greene.

Miss Dimock was a very good swimmer and was possessed of considerable courage, and it is possible that these companions may have survived the terrible disaster and landed on one of the islands.[9]

But the body of Susan Dimock lay that very evening in a disused store, temporarily the mortuary for hundreds of *Schiller*'s victims and situated at the end of a stone-built pier at Hugh Town on the Isle of St Mary's.

Hugh Town pier showing warehouses – one of which was used as a mortuary in May 1875. The pier was extended in 1889. Photographed c.1910.

NOTES

1   *New York Times*, 9 May 1875.

2   *Daily Bristol Times and Mirror*, 11 May 1875.

3   *Daily Bristol Times and Mirror*, 10 May 1875.

4   *The Argus*, 8 May 1875.

5   *New York Times*, 9 May 1875.

6   *New York Times*, 10 May 1875.

7   *The Davenport Democrat*, 8 May 1875.

8   *New York Times*, 11 May 1875.

9   *Boston Evening Transcript*, 10 May 1875.

A salvor's warrant completed by the Receiver of Wreck on the recovery and delivery of Susan Dimock MD's body to the pier-head storehouse at Hugh Town.

PUBLIC RECORD OFFICE

CHAPTER 14

◆

Safe

'Safe, send letters to Berlin. Sterne.' This cable was sent from St Mary's to Sterne's friends in New York city on Saturday evening. But for the few who were safe, that first night ashore brought them little sleep. Exhausted though they were and in warm, dry beds at the two inns at Hugh Town, many could not erase the terrible events of the previous night's ordeal from their minds. The cries and shrieks of women and children still rang in their ears. Most had suffered bereavements of friends and loved ones in the most horrendous manner. For Leo Weste and Louis Reiderer there had been the additional ordeal of identifying their lost wives among the dead brought ashore that day. Mrs Reiderer was found holding tight to a dead child in her arms – the couple's little daughter Lulu, aged about six.

The majority of the survivors were taken to Penzance early on the Sunday morning. Thirty-two of them boarded the *Lady of the Isles* at St Mary's pier, escorted by second mate Erwin Polemann. The two other surviving ship's officers, Hillers and Heintze, remained in Hugh Town, as did Leo Weste, Louis Reiderer and those who were still too ill to travel – Williams, Percy, Schnellenberg, Jantzen, one steward and a sailor.

When the *Lady of the Isles* had finally puffed her way against the still heavy seas to reach Penzance, it was late morning. At the pier-head there was a gathering of hundreds of people, who despite it being a Sunday were there to see the survivors of one of the most disastrous shipwrecks ever to have occurred around the coastline of Britain. Above all else they wanted to get a glimpse of Mrs Joens, the only woman to have been saved.

There to receive the party officially were Thomas Jones Stevens, the Eagle Line's Plymouth agent; Mr Uren, the Penzance Postmaster, straight from the much over-worked telegraph office; and the local stationmaster – for the survivors were soon to join a train for Plymouth. A large gathering of newspaper reporters awaited them too:

none had so far managed to make the crossing to the Scilly Isles, what with both steamers being at St Mary's and the 25 miles of sea between being still too rough for smaller craft.

Erwin Polemann led the way from the steamer up the pier stairs, impressing one journalist to describe him as:

…a fine-looking German, about thirty, every inch a sailor.[1]

The other survivors followed Polemann in a less dignified manner, looking rather dejected as they walked through the crowds. People who had patiently awaited their arrival now respectfully fell back to watch in silent awe, allowing a passage through their ranks for those who had endured such traumatic experiences. Physically, they were a strong and healthy looking bunch taken together, what with most of them being sailors, but many bore visible scars. Almost all had faces ravaged from over-long exposure to wind and sea; some had cuts and bruises from swimming among wreckage and rocks; and all of them had an aura of melancholy from having witnessed the deaths of so many of their companions on that terrible night.

The main focus of interest for the curious came last in the long line. Christine Joens walked slowly and very despondently, clutching the arm of her husband and looking careworn and ill. Although the waiting reporters questioned her she was able only to give a short account of her ordeal, just a few sentences summarising her and her husband's actions during the wreck and their subsequent hours in the ship's lifeboats. She concluded by saying:

I cannot tell you what has happened, I feel as if I were out of my mind.[2]

John, her husband, was so badly affected by shock he could recall nothing of what occurred that night.

Few survivors spoke English, but those who could and were willing gave reporters their version of the wreck. Most of the crew spoke only their native tongue, but Polemann once more impressed the representatives of Fleet Street, speaking English 'admirably'. He explained to the waiting reporters:

Today, I've brought those people able to travel here and will go back tomorrow to do my best to find the Captain and arrange his funeral. I hope I will succeed.[3]

The survivors landing at Penzance: John and Christine Joens of Luzerne, Iowa, in centre.

ILLUSTRATED LONDON NEWS

The long-term American domiciled, like Sterne, Hexter and Powitzer, also had no linguistic difficulties, although Johannes Rink's few years in New York had given him just the basics coloured with 'a decided Yankee tinge'. Henry Sterne's clear and perceptive narrative of the events on board the *Schiller* was later awarded the most prominence in any press coverage of the disaster; but he made claims in an interview with a *New York Herald* reporter which were to greatly offend his fellow travellers when they came into print.

The survivors were next taken by Stevens to the Queens Hotel on the Esplanade, where lunch had been prepared for them. Previously, the Eagle Line's directors had telegraphed from Hamburg telling Stevens to spare no expense in caring for them and attending to their comfort. After the meal, large crowds again witnessed the survivors' departure at Penzance railway station and there were yet more curious onlookers to greet their arrival at Plymouth. It was intended that those who required it would continue their journeys to Cherbourg or Hamburg on the Hamburg-Amerika *Pommerania* – the vessel on which Captain H.F. Schwensen was about to complete his centenary of voyages. She was due to dock there that Sunday.

Schwensen's arrival, at around two in the afternoon, was a cause of great celebration for some. Bullion dealers, merchants and underwriters from the City of London were all gathered at the pier-side to honour the elderly commander's achievement. They presented him with a congratulatory address and a purse of gold to mark his 100 transatlantic voyages without serious incident. But for Schwensen the occasion was tragic, marred by news of the *Schiller* disaster and the death of his Eagle Line friend Captain George Thomas, whom he had last seen at the celebratory banquet in New York on what was his last ever night ashore.

The *Pommerania* had left for Cherbourg by the time the survivors' train arrived at Plymouth. Eagerly awaiting them though, were more reporters. One, a Reuters correspondent, later telegraphed Hamburg that the rescued were united in praise of the Captain, both for his bravery during the wreck and the manner in which he had pursued his duties during the passage across. When for three days he could not get an observation from the sun, he was, they said:

> *…indefatigable in successive attempts with the lead.* [4]

This, as was later proved, was not entirely accurate.

Passengers Sterne, Kuhn, Powitzer, Hexter, Charles Frahm and the Joenses, then took the train to London aiming to complete their journeys to Hamburg in a day or so. The remainder, mostly crew members but including Johannes Rink and Joseph Legenore, were taken to the Sailors Rest Home operated by the Shipwrecked Mariners Society in Plymouth. There they were to be provided with food and accommodation until the arrival of the Eagle Line steamship *Lessing* on Friday, on which they were to embark for the final leg of their tragically interrupted passage. After their meal that evening the Rev. W. Oxland read to them from a German Testament in which were several repetitions of the phrase, 'One shall be taken, and the other left.'

It was thought to be a most appropriate text and was said to have struck home with great force upon the men – although the ratio of lost to saved was very different in *Schiller*'s case.

On the following day, Monday 10 May, some of the German-speaking sailors gave press interviews at the Sailors Home. Goldberger, Wallis, Peck and Blohm were among those who told how they had survived to visiting journalists, with Goldberger's harrowing account gaining the most column inches in newspapers. Almost all the men were destitute, owning only the clothes they stood up in, but publication of their stories brought them much sympathy. A few days later the secretary of the Sailors Home received a donation of £5 from the Duke of Marlborough. This was followed by a visit from Admiral Sir W. Ring Hall, who handed £48 to them; this sum having being collected among officials and shipyard workers at Devonport.

On Tuesday the *Lady of the Isles* left St Mary's for Penzance taking eight more of the survivors with her. Polemann, who along with two stewards had returned to the island on Tuesday, now accompanied Weste, Reiderer, and the four passengers, one steward and a sailor who had been in too bad a condition to make the journey on the previous day. Before leaving St Mary's, Leo Weste made a statement criticising Captain Thomas for telling the women in the saloon that the tide was going down, blaming him for the deaths of his wife and daughter. His was the only dissenting voice among the survivors, who so far had expressed only praise for Captain Thomas's efforts to save them on the night of the wreck.

Arriving at Penzance, Louis Reiderer appeared to one of the onlooking journalists as being 'completely crushed' by the misfortune of losing his wife and child. The small band of survivors was escorted by Stevens to the Queens Hotel for refreshments prior to journeying on to Plymouth by train, as were their predecessors. Before they caught the train there was a body for them to identify – a traumatic experience for some.

Of the passengers who had journeyed to London on the Monday, Hexter, Powitzer, Charles Frahm and Mr and Mrs Joens arrived by the steamer *Libra* at Hamburg on Friday. They were first taken to the city's stock exchange for interviews with the German press, where once again they issued only favourable reports on Captain Thomas's conduct before and during the wreck. Afterwards, Eagle Line representatives gave them money to continue to their destinations.

Lessing, the last Eagle Line steamer, as yet not taken over by Hamburg-Amerika, had sailed from New York on 4 May to complete what should have been the line's 31st and last ever, round voyage. On Saturday 15 May, she arrived at Plymouth. Captain Toosberg, her crew and the passengers on board, were severely shocked to hear the fate of the sister ship which had preceded them across the Atlantic. Officers on both

Eagle Line S.S. Lessing, *built by Alexander Stephen & Son: a sister ship of the* Schiller *and last of the line – here in Hamburg-Amerika livery with all-black funnels.*

NATIONAL MARITIME MUSEUM

vessels were on very friendly terms and some passengers knew people or had friends among those on the *Schiller* – one had a brother among the victims. A relief fund was soon arranged and a total of $700 collected for the survivors.

The 25 survivors still residing in the Sailors Home at Plymouth were then embarked on *Lessing*; Joseph Legenore for Cherbourg and the rest for Hamburg and the seamen's home and hospital there. Only Hillers, Polemann and two stewards were left behind on St Mary's, for fourth mate Richard Heintze had joined those of the crew who were leaving for the Fatherland. They were taken out to *Lessing* in the steam tug *Volunteer* accompanied by Eagle Line agent, Thomas Jones Stevens. Passengers and crew of the last ever Eagle liner warmly welcomed them aboard and then, as the tug moved off, Stevens got a round of rousing and prolonged cheers from the *Schiller*'s survivors.

NOTES

[1] *The Cornish Telegraph*, 12 May 1875.

[2] *Manchester Guardian*, 10 May 1875.

[3] *Hamburgischer Correspondent*, 13 May 1875.

[4] *The Cornish Telegraph*, 12 May 1875.

CHAPTER 15

◆◆◆

Under a Beautiful Row of Palms

The first of the many salvor's warrants: this one issued for the body of the dead quartermaster brought in with survivors from the Schiller's foremast by the Sennen lugger Rapid.

PUBLIC RECORD OFFICE

The beginning of what was to become a grisly day-to-day duty for the people of the Isles of Scilly started soon after the wreck of the *Schiller* became known. Jacob Deason and the Sennen men landed the bodies of two crewmen among those picked up from the fallen foremast. The ship's quartermaster whose lifebuoy Hillers had clung to was dead already, while the sailor in an insensible state died later in spite of all efforts to revive him. Then, just after 11am, another St Agnes boat reached St Mary's with the bodies of four men and two women – one holding a dead child in her arms being later identified as Mrs Reiderer. A further three bodies were brought ashore mid-afternoon and in the hours following the total climbed to 24 for the day. But that was only the beginning: there were hundreds still in the sea around the islands or being washed up on their shores.

A fishing boat from Mousehole, the *Robert*, had left St Mary's for her home port at ten that morning, it being usual for the Cornish fishermen to return home in time for Sunday. When just two miles west of St Mary's, she sailed into a large area of floating luggage, mailbags and bodies, all drifting slowly westwards with the receding tide and south-westerly wind. There were no fewer than 200 bodies there, according to the master of the *Robert*, and several were those of children. All were wearing cork life-jackets but their faces were hidden for they floated face downwards in the sea. The crew tried to retrieve some but as the wind and tide threatened to carry them on to a lee shore, that of the unin-habited island of Samson, they gave up the task. Eventually, after picking up three mail-bags, some bundles and a passengers bag, they left the scene and made for Mousehole, from where the bags were sent to the Receiver of Wreck in Penzance.

During the next week large numbers of the victims' bodies were to be brought into St Mary's by a succession of pilot boats, gigs and fishing boats. Once taken up from the sea, the rocky foreshores, or the sandy beaches around the islands, the sorry cargo would be laid reverently in the bottom of the boat and covered over by a sail until the pier at St Mary's was reached. Retrieved bodies were then brought into the disused pier-head storehouse, which Dorrien-Smith, the owner, had placed at the disposal of the authorities. There they were numbered and examined for possible identification. Notes were taken of their dress, markings such as initials on clothing, jewellery, papers found upon them, the contents of their pockets, facial and physical character-istics or tattoos. Many had large sums of money in coin or banknotes, bankers draughts, expensive jewellery and watches upon them. Every possession was regis-tered and placed in the care of James Handley, the Receiver of Wreck, or his clerk, for eventual return to relatives of the dead person.

Corpses were laid out and wrapped in calico winding sheets behind a screened-off area of the storehouse loft. This work was the preserve of two elderly St Mary's widows, who were no strangers to tragedy, having lost their husbands through drowning 30 years beforehand. The wooden coffins into which the dead were con-signed were of simple construction, deal stained black, and these were made in quan-tity and at some speed by men in the employ of Dorrien-Smith. The lids were not screwed down, to facilitate identification at some later time. Some bodies were never identified. Their only epitaph would remain a number and a word or two of descrip-tion in the search register, as were:

…men… 6- Anchor, left hand; A.P., right hand. 12- Silver sleeve studs, A.W., two Masonic emblems.' and *'women… 5- Chemise, initialled L.B. 13- One gold ring, H.J.*[1]

Among the identified passengers on Saturday, along with Leo Weste's wife Hermine and Mrs Reiderer and her daughter, were the bodies of Mrs Ridgeway, Mrs Becker and a man thought to be George C. Leonhardt, the Augusta, Georgia, jeweller. The dead brought ashore the following day included Susan Dimock MD; the New York shirt manufacturer's wife Clara Just; and the young newly-weds Mr and Mrs Munte.

Augustus Munte and his bride of 12 days, who had made their vows to each other only hours before the *Schiller* sailed, were picked up by separate boats and landed within an hour of each other. Having then been identified by their twin, engraved wedding rings, the marriage certificate in Augustus's pocket book and the gold locket around his neck containing his wife's picture, they were laid out side by side in the improvised mortuary.

Two children's bodies were also recovered that Sunday. One was a baby of seven or eight months, said to be 'looking as if it were in peaceful slumber'. It was found near Peninnis Head, where a woman's body was also discovered. About half a mile away, the body of a little girl was brought ashore by a fisherman living in Old Town Bay shortly after he had set out on a fishing trip. She was later identified as Georgina Duckfield, the four-year-old youngest daughter of Susan Duckfield and her New York shoemaker husband George.

Peninnis Head. Its lighthouse replaced the St Agnes lighthouse in 1911.

By Monday morning the recovered bodies of *Schiller* victims numbered 52; 22 men, 17 women and girls, and three boys. At 10am an inquest on them was opened at the Court House in Hugh Town, under the Coroner T.L. Hall JP. Prior to it, the *Schiller*'s first and fourth mates, Hillers and Heintze, had identified the dead from Saturday and Sunday's haul as best they could. But they could not be expected to have known everyone on board the ship by name, not even their crew of 120, so the definite identifications came to only 13 of the total. One, initially thought to be that of George C. Leonhardt, was discovered to be Dr Sanders, the ship's surgeon from the Holland-America *W.A. Scholten*. He was wearing an overcoat with Leonhardt's passport and a considerable amount of money and valuables in the pockets.

At the Court House both officers made formal identifications that all the dead were passengers or crew from the *Schiller* before the Coroner and jury. A verdict of 'found drowned' was then recorded, after which the Coroner felt bound to recommend that telegraphic communication between the lighthouse and the shore should be established. If it had been installed already, he suggested, then the result would have been the saving of all of the lives lost. Hillers and Heintze both concurred with his statement.

If they could have been there, then it is likely that the lighthouse keepers themselves would have been in full agreement too. Much later that day, senior keeper James Daniel wrote to his wife from Bishop Rock:

On Sunday three bodies floated past us, and this afternoon more have passed close by to us. No one knows what was felt in this house by all hands to see so many of our dear fellow-creatures suffering and dying so near to us.[2]

Lady of the Isles left Penzance at 10.30 on the Monday morning to make her return to St Mary's. The little steamer had been specially chartered on behalf of the Eagle Line. On board were Stevens, the company's Plymouth agent; Erwin Polemann and two ship's stewards returning from escorting survivors the previous day; a Captain Lodge, who was to assess the wreck for salvage operations; some representatives of the marine underwriters; and several journalists. The heavy swell of the previous few days had now subsided and the cloud lifted to allow a pleasant crossing under a sun shining bright in a cloudless sky. The mood of those on board was by contrast sombre as befitted their mission, and if any individual's thoughts turned for a while to lighter subjects, the realities of the tragedy soon brought them back.

Not far beyond the Rundlestone they encountered increasing amounts of floating wreckage. There were two large boxes, the fittings of a cabin and one of *Schiller*'s upper yards. A mail bag was harpooned and brought aboard, but contained only New Zealand newspapers. Then a seaman shouted to Captain Gibson,

'There's a body, Sir!'

It was floating about 200 yards away and would have remained unseen had it not been for the white of its lifebelt. The paddle steamer hove-to and a boat was lowered. It returned in minutes with the body laid so that the feet, white and lifeless, stuck out over the stern. The man, as it proved to be, was wearing a life-jacket and had $150 in his pocket, but there was no other means of identification. With her flag lowered to half-mast as a token of respect for the dead man, the steamer continued towards the islands, appearing, as one journalist put it:

…to be slumbering beneath the beams of a bright May sun.[3]

But for the Scillonians too, this day, however bright, was to be one of the most profound melancholy.

Old Town Church, St Mary's.

The first mass funeral for the *Schiller* victims was to take place at 4pm that day. Preceding it by two hours was the private funeral for Hermine Weste. Only her husband Leo, the three ship's officers, two stewards and the sailor still on the island were in attendance at the graveside. It was situated 'under a beautiful row of palms' in the islands' burial ground at Old Town churchyard.

Here, less than a mile from Hugh Town at a small hamlet which once had been the island's main settlement, was a small, low-built stone church with a bell-less bell turret. In early times it had formed the chancel of a much larger Norman church, which falling into ruin was reconstructed in its present form in 1660. It had been superseded as a place of worship more than 40 years before by a new church at Hugh Town, but was still in use for funerals.

The stone-walled churchyard in which it stood began almost at the rocky beach of Old Town Bay and rose up in a series of small terraces towards the high ridge leading from Hugh Town to the granite buttressed promontory of Penninis Head. It boasted one large monument; a rough hewn obelisk dedicated to Augustus Smith, the Lord Proprietor of the islands who had died three years beforehand. Yet however unimpressive the church architecture, or the churchyard's lacking in splendid monumental masonry, it was a scene not without considerable charm. This was partly due to its location at the bay-side, but also because of the flora with which it abounded. A journalist noted:

> *Where else in the Kingdom could we find a God's acre where the straggling stone cross give place to the luxuriant mesembryanthemum, and where, side by side with the broom and elder, flourish in rich exuberance the aloe and the New Zealand flax.* [4]

In the churchyard close by the little stone church, two long trench graves had been prepared to receive the remains of those who had perished at sea. Each one was 25ft long and occupied a considerable portion of the lower terraces. With the sub-stratum of the islands being of granite covered only by a shallow layer of topsoil, the men employed in digging these graves had sweated and strained to remove huge boulders found beneath the surface. They had even been forced to resort to blasting away the bedrock in some places. Two regular size graves had also been dug some way apart from the long trenches: one for Mrs Weste and the other awaiting Mrs Reiderer and her daughter Lulu.

At 4pm the main funeral procession left St Mary's pier-head. All the vessels in the harbour there flew their flags at half-mast in respect for the dead, while the pier itself

Preparing graves for the Schiller *victims at Old Town Church. Stakes and identification numbers mark the position of those already interred.*

GIBSON OF SCILLY

A mass funeral procession makes its way along Hugh Town pier, St Mary's.

ILLUSTRATED LONDON NEWS

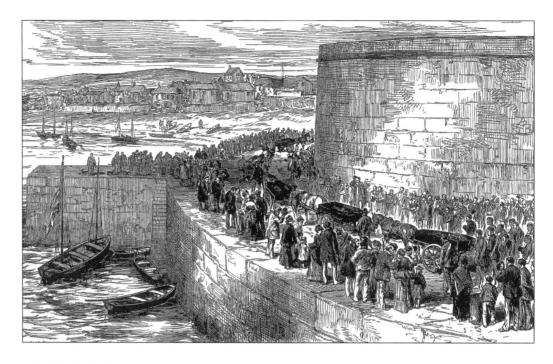

Mass funeral procession entering Hugh Town from the pier.

GRAPHIC MAGAZINE

was thronged with islanders. Death by drowning and the disposal of the mortal remains of seafarers was no uncommon occurrence on these islands with their long history of wrecks. Yet because of the number of fatalities, and with so many women and children among them, there was no Scillonian unmoved or unwilling to pay their respects. Having had this onerous duty thrust upon them through the misfortune of others, they rallied without exception to perform the last rites with the utmost courtesy and sympathy for people, although unknown to them and of foreign nationality.

None of the usual funereal trappings of that era were to be seen: no tall-plumed, jet-black horses, no crêpe, no hearses or mourning coaches. All that stood for the solemnity of the occasion was the black of the 37 painted deal coffins. These had been placed in pairs upon small, two-wheeled carts of varied descriptions drawn by horses and shaggy-coated ponies, brown, black or grey in colour. There were flowers in abundance though: each coffin had floral tributes laid reverently on its lid as a token of heartfelt condolence by the people of the Scilly Isles.

The long procession moved off from the pier-head storehouse, each horse or pony led out by its driver to follow one behind the other. As the little carts and their sad freight passed through the silent ranks of islanders, men removed hats respectfully while some of the women hid their tear-stained faces with handkerchiefs. Trailing behind one of the carts looking desolate and heartbroken, Louis Reiderer took a last, leaden-footed walk with his wife and daughter. A few carts behind him was another followed by a group of young men wearing the regalia of a friendly society, the Order of Good Templars. In the coffin on the cart before them was a brother member of their order, identified as such by a small card carried on his person. He was a total stranger but still a brother, and the Good Templars of the islands paid their respects dressed accordingly.

When all the carts had passed along the pier, the islanders fell in behind them, spectators no longer but participating as mourners. Along with them came the survivors of the *Schiller* who had remained on the island, Stevens the Eagle Line agent and several local dignitaries, among whom were Algernon Dorrien-Smith, John Banfield, T.L. Hall JP, James Handley, the Receiver of Wreck, and the Revd J.H. White, who was to conduct the burial services.

The long cortège wound its way through the narrow, twisting streets of Hugh Town, which were otherwise deserted. Each home and each little shop had curtains or blinds drawn and shutters closed. From there, the funeral procession followed a rough-surfaced road, snaking over Buzza Hill with its views of Hugh Town huddled

Right: *View over Hugh Town; the harbour is on the left and Buzza Hill with its Napoleonic gun tower is on the extreme right.*

Below: *Panoramic view of Hugh Town; the harbour is on the right and Lloyd's signal tower can be seen above Porthcressa beach on the left.*

on a sandy spit with the sea upon either side, before a short descent brought it to Old Town and its tiny church. There, the coffins were stacked upon each other beside the long trenches.

The burial service which the Revd White conducted was of some duration. While he was proceeding, telegrams from relatives of two of the dead were received on the island requesting that they were kept back for embalming. These were singled out and returned to the pier-head. The remaining coffins were then lowered into the trenches and arranged two deep. A stake placed at the head of each pair carried a small white plaque with the number attributed to the dead persons lying below

The burial of Schiller *victims in mass graves at Old Town Church.*

ILLUSTRATED LONDON NEWS

painted in black: this in case of the need to remove them later for interment elsewhere. Thirty-five of *Schiller*'s unfortunates were laid to rest in the mass graves that afternoon.

A problem arose out of the requirements of some relatives for the return of remains – there was no embalmer on the islands. John Banfield had at first telegraphed to Knauth in New York to say that it could not be done; they would have to bury them all. But he later sent off to London and employed two embalmers, who arrived in St Mary's on the Wednesday. In the meantime, yet more victims of the wreck were recovered. On the Monday evening, having that afternoon interred 38 all told and with several more in the makeshift mortuary awaiting the embalmers, another ten bodies were brought ashore.

Corpses of the victims were being dispersed by tide and wind over a widening area. Of those collected on Monday, several came from locations all around the islands. A six-month-old baby was recovered from Melledgan. The body of Johanna Zach, wife of the German Consul at Havana, had been found floating off Maiden Bower, 6½ miles north-west from the scene of the wreck. Two more females were discovered at even further distance. One washed up on the isle of Tean, among several small islands to the north of St Mary's; another was brought in by a Falmouth pilot cutter having been taken out of the sea eight miles to the south of Scilly.

Most of that day's dead were identified. Along with Mrs Zach were Annie Zinkeisen, the 19-year-old daughter of the Milwaukee stockbroker; Henry Friend of Friend & Bros of the same city; Elise Neo, the music teacher from Hoboken; Anna Meisner, the mother of seven from Jersey City; Mrs Augusta Deckritz, wife of the Brooklyn architect; Carl Schmidt, the New York jeweller; Herman Stoelting, the assayer from Colorado, and Dwight Klink, younger brother of New York port's deputy surveyor. Further still from the islands that Monday evening was the body of a young man picked up six miles west of Land's End by the Lowestoft fishing lugger, *Coleen Bawn*, and taken on to Penzance. He was thought to be a German by his looks and about 22 years old. His pocket book contained an address card printed 'Richard Feederle, Akron, Ohio'.

Almost without exception the bodies recovered were wearing life-jackets. Many, however, were fitted badly or the strings attaching them were broken. While the majority appeared to have died from exhaustion or exposure in the cold, heavy seas of that night after some time spent in the water, there were those whose life-jackets had ill-served them. Numbers of corpses had been found floating face down, or even upside down with legs in the air, because the life-jackets were incorrectly fitted and they had not enough strength to right themselves.

Several of the men who died did so with their arms outstretched and fists tightly clenched, as if in a desperate struggle to hold on to life. In being laid out by the two widows, arms had to be tied down beside bodies before they would fit into a coffin. Most men were fully dressed but a large proportion of women had obviously been in bed when the vessel struck the rocks, wearing only underclothes or nightdresses under their life-jackets. One of those recovered on Monday wore just a 'chemise, silk stockings and drawers' and another a flannel night-dress; while one poor woman recovered on Tuesday was utterly naked – and, as the reporter coyly put it:

Her condition was such as to indicate a double loss of life. [5]

When, on the Tuesday the last of the surviving passengers arrived at Penzance on the *Lady of the Isles* to take the train on to Plymouth, one final identification awaited them.

Before boarding it they were taken to the morgue there in the hope that someone could identify the body of the young man brought ashore by the Lowestoft lugger during the previous evening. The ordeal caused three of them to lose the dinners they had just eaten at the Queens Hotel.

The man's face as he lay there under the morgue gaslight was a little swollen, but with its light, gingerish hair, blue eyes and still smiling, looked handsome even in death. When found, a silver Geneva watch which hung on a gold Albert chain across his barrel chest was stopped at 3.30. In his pockets a small pocket book contained three two-dollar notes and the card printed with the name 'Richard Feederle, Akron, Ohio', and the same name written in pencil on the reverse side with an address at Schwartzwald. The survivors were asked if this was Richard Feederle. They recognised him instantly. 'De bruyer, de bruyer!' they exclaimed. The Coroner's men did not understand. The survivors continued in words and actions – as a local newspaper told the tale:

> 'He was de bruyer from oh! vat its name? Vat vas his name! En-n-n-n-n!' But the name would not come. 'He vas big man, gross man, fery stout he vas – de bruyer.' (Pantomimic portraiture of a big man, thick at the chest and portly at the waist. Also of quick work with knife and fork, and rapid eating.) 'He vas twins. He had a twin bruder that is saved.' Then all discoursed volubly about the twin brothers who were as big as their own casks of lager beer, and who were well known all over the Schiller.

The body was not Feederle, this was William Frahm, who last accompanied his twin brother Charles when they were washed off the deck of the ship together. Now he never would follow his father Matthias in the family brewing business at Davenport, Iowa.

The second of the mass funerals was to take place on St Mary's on the Tuesday afternoon, following a formal inquest as before. Owing to the volume of work at the improvised mortuary, with another 16 bodies landed that day, the Receiver of Wreck and the two widows could not prepare in time. They had several assistants, among whom was a lad of 12 engaged in errands. On seeing the corpse of a boy his own age in the loft, with the ball he had been playing with on board ship still in his pocket, the lad ran home to fetch some flowers, and returning, placed them on the dead boy's chest as a tribute.

The funeral cortège finally left the pier-head at six in the evening. The coffins were interred in the long trenches at Old Town churchyard as on the previous day, but on this occasion they were strewn with flowers sent over especially from Tresco by Dorrien-Smith's recent bride Edith. By the end of the day the total of dead recovered and brought to St Mary's had risen to 78; 40 men, 26 women, and six children.

Among those brought ashore to the improvised mortuary that Tuesday, were the bodies of passengers Morris Harrison of Hawkinsville, Georgia; Frederick Uhlmann, the bookseller from Columbus, Ohio; Godfred Altmann, the young marine artist, and Chicago bank clerk, J. William Metzger. Laid beside each other on the storehouse floor were two dead from *Schiller*'s crew, Augustus Felkstow, the chief steward of second cabin and his stewardess wife Maria. Mrs Frances Friend of Milwaukee, the wife of Henry, who had been recovered on Monday, was found that day too – a large reward had been offered for finding her body.

Others were not identified. Charles Walter, the widower son-in-law of Mrs Ridgeway, was almost included among this group. There was nothing upon the body to identify him, in his pockets a comb and penknife. Yet fourth mate, Richard Heintze, recognised him instantly: the corpse was that of the rather nervous man who had regularly asked him about the safety of the ship.

Supplies of wood for the coffins were running low by the Wednesday and large numbers of made up coffins were brought over from Penzance on the steamer during the morning for the main, mass funeral later that day. Before it, in the early afternoon, the body of Mrs Zach, wife of the German Consul at Havana was buried in a private service at the churchyard. This was at the request of the German Ambassador in London. Her coffin was of mahogany rather than the black-painted deal, and bore a black plate inscribed simply, 'Johanna Zach, aged 37, died 7 May 1875'. She was borne by eight mourners to the separate grave where she was to lie. The mourners included John Banfield in his role as German Consul at Scilly, the coffin being preceded by 12 men dressed in black.

Another woman buried separately that day was Clara Just, the wealthy shirt manufacturer's wife from Broadway, New York. Laid beside her was her small son Edward – her daughter Else was not found. Nineteen more victims were interred in the long trenches during a mass funeral that took place at 5pm. During that Wednesday the total number of bodies brought into St Mary's had risen to 91.

The pitiful remains of the *Schiller* victims were turning up over a more widespread area and at all points of the compass as the week progressed. Men on the Seven Stones lightship, 20 miles from Scilly towards Land's End, reported seeing upwards of 50 bodies passing on their north-easterly side on the Tuesday. Ten miles to the west of the islands, a fishing lugger *Tempus Fugit* found and buried at sea the body of a ship's steward that same day. In the evening, French fishing boat *St Marie Mare de Dieu* came into Penzance bearing the corpse of C. Putfarken, the *Schiller*'s chief steward of first cabin. It had been recovered from the sea five miles south-east of Scilly. Three bodies were washed ashore at Mousehole on the Wednesday. Then on Thursday afternoon when making passage for Penzance, the *Lady of the Isles* picked up the body of a well-dressed and bejewelled woman wearing a gold watch and chain around her neck but no life-jacket. At Penzance Polemann identified her as Maria Reichlin, a second-cabin passenger and mother of four children from Detroit.

With many of the dead carrying expensive jewellery, gold watches or sums of money – enough of value in some cases to cover the wages of a poor fisherman for a lifetime – the temptations were not always resisted. There seem to have been few doubts expressed about the honesty of the Scillonians. Bodies brought to St Mary's apparently had all their possessions intact for the Receiver of Wreck to take charge of. There was a story that some of the dead washed ashore at St Agnes had jackets bulging with bundles of dollar bills, which were carefully dropped overboard by boatmen for retrieval later as the bodies were brought into St Mary's. Unfortunately for them, their hoped-for ill-gotten gains were dispersed by the tide and picked up by others elsewhere. Sometime later, two dealers were said to have visited the islands, buying up salvaged dollars at a cheap rate.

As the corpses drifted much further afield, well beyond the sight of land or other vessels, the temptation to take what the sea and providence had offered up in easy pickings was not always resisted. Stories of bodies discovered with rifled money belts abounded, as did those of life-jackets found with no one inside them, where the occupant had been robbed, weighted down and sunk. Among the floating wreckage were passengers' trunks and sea chests with the potential for valuables being found among the personal items inside: these too were not always handed over to the Receiver of Wreck.

The possessions of one dead man signified a remarkable coincidence to the master of the vessel which took his body from the sea. The corpse of this elderly man was recovered six miles south of Scilly on Friday evening by the crew of a Newlyn fishing boat, *Argo*. Upon him was a gold watch and Albert chain, and stitched inside a pocket of the merino vest he wore was £450 in Bank of England notes. His pocket handker-chief and shirt were marked 'Edward Ball'. There was also a diary, completed up to the *Schiller*'s arrival at Plymouth, but with the time left blank, and a card with the name and address of his son, also named Edward, at Birmingham. Strangely, the boat's master, Captain Harvey, knew the son. During a holiday the previous summer the younger Edward Ball had lodged with Harvey's relatives at Newlyn, and he had made many friends in the area. The *Argo* landed the body of the elder Mr Ball at Penzance.

There were funerals for *Schiller* victims on the mainland that afternoon. Two of the crew were buried at Mousehole and another two at Penzance. The oak coffins of ship's purser E. Schmettan and of Krender, the chief baker of the ship, were carried in procession through the narrow streets of Mousehole to St Paul's Church, where the burial-ground overlooked the sea. Each coffin was draped with a small flag provided by the town's coastguards and they were followed by most of its inhabitants, all of the women being dressed in mourning. In Penzance, the last remains of *Schiller*'s chief steward of first cabin, C. Putfarken, together with those of a second-cabin steward named Holm, were laid together in rest at the cemetery. The hearse was preceded by Messrs Matthews the undertaker's workmen and pilots from the port.

Still more corpses were brought ashore. On Saturday the body of a woman thought to have been a stewardess on the *Schiller* was landed at Penzance, and one of the last of the victims recovered near Scilly was brought into St Mary's that afternoon. Among the identified dead on the island that Friday and Saturday were George C. Leonhardt, the jeweller from Augusta, Georgia, and Leonard Fahrig, the *Schiller*'s chief engineer. Unidentified for a time was a woman wearing a ring marked 'Hermann Zinkeisen'.

By the weekend the state of some corpses discovered was such that rather than bring them ashore, they were stripped of valuables and any means of identification, sewn up in a blanket or sailcloth, and after the last rites had been read over them, weighted down and sunk. On Sunday morning a Newlyn fishing boat picked up the body of a woman ten miles west of Bishop Rock. She appeared to have been a fine young lady of some wealth. She wore a seal-skin coat and her jewellery was expensive – gold rings set with diamonds and amethysts, and a gold bracelet with a gold pencil case attached. All these were handed in to the coastguard station at Penzance; but the body, though well-preserved, was wrapped in a sheet and sunk where it was found.

This practice did not please everyone. The captain of a Porthleven fishing lugger sighted a body 15 miles off Scilly on Monday the 17th. It too was that of a woman, only in a very decomposed condition. Having relieved it of money, rings and a memorandum book which gave the lady's identity, the crew then committed the body to the deep in time-honoured fashion. Yet when they carried her belongings to the Receiver of Wreck at Penzance, to their surprise he was most curt with them and rebuked the captain for not bringing the poor woman's remains ashore to be identified by relatives who might be waiting there.

One of the last funerals of *Schiller* victims to take place on St Mary's was held on Sunday the 16th. Shortly after the body of the woman wearing the ring inscribed 'Hermann Zinkeisen' was recovered on Friday, a man arrived from Europe who was able to identify her as his late sister-in-law, Celine, wife of his brother Hermann Zinkeisen. His body had not been recovered, but that of Annie, their 19-year-old daughter, had and been interred on Thursday the 13th. A side-by-side burial was arranged for mother and daughter.

With the funeral being on a Sabbath, the procession from Hugh Town was led by large numbers of Sunday-school children. Along with the many St Mary's inhabitants in the long cortège were German Consul John Banfield, Heinrich Hillers, Erwin Polemann and two stewards of the *Schiller*. After a service by the Revd White, the coffin containing Mrs Zinkeisen was laid beside that of her daughter and the children threw flowers into the grave. Mr Zinkeisen, the brother-in-law, then made a speech of thanks:

> *Mr Banfield, allow me to express on this sacred spot my heartfelt thanks for the way in which you have treated the remains of my dear friends. It will be a great alleviation to the misery of the friends of the dead when I tell them in what a considerate and kind way the remains of their friends have been treated by you and the inhabitants of Scilly.*[7]

The funeral of Edward Ball was arranged for Monday at Penzance. Having had no previous knowledge that his father was on his way to visit him, it came as a complete shock to the younger Edward Ball when earlier in the week he received a telegram from his brother in America, asking him to go to Penzance in the hope of finding his father's body. The news made him ill, and he was only able to make the journey from Birmingham when another telegram arrived informing him that the body was found. He brought with him to the funeral one of his father's old friends who wished to pay his final respects. In Penzance, he soon renewed his acquaintanceship with the Newlyn people with whom he had stayed on holiday the previous year, including the captain of the *Argo*. But when he offered the captain and his crew £40 for finding his

Right: *The burial of* Schiller *victims – possibly on Sunday 16 May when Sunday-school children were present. Note the three men wearing peajackets and peaked caps and one other in a sailors' hat with bobble. These are most likely* Schiller's *officers; Heinrich Hillers, at the foot of the coffin; Erwin Polemann, the taller man; and two stewards.*

GIBSON OF SCILLY

Above: *Highlighted from the main image, these four men are almost certainly German sailors.*

father's body, he caused offence and the money was refused in no uncertain manner. As in previous Penzance funerals of *Schiller* victims, the cortège left the undertakers premises led out by their workmen and several pilots. Two others were interred at the same ceremony; one unknown woman and the other, John Jacob Brunner, head of a long-established firm of importers from New York. His coffin was followed by one of his London business associates.

Two more *Schiller* victims were found the following Wednesday. One, appearing to be that of a petty officer of the ship, was brought ashore by some crab fishermen and later buried at Penzance. The other was that of a woman discovered by the crew of the *Nellie,* a fishing boat from Porthleven. Her corpse was so decomposed that it was weighted down and sunk where it was discovered, after the removal of a gold ring and a pouch which might help give her identity.

The tally of bodies recovered amounted to 130 by Friday the 14th, with the final total mounting to well over 100 at St Mary's and several dozen in other places on the mainland. Fourteen of the St Mary's haul were embalmed, placed in lead-lined, airtight coffins and returned to relatives in America. These included Mr and Mrs Henry

Friend, Morris Harrison, Charles Walter, Frederick Uhlmann, Mrs Kornblum, Carl Schmidt, Mrs Deckritz, Dwight Klink, Miss Dimock, and Mrs Becker, who had to be exhumed from the mass grave for embalming. Two bodies were returned from Penzance; Maria Reichlin to Detroit and William Frahm to Davenport. All of the remaining St Mary's victims were interred at Old Town churchyard, only 34 passengers and 17 crew among them identified, while the remainder were buried in anonymity.

Susan Dimock was embalmed specially by a Dr Hoggan, the house surgeon at Mrs Garrett Anderson MD's college in Boston. An earlier telegram to St Mary's from this lady indicated that she would come to the islands to pay her last respects to her sister doctor. In the event, she sent Dr Hoggan and a Miss Duhms, who were in London at the time, to represent her.

The immense cost of the whole undertaking on behalf of survivors and victims alike was borne by the German Government. Prince Bismarck himself had sent a telegram to German Consul John Banfield early on Tuesday the 11th, instructing him to render every assistance possible to the survivors. All consuls of the German empire in Britain were instructed to provide clothing or money for the journey home on request by any survivors. Burials on both Scilly and the mainland were conducted at German expense. The property taken from bodies recovered or buried at sea was forwarded by John Banfield to the Eagle Line at Hamburg, from where it was returned to relatives. Only the cost of embalming and returning some of the dead was paid for by relatives.

A large reward had been offered for recovering the bodies of Mr and Mrs Henry Friend of Milwaukee, and both were found, embalmed and returned to their home city and 11 grieving children. They were buried together in a Reformed Jewish Church ceremony at Milwaukee's Greenwood Cemetery on 2 June.

A memorial service for those who had perished in the *Schiller* was held at the St John's Lutheran church in Christopher Street, at the heart of the German quarter of New York, on 24 May. It was conducted by the Revd Held before a large gathering of people. In the congregation were many of the family and friends of those passengers who had died in such tragic and terrible circumstances that night.

The many crew who died were not forgotten in Germany, where most had homes. An appeal was launched to provide for the widows and orphaned children of the 91 crew members who would not be returning. By 23 May the sum collected had reached over 23 600 marks. Sympathetic people from all walks of life, senators, businessmen, housewives and schoolchildren, contributed sums ranging from hundreds of marks to pocket-money amounts. A collection was made at the table d'hôte of one large hotel and the entire proceeds of a night's performance at a Hamburg theatre were given over to the fund. Many a ship's captain and crew numbered among the donors; for they were only too well aware of the potential sufferings of a seaman's wife and children in such tragic circumstances. From his home in Strinton Place, Blackheath, Charles H. Martin forwarded £10 for the dependent relatives of those who had shared their Captain's – his brother-in-law George Thomas's – fate.

NOTES

[1]   *The Cornish Telegraph*, 19 May 1875.

[2]   *The Times*, 13 May 1875.

[3]   *Daily Bristol Times and Mirror*, 11 May 1875.

[4]   *The Cornish Telegraph*, 19 May 1875.

[5]   *The Cornish Telegraph*, 19 May 1875.

[6]   as above.

[7]   as above.

An appeal for the widows and orphans of 91 dead crew members with names of donors and amounts suscribed; a full broadsheet page in length in the Hamburgischer Correspondent, *23 May 1875.*

HAMBURG STAATSARCHIV

CHAPTER 16

◆

Fame and Infamy

Capt. Thomas, of the ill-fated steamer Schiller, died like a hero on the post of duty… High above the cries and shrieks of his panic-stricken passengers and crew his stern voice was heard at the supreme moment of danger, commanding his sailors to duty, and even using his revolver in enforcing his orders. Let his name be written on the roll of fame.[1]

Newspaper columnists, like the writer of the above in Augusta, Georgia's, *Daily Constitutionalist*, were inclined at first to highlight the heroic qualities of Captain Thomas's last hours. There was no doubt that he had been resolute and steadfast in doing his duty to the very end, even maintaining a confident demeanour in an attempt to reassure the frightened passengers. Several of them attested to his courage. Henry Sterne said:

Captain Thomas behaved with the utmost bravery… and throughout the terrible and trying scene acted with marvellous coolness and bravery.[2]

For the first two days after the wreck it was the Captain's courageous stand against cowardly men and his death at the height of the storm which coloured newspaper stories. In many, Sterne's version became yet more dramatised in the retelling. Relating how Captain Thomas fired his revolver over the heads of men crowding the number 5 lifeboat, Sterne voiced the opinion that had he been in the Captain's place he would have shot at them. In several newspapers on both sides of the Atlantic this became fact: Captain Thomas first fired over their heads and then at them as well. One version had him expending all his cartridges in this way and then sending for his sword to make some examples among the cowards. Even without such exaggeration, the very mention of the Captain in editorials was likely to include something along the lines of, 'The gallant Captain, who had never departed his post'.

Yet while the *New York Times* of 10 May was commending his 'cool and resolute' actions in its editorial columns, a caustic letter within was raising serious doubts. Signed 'Seventy Voyages', it condemned the paper's statement of the previous day that the wreck was due to 'no fault which human skill could correct'. This, and the glowing testimonials to the Captain, left no room for attributing the loss of his ship to 'ignorance, carelessness or recklessness', he complained. On that same morning, other newspaper editors were demanding an investigation into who, if anyone, was to blame. By evening, one at least was indicating where the culprits might be found:

> *The fact that the vessel was sailing in a dense fog under a heading sufficiently to dash her hopelessly on the rocks causes general condemnation of her management.*[3]

Accusations of recklessness were at first attributed more to the shipping line than the Captain himself. The 'Seventy Voyages' letter had stated already that the demand by shipping lines for fast passages was the root cause of reckless behaviour, when captains, worried in case the line's reputation for speed should suffer, pressed on regardless in thick fog relying solely on their steam whistles to avert danger. In Britain, concerns over the speed of the *Schiller* were similarly expressed through letters to *The Times*. The inter-line rivalry made commanders reckless of their own, their passengers and their crews' lives, while owners were safe and well insured, stated one.[4] The weekly illustrated newspaper *Graphic* suggested that fines should be levied on owners for each death in such disasters. They placed the owners squarely at fault for instructing their captains to push on in thick fog to save time:

> *The loss of the Schiller was due, not to the inevitable perils of the sea, but to culpable human rashness.*[5]

Outright condemnation of Captain Thomas himself came slowly in some quarters. In Augusta, where the *Daily Constitutionalist*'s 'roll of fame' eulogy was published on Wednesday, its rival daily, *The Chronicle*, still displayed an unwillingness to censure the 'hero' with harsh words even on the following Saturday:

He acted in a most gallant and heroic manner... But his heroism came too late and a little prudence two hours earlier could have rendered its display unnecessary.[6]

No such reluctance to apportion blame was by then to be found in any New York newspapers. Thursday's evening *New York Post* reminded its readers of the Captain's valiant end but bluntly added that the disaster was no accident:

It was the result of recklessness and bad seamanship.[7]

This reversal in the dead Captain's reputation was echoed in Britain too. Monday the 10th's edition of *The Times* had carried Sterne's glowing words, 'a more clever gentleman and a better sailor than the Captain could not be'. But by mid-week, George Thomas's skill and seamanship were being questioned severely. His undoubted courage was soon overshadowed by reports of his culpability. Theories about the extent of his error, bad seamanship or sheer recklessness came from all quarters.

The opinion of one officer of a British steamship docked at New York inclined towards error. His suggestion was that, having been unable to take observations for several days, Captain Thomas was far out of his reckoning and much further advanced than he thought he was. In such fog he was on the rocks before he was aware of the proximity of the islands, he said. When pressed to state what precautions should have been taken in those circumstances, he would not say, as if by so doing he might condemn a fellow officer. His reply was that he had no doubt that the Captain had done everything necessary, as he would not wantonly run his vessel into danger.

Others who volunteered their expertise in letters to newspapers were more specific about the precautions Captain Thomas should have, but had not taken. Pilot Commissioner Blunt of New York Harbour drew attention to Rennel's current, running northward across the mouth of the English Channel at approximately 24 miles a day. A careful navigator would allow an extra ten miles a day for error, he claimed, and estimate himself to be this much nearer to land than his reckoning had given him. The Captain was so anxious to make a quick passage that he sacrificed every other consideration, 'but he died at his post, and a man can do no more'.

Blunt thought that taking soundings would not have saved the *Schiller*, where there can be 40 fathoms close in to the shore of the abruptly rising English coastline. Yet in

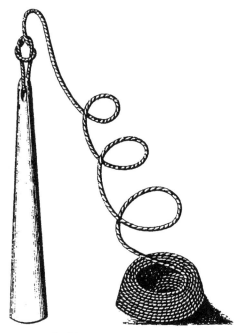

Deep-sea lead-line.

the same day's *New York Times*, 'Old Navigator' argued to the contrary, stating that if soundings had been taken, the *Schiller* and all aboard her would have been saved. The variation of sea-bed deposits between the mid channel 'Fairway Track' of 60 to 90 fathoms, and those on the north side in a direct line with Scilly, where the depth shoaled from 40 to 30 fathoms as the shore was approached, should have shown him his error. In mid-channel it was fine sand and shells, while to the north there was mud and coarse gravel. A careful master would have coated the end of the deep-sea lead-line with tallow to sound the depth and take a sample of the sea bed at the same time, from which to judge where he was in his approach to the Channel. However, the main drawback of taking soundings way out at sea was that the operation required having the ship hove-to with her head to the wind, while a large proportion of the ship's crew heaved the ponderous deep-sea lead-line. 'Old Navigator' recognised this when he wrote:

> *Partly from professional pride, and partly from an unwillingness to lose time, they too often neglect the lead, by the use of which the stranding of any steamship on any coast is well nigh impossible.*[8]

Letters to *The Times* in Britain also addressed the question of taking soundings. One from 'Leadsman,' of the Royal Naval Club, Portsmouth, quoted the official Naval Channel Pilots' Book, where it clearly stated that in thick weather:

> *No ship should approach the Scilly islands to a depth of less than 55 fathoms.*[9]

Another, from Captain Madden RN, echoed 'Old Navigator's' claim that if in the *Schiller*'s last half-hour, the lead-line had been 'armed' with tallow, the ship's position would have been known accurately and disaster averted. A newspaper correspondent telegraphing from St Mary's on Tuesday night, summarised Captain Thomas's neglect thus:

> *The fault of the Captain appears to have been in not heaving the lead; had he done so the peril of the ship would have been manifest, and the shipwreck prevented. As it was Captain Thomas pushed on in the fog, having had no observations for three days, and being as events proved woefully out in his reckoning, which was not unnatural seeing what the winds and currents were.*[10]

Some less well-informed contributors offered the opinion that rather than steam ahead in thick fog, Captain Thomas should have brought the ship to a stop:

> *It was clearly his duty to have stopped the engines altogether and to have kept the steamer stationary until the fog lifted or until the ship's reckoning was regained.*[11]

Others argued he should have avoided Scilly altogether. Those more knowledgeable in maritime matters then pointed out that unless some headway was kept, the ship would not steer at all and drift uncontrollably with the wind and current. Also, in approaching the English Channel some guiding light had to be steered for, and if not the Bishop Rock, then the Lizard or Eddystone had no less sharp rocks adjacent to them.

As newspapers on both sides of the Atlantic castigated the dead Captain for recklessness, a Liverpool newspaper hinted that what had happened was not entirely out of character:

> *It is perhaps, a little remarkable and worth noting, that the Schiller in her first voyage, ran on to a sand bank in dense fog.*[12]

One Cornish contributor exceeded the generally mild tone of most British condemnation, writing that the navigation of the *Schiller* was of the most 'reckless and culpable kind'. A delay of ten minutes while casting the lead would have saved 350 homes from being darkened by the shadow of death, he stated, adding:

> *Captain Thomas may have earned a reputation with his employers and the Atlantic travelling public for smartness and punctuality. Cracking on is all very well until you crack off.*[13]

Generally, concern in Britain over the wreck revolved more around the measures taken to save life afterwards than how it might have been avoided in the first place. The misuse of signals was one of the most hotly debated topics. A letter from Dorrien-Smith to *The Times*, published on the Tuesday, condemned the practice of signalling by guns when passing the islands and mentioned the 1873 international agreement on uniformity of signals allowing their use only in times of distress. In it, he claimed:

> *The North German steamships have been in the habit of firing rockets and guns as signals when they passed at night or in thick weather.*[14]

If the one gun heard on St Mary's that night had been interpreted as a distress signal, then the lifeboat would have put to sea at daybreak and many people saved, he stated. In a letter to the Admiralty in London, James Bulley the Divisional Officer of Coastguard at Scilly went further still and blamed the Eagle Line ships specifically.

It is the practice of this company's steamers to sight Scilly and signalize to Lloyd's agent by firing guns and letting off rockets for the agent to telegraph the ship as passing alright...[15]

More letters to *The Times*, this time refuting such statements, quickly followed. North-German Lloyd's Southampton agents wrote that their vessels had not used guns or rockets for 'private use' since the Act of 1873 limited their use to distress situations. Hamburg-Amerika's London agents retorted in the same vein, adding on behalf of the Eagle Line, whose ships first sailed after the Act had been passed:

We cannot for a moment believe that guns fired from the Schiller, *or any vessel of the Eagle Line, has ever been used, except as a signal of distress.[16]*

Later contributions to *The Times* latched on to the remarks made at the inquest on 10 May, when the St Mary's Coroner stated that telegraphic communication between the lighthouse and the island would have saved almost all on board the *Schiller*. Reiterating this claim were J.G. Uren, the Penzance telegraph superintendent, and Algernon Dorrien-Smith. Dorrien-Smith took up the matter with Pendarves Vivian MP, who aimed to get Parliamentary approval for such links to be made from all isolated lighthouses to the nearest land, even if the line could only be used for a simple 'call' bell at the nearest lifeboat station and not for transmitting messages back and forth.

The reputation of *Schiller*'s crew was inevitably to suffer, considering there were 28 of them saved against only 15 passengers. In Britain's Monday-morning newspapers was an account, attributed to 'A passenger,' which suggested that on the fateful Friday night there had been some 'birthday celebrations' for one of the ship's officers. It went on to state:

The darkness was intense and a great deal of confusion prevailed, as a great many people, both passengers and crew, were intoxicated.[17]

Later that same day, when some of the surviving sailors gave press interviews at the Sailors Home, Plymouth, they were incensed by this claim. All that were there, sailors and steerage passengers, added their voices to a statement refuting the charge:

> *There was no drinking or drunkenness, nor any opportunity for getting intoxicated; nor was there any more confusion than under such awful circumstances was natural and inevitable.*[18]

But this was not strictly correct.

The author of the accusations was Henry Sterne. In interviews he had given to British reporters on the quayside in Penzance and published with his own name, he made no such claim. Yet, this slightly different but more damaging version, voiced there to a *New York Herald* correspondent and attributed to 'A passenger,' was syndicated by their London agents and so appeared in several British newspapers. This account mentioned the drunkeness and additionally accused chief boatswain Simon Jensen and the sailors in number 7 gig of acting in a cowardly manner, having not stayed alongside the *Schiller* to take passengers on board. Sterne did have ample opportunity to make such allegations official when he was the only passenger required to make a deposition on oath before the Receiver of Wreck on St Mary's, along with ship's officers Hillers and Heintze. However, he had not done so then.

In America, there was little reservation about condemning the crew as drunkards or cowards and the *New York Herald*'s publication of Sterne's 'A passenger' account had a far greater impact than in Britain. A general report in Monday morning's *Herald* set the scene; one of the sub-headings for it reading in large capitals, 'THE COWARDLY CREW RUSH FOR THE BOATS'; and beneath it the emotion grabbing line, 'A child's cry the last word from the ship'. On Tuesday, the full 'A passenger' account was published under Sterne's own name, with no indictment spared.

Having, it seemed, not only been negligent in navigation but also failing to exert the proper authority over a crew that was his to command, Captain Thomas was thus further to blame. The once dramatised hero of the American press fell rapidly from grace, his descent particularly abrupt in that district about the Eagle Line's dock where he was well known. Under the influence of Sterne's remarks, the leader writer of Wednesday's Jersey City's *The Argus* compiled a lengthy catalogue of Captain Thomas's wickedness with scant regard for accuracy. No lead was cast and yet the vessel was obviously approaching Scilly, for had not Mr Sterne been out on the foredeck looking for its light? And if he and other passengers knew they were nearing the islands, why did the Captain not know? Many of the crew and passengers were intoxicated because one of the officers was celebrating his birthday: did this mean that the *Schiller*'s officers were in the habit of 'hobnobbing with the crew?' And were passengers on terms of 'undue familiarity' with them as well? It was this lack of discipline which, said the writer:

> *...developed into open disobedience of orders and the crew degenerated into a mob that even the Captain's revolver could not control.*[19]

To cap it all there was the 'defective signalling system' and the lack of ordinary means of saving life on board, for as Mr Sterne had said, he and other persons had distributed the life-jackets until all were gone.

An element of truth in Sterne's initial remarks to the *Herald* reporter at Penzance came out a week later. On 15 May, a London daily newspaper, *The Standard*, reported an interview given by an unnamed officer from the ship still on St Mary's, almost certainly Heinrich Hillers. This officer did agree there was some drunkenness. He told how directly after the ship struck, the ship's fireman and many steerage passengers gathered all the spirits they could find, got hopelessly drunk, and then lay helpless until swept overboard by the waves. But these were a relatively small body of men who became drunk in the time-honoured, fatalistic way of sailors when facing impossible odds – not quite the slant Sterne (or the *New York Herald*'s reporter) had put on the story, implying that drunkenness was widespread and interfered with the lifesaving procedures.

Yet rumours and exaggeration were inevitable outcomes of such a disaster. Only the previous day, the same newspaper had printed a story said to be gaining currency on the Isles of Scilly. This was, that during the night of the wreck women and children were locked in the *Schiller*'s main deckhouse, the pavilion. The officer interviewed utterly refuted this. The doors were not locked, just closed to keep the water out, he explained somewhat bewilderedly to their reporter.

Outright condemnation of Captain Thomas was less harsh in Britain than in America, where the victims had relatives and friends to mourn them. The most virulent recriminations against him expressed in British newspapers were from West Cornwall. 'Our Boy Jack', writing in the *Western Counties Herald* gave this reason:

But for many it needed the actual sight of death's victims and the piles of coffins on the steamer's deck (being sent from Penzance to St Mary's) in order to realise the havoc caused on the Retarrier Ledges.[20]

Reporting the identification of William Frahm's body in the same newspaper, another journalist wrote:

And this is but one out of three-hundred and fifty. Oh! Capt. Thomas, Capt. Thomas. Perhaps it is as well that thou art among the number. Now, men shrug their shoulders and say you are before the highest tribunal. Here, every man's hand would be against thee, judging by what I hear.[21]

NOTES

[1]   *Daily Constitutionalist*, 12 May 1875.

[2]   *Daily Bristol Times and Mirror*, 11 May.

[3]   *Boston Evening Transcript*, 10 May.

[4]   *The Times*, 15 May.

[5]   *The Graphic*, 22 May.

[6]   *The Augusta Chronicle*, 15 May.

[7]   *New York Evening Post*, 13 May.

[8]   *New York Times*, 11 May.

[9]   *The Times*, 18 May.

[10]   *The Cornish Telegraph*, 19 May.

[11]   *The Augusta Daily Chronicle*, 15 May.

[12]   *Liverpool Weekly Mercury*, 15 May.

[13]   *The Cornish Telegraph*, 16 May.

[14]   *The Times*, 10 May.

[15]   *The Cornish Telegraph*, 26 May.

[16]   *The Western Morning News*, 13 May.

[17]   *Manchester Guardian*, 10 May.

[18]   *Daily Bristol Times and Mirror*, 11 May.

[19]   *The Argus*, 12 May.

[20]   *The Cornish Times*, 19 May.

[21]   as above.

CHAPTER 17

•◆•

Entire Neglect

A letter to *The Times* from 'Commander RN,' had suggested that blame should be appointed only after a full and impartial investigation. At first, several British newspapers were of the opinion that there would probably be no inquiry into the wreck at the Board of Trade as the vessel was owned by a German line. Rumours abounded that the Germans would rather have the whole affair hushed up and forgotten. But by the second week, the Foreign Office was reported as being in communication with the Imperial German Government with a view to holding an inquiry in Britain. Foreign Secretary to the Disraeli Government, Lord Derby, finally got both the German Government and Hamburg Senate to agree to one, as the wreck had occurred within Britain's three-mile limit.

No marine or judicial inquiry was to be held in Germany itself, but contrary to the somewhat hostile, xenophobic inferences in English newspapers, there was no reluctance to discuss the *Schiller* disaster there. One newspaper, the *Hamburgischer Correspondent*, conducted a kind of inquiry on its own. This was based on statements taken from officers and passengers and a letter sent by Erwin Polemann to the Eagle Line, which they had published on 13 May. On the 21st they printed a lengthy article in which the writer, an experienced mariner, tried to establish what the ship's course and positions had been and why she struck the Retarrier Ledges. He argued that Captain Thomas had done his duty thoroughly and concluded that, with the information available, he was beyond reproach.

Unfortunately, the information the writer was working with was not entirely correct. The *Schiller*'s noon position, stated to be 49° 49' N latitude, 9° W longitude, seems to have originated with the omnipresent Henry Sterne rather than the ship's own officers (who were later agreed upon 49° 50' N; 10° 23' W). Assuming then that the ship was travelling at only ten knots, he carefully calculated that the east-by-south course steered would have brought her in sight of the Bishop Rock light at 9pm, with 11 miles south to spare. But with the fog descending at 8.30pm, and Rennel's current at its strongest in a westerly or south-westerly wind, he thought Captain Thomas would not then be sure if he was north or south of the lighthouse.

'He had been tireless in his depth taking,' wrote the journalist, repeating what some passengers had previously quoted. Yet to the north-west and again south of the Bishop, there is the same depth and the same type of sea-bed deposits, so he had no way of knowing to which side the *Schiller* was positioned. That was why he changed course to south-south-west at 9.30pm. But he had no idea that he was much more westerly than calculated, and the manoeuvre was already too late. With the Bishop Rock light invisible to them through the fog and its bell not heard above the violent sounds of wind and sea, 'Demonic forces had dedicated the ship to its ruin.'

There was also criticism of Captain Thomas in German newspapers; some of which should have had the weight of authority, considering its author. That unfortunate survivor, Louis Reiderer, whose wife and six-year-old daughter were lost in the wreck, contributed to an article published in the *Frankfurter Zeitung* on 3 June. As he still had in his possession the sheets providing passengers with a daily record of the ship's run and noon positions from 3 to 7 May, he argued that survivors claiming calculations were not made because of the fog must be wrong. Captain Thomas knew exactly where the *Schiller* was positioned, he stated, arguing there was negligence. He included comments that the sea was 'calm' for the first hour and a half after the wreck; that the lifeboats were difficult to launch, 'immovably fixed in position' by a thick coat of paint which covered even the ropes and pulleys; and there were not enough life-jackets.

The *Hamburgisher Correspondent* was incensed that any German newspaper should accept such an article. Already in foreign newspapers there was 'unpleasant and wide ranging criticism', they wrote. It was obvious that Reiderer was confusing ship's positions gained from celestial observations with those ascertained by dead reckoning, and attributing a degree of accuracy to the latter which no experienced mariner would dare do. The 'calm' sea, as it might have seemed to a layman, had nonetheless a sufficient swell to smash lifeboats and later still the *Schiller* itself to pieces. None of his criticisms, they wrote, were supported by a single official statement from crew or passengers taken in Hamburg; and the British Board of Trade Inquiry, currently sitting, had already maintained that the ship and its lifesaving apparatus was in an 'exemplary' condition.

The British Board of Trade Inquiry had opened on 1 June at Greenwich Police Court. It was headed by J.H. Patteson, stipendiary magistrate, assisted by two nautical assessors, Captain Henry Harris and Captain Charles E. Pryce. At its very outset, the legality of the proceedings were questioned. Appearing for the Eagle Line's solicitors, Mr Mansel Jones asked how it was that the Board had power to order an inquiry on a foreign vessel. Mr Charles Bowen, for the Board, answered by stating that it had been ordered under the 1854 Merchant Shipping Act, and that there was a precedent in an Inquiry held after the U.S. vessel *Endymion* was burnt in the River Medway in 1860. Mansel Jones then asked if the German Government had agreed to the Inquiry, rather than one held in Germany. In reply, Mr Bowen produced a despatch from Germany which read:

> *We thoroughly acquiesce in this inquiry on the part of the Royal British Authorities and it will be of great interest to the Imperial German Government to learn the result.*[1]

The Germans also reserved the right to hold an inquiry of their own.

With this established the proceedings commenced. The Court was to address five main questions: how the ship got into her position? what precautions were taken in the thick fog? why the Bishop Rock fog bell was not heard? why so many of the passengers and crew were not saved by either the ship's own boats or boats from the shore? and if communication between the lighthouse and the shore would have prevented the heavy loss of life. They were also to discover why the ship's signal guns were ignored by people on the shore and if this was because they were frequently used to signal shipping line agents.

First to take to the witness stand was Heinrich Hillers, the *Schiller*'s first mate. Speaking in German, he related all that had happened of which he was aware from noon on 7 May, almost without interruption. He concluded the first day's hearing by stating that the ship's crew had been a good one, the Captain 'steady, sober and well-conducted', and that discipline had been maintained until the last. He thought the Captain had done all he could have done.

On the second day, Hillers changed some of the evidence he had given the previous day – his memory had not been too good since the wreck, he explained. Then, when the ship's course was under investigation, Hillers and second mate Erwin Polemann gave differing accounts, with Polemann, said to be 'a very intelligent witness', speaking in excellent English. Both were agreed that the noonday position on the 7th, calculated from the previous day's dead reckoning, was 49° 50′ N latitude, 10° 23′ W longitude. Both men also claimed that Captain Thomas's reckoning was always very accurate, Hillers saying:

> *He had never before found the Captain to be more than a mile and a half out in his reckoning, and that was only after a bad observation.*[2]

Where they differed was in their estimates of the vessel's true course as opposed to the course steered by the compass. Until 9.30pm that evening the *Schiller* was steered E 30° S (or SE by E). Hillers, working on a compass variation of 31° W, thought this would give them a course one degree north of east, and estimating the drift of current would take them some way south of this, reckoned their true course as E 3° S.

Polemann had taken an azimuth reading when the sun showed at around 6pm, and this corroborated his belief that the magnetic variation from true north was 27 degrees. From this he calculated their course as S 87° E, to which he added three degrees for the northward drift of the current. This gave him a true course of due east.

Questioned closely by Captain Harris, Hillers explained that he had since realised his allowance for compass variation was wrong and that it should have been 27 degrees. Captain Thomas had told him it was 31 degrees, he claimed. He was dumbfounded to learn that his estimate of a three-degree southerly drift of current was totally incorrect. Harris pointed out that Rennel's current runs diagonally north-west across the mouth of the English Channel – 'as everyone should know' – and they should have steered south to counteract it. They had got it back to front, he said. Polemann's calculations were near to correct. Had the noonday position been right and their true-course been S 87°E, they should have passed seven or eight miles to the south of Bishop Rock. Unfortunately, neither their position at noon, nor the heading they thought they were on, were accurate.

Added to these errors was a lack of precise knowledge as to where the Bishop Rock was positioned. Harris queried Hillers on this topic. He instructed the interpreter,

'Will you tell him that having observed the 49° 0′ (north latitude) he was only two miles south of Bishop Rock.'

'All I know is that the lighthouse was in 'latitude 55', replied Hillers.

'49° 55'?' Harris asked him.

'As such as I know.'

On being shown a chart, Hillers was forced to admit that the lighthouse was in latitude 49° 52′ N.

'Was he aware at that time that his dead reckoning only gave him two miles south of Bishop Lighthouse?'

'I knew that, and in effect it must have been so.'

After this odd answer, Dr Mühlberg, the German Vice-Consul, intervened and questioned Hillers, obtaining a correction,

'But I did not know it on the 7th,' he explained.[3]

Had all their calculations of position and a heading of due East been correct, then they would have passed the Bishop Rock by only two miles, not seven or eight.

In fact, they were well to the north of their supposed noonday position and much further eastwards, where the Schiller had greatly over-run the distance which the chronometers and log indicated. In dead reckoning from the previous day's dead reckoning on three successive days they had magnified their errors until they had a totally false opinion of their position on the chart. Yet if it had not been for the thick fog, they would have almost certainly had the opportunity to avoid the islands and their treacherous rocks.

At what time the fog descended upon the vessel was never fully clarified. Few witness accounts corresponded on timing. Hillers stated it was thick at 8pm when his watch began and Fritz Beckhaus, the forward lookout, agreed. Yet Polemann, who first noticed the fog at 6.30pm, claimed it was not dense at 8pm when visibility was up to five miles. Fourth mate Richard Heintze, by contrast, claimed it was dense at 6pm and that by 8pm he could not see all of the ship's length. Some of these discrepancies were no doubt due to the foreign tongue in which some witnesses were examined, although Captain Harris pointed out that varying descriptions of weather conditions were quite normal in nautical matters.

There was little about the precautions taken in the face of the oncoming dense fog which found approval among Board representatives. Captain Harris asked Polemann if it had been prudent to aim at passing the Bishop by seven miles in such foggy conditions. Polemann's defence was that the dense fog only came on at night – after his watch had ended. Hillers, in whose watch the worst of the fog and the wreck occurred, admitted that apart from sounding the ship's fog whistle at half-minute intervals from 8pm, and the usual two lookouts posted forward at dusk, the Schiller was run at her full speed of 14 knots until 9pm. They had begun furling the sails at 8.30pm, but this and a slowing to half-speed of ten knots was all that was done until their course was changed from E 30° S to SSW at 9.30pm. The course change was at his prompting, he claimed, and when asked the reason by Captain Harris he said:

> *In order not to run on to the shore and let the night pass. We did not want to go further until daybreak.*[4]

After the course change, the vessel was slowed first to quarter speed and then to dead slow, according to the accounts of other survivors.

When asked why soundings were not taken, Hillers replied that he was occupied with the taking in of the sails and that Captain Thomas had not ordered him to do so. The Captain was eccentric in this respect, he claimed, and orders to use the lead-line came from him only. He could give no reason why the ship was not stopped at 8pm for soundings to be taken. Although the deep-sea lead-line was laid out on deck ready for use, it never was used, and had not been for three days, he said. He had made no suggestions to the Captain that they should take soundings.

Mr Bowen, representing the Board, then read out a translation of the instructions given to captains in the service of the Eagle Line with reference to soundings:

> *The loss of the* Atlantic *and* City of Washington *have shown how important it is to take soundings near the land, particularly in the night and in foggy weather, and in doing so not to neglect anything. Even so, if you believe you are going safe according to your prickings of the chart but have not had any pure observation, it is your duty to assure yourself that you are at that spot which the pricking of the chart has shown.*[5]

This also stated that, if in doubt, the captain was expected to consult his officers. These instructions had been on board the *Schiller* along with a set of directions for approaching the English Channel, warning all navigators to guard against the northerly drift of Rennel's current when approaching Scilly and urging then to use the lead-line in thick weather. Captain Thomas had clearly neglected them both. Hillers claimed to have seen the Eagle Line's instructions on the Captain's table but he had never read them. 'They were for captains,' he explained.

The court then heard that it was common practice for vessels to come in close to the Isles of Scilly in all weathers. James Daniel, the senior lighthouse keeper on the night of the 7th, gave evidence of ships coming to within a half a mile of the lighthouse in thick weather so they could signal. For the Eagle Line, Mansel Jones pointed out that masters wanted to make Scilly to signal their imminent arrival at south-coast ports to the Lloyd's agent there. There was also a recommendation in the British Channel Directions for ships to make Scilly before coming up the Channel, he said.

Countering this, James Nicholas Douglass, chief engineer of Trinity House, argued that ships were not advised to come close in thick fog. The use of the lead-line was recommended, he said, even in the most favourable circumstances, and was crucial when celestial observations had not been made. Captain Pryce and both Jacob Deason and Stephen Hicks, the Trinity House pilots of St Agnes, were all agreed that in the circumstances, soundings should have been taken.

All witnesses from the *Schiller*'s crew were questioned about having heard the Bishop Rock fog bell, and each one said they had not heard it at all from the ship. Only Polemann and chief boatswain Simon Jensen had heard the bell faintly when near to the lighthouse in the lifeboat during the night. That the lighthouse keepers had rung the bell was corroborated by the evidence of mechanic Thomas Cole, who had been on Bishop Rock that night.

Following on from this came the question of how to ensure that some warning of fog was better heard in the future. Hillers stated that if the Bishop Rock lighthouse had such a foghorn as was used at Sandy Hook, audible up to five miles, they would have heard it on the *Schiller*. Mansel Jones remarked on the difficulties of hearing a bell above the noise made by a steamship's engines. Both he and John Banfield advocated a steam foghorn on the islet of Rosevear: there was certainly no room for one situated beside the lighthouse itself. However, Daniel and Douglass were of the opinion that Rosevear was unsuitable too; for if the wind blew from the south-west, as it did on the night of the wreck, it would not be heard to windward. Crebawethen was then put forward as a likely site by Dorrien-Smith, but nothing specific came of the discussion.[6]

Having established that the *Schiller* was off-course, soundings had not been taken and neither the light nor fog bell at Bishop Rock been seen or heard, the Board turned their attention to the saving of lives in the aftermath. First, there was some disagreement about the lifesaving equipment on board the *Schiller*. Hillers claimed that the lifeboats could hold 80 to 85 people in each and the gigs 40, but later admitted he was guessing. Stevens, the Eagle Line agent, gave them a total carrying capacity of 400, but then stated that the vessel was equipped with 'Cliffords patent lowering apparatus'. This point was denied by Hillers who maintained that it was not 'Cliffords' but just block and tackle hung on davits. Captain Harris commented that the only two

Steam fog-horn of the type being tested by Trinity House, mid-1870s.
ILLUSTRATED LONDON NEWS

boats to get away successfully were gigs and that the much heavier lifeboats proved difficult to raise because of the lack of a patent lowering gear. Otherwise, with eight lifeboats, 12 lifebuoys and 800 life-jackets on board the vessel, it was quite well-equipped.

There were no questions asked about the condition of the lowering gear, the manner in which the lifeboats were launched, or criticisms made of their manning by the crew. The owners had given proper instructions to their officers, declared Mr Patteson the Magistrate, and it seems that the Court was satisfied that they did their duty to the best of their ability under trying circumstances. Comment was made that many of the life-jackets had been 'unskilfully used'. When queried about locked doors, Polemann said that the fore cabin and quarter-deck doors were open and never locked, day or night.

Almost all of the court's concern over the lifesaving measures revolved around the question of the signals used by the *Schiller* in passing the islands and the firing of guns by German steamers for this reason. When interrogated closely on this issue, both Hillers and Polemann replied that the *Schiller*'s night signals were always the same; a blue light, a rocket and a fire-ball, in that order. Guns had never been used on either the *Goethe* or the *Schiller* while he was on them, said Hillers. Polemann mentioned a night in November 1874 when in passing the islands in thick weather, *Schiller*'s signals were repeated three or four times with no answering signal forthcoming (this possibly the incident for which Banfield was reprimanded) – yet they did not resort to using guns. Their evidence of the night signals used was corroborated by Stevens who also quoted an Eagle Line rule stating that 'under no circumstances' were guns to be used for signalling, as it was by order of the German Government.

Signal gun from Schiller.

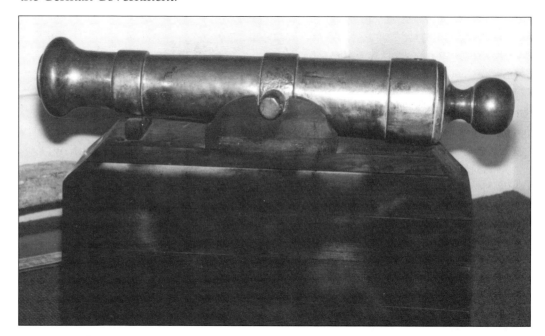

Nonetheless, there was evidence that this had been done by one German steamship, in contravention of the International Agreement of 1873. A Hamburg-Amerika vessel had been observed to fire a gun in signalling her arrival early in 1874, said John Banfield. He gave several instances of guns heard from out at sea but said that no Eagle Line vessels had ever fired them. His nightwatchman had not believed that the gun heard on the night of the wreck was *Schiller*, he added. The United States consular agent on Scilly, Thomas Johns Buxton, then gave evidence about an incident on 14 February that year, when loud guns were fired during the night off Porthcressa Bay. He, like many other islanders, had left their beds expecting to have to help save lives, but no vessel was seen and it was ultimately assumed to have been a ship's passing signal. Both Jacob Deason and Stephen Hicks, the Trinity House pilots, gave other instances in which they had put to sea after hearing guns, when as Hicks put it, 'All I got was a wet shirt.'[7]

That there was reason to suspect some German steamships of using guns illegally, was admitted by the German Vice Consul, Dr Mühlberg. Hamburg-Amerika ships had official instructions not to use guns that way in spite of the incident mentioned. North German Lloyd captains had been barred by the company from doing so since 1867. After the *Schiller* disaster their captains had been questioned on this matter and only one had admitted infringing the rule – and that was in salute to the German Crown Prince the previous year. The *Schiller*, however, was not among the culprits, he said. In summing up the court were moved, in justice to Captain Thomas and the Eagle Line, to exonerate them completely from any misuse of signals.

On the final question of communications between the lighthouse and St Mary's, Dorrien-Smith mentioned that a telegraph link between the two would have helped save more lives. Although the weather was too rough to go out at night, the lifeboat could have left at 6am and saved the people from the ship's masts, he said. A line laid between the islands could have had the same result, with the wreck being known of on St Agnes so early in the night. He also commented that the privately owned line in use would be better maintained in Government hands. Trinity House engineer Douglass was of the opinion that a line could not be kept up to the lighthouse as any cable would be soon worn away against the rock on which it stood. By way of an example he mentioned that a 1½in-diameter mooring chain there had been worn away completely over one winter. The Court ultimately decided not to offer an opinion on the issue.[8]

No credence was given to stories in the press about drunkenness and disorder among the crew and passengers on the night of the disaster. Both Hillers and Mr Bowen stated categorically that there had been no celebrations on board the ship on the 7th. Neither were the accusations of cowardice levelled at chief boatswain Jensen and the sailors under him in gig number 7 by Henry Sterne brought into court. In his own evidence Jensen merely stated that he had cut the rope because he could no longer remain safely alongside the *Schiller*. That he had also apparently ignored an order from Captain Thomas to return to the ship and take on passengers was never mentioned.

The speed at which the *Schiller* had been travelling obviously concerned some in court. Captain Harris asked if the Eagle Line were bound by any penalties under their mails contract which might induce captains to take risks. Stevens declared that he believed there were no penalties imposed for late arrival of mails. This was to be confirmed later in an examination of the contract.

Mr Batten, defending Captain Thomas and instructed to appear on behalf of the Captain's sister, Elizabeth Martin, addressed the Court at considerable length on the third day of the hearing. Several testimonials referring to George Thomas's conduct during a career spanning the years 1851 right through to his resignation from P & O in December 1872 were read out. Most were from masters of P & O ships on which he had served; two were from Captain J.S. Castle, under whom Thomas had served as first officer on the *Mongolia*; another was from Captain Mitchell of H.M. Bengal Brig *Kedgeree*, on which he served before joining P & O.

Batten was all out to refute any charge of negligence which might be levelled at his client's late brother. He reminded the Court:

'During the last days of the *Schiller*, the evidence was that he was most sedulous. He almost slept in the chartroom.'

He was confident in his and his mates' reckoning, and, being certain that he was still 28 miles from the Bishop, he ordered the fog-whistle to be sounded, said Batten.

'The lead was got ready. Everything was ready to be done when the sails were furled, but the whole of the watch were occupied at the moment she struck in furling sails.'

Having tried to establish Captain Thomas had every intention to take soundings, Batten next turned his attention to the ship's speed.

'Why did he go at that rate in the fog?' he asked rhetorically.

If there was a fog 150 miles out, it did not necessarily mean there was fog at Scilly. When he realised he could not sight the islands he altered his course, believing he would be able to sound and feel his way up Channel. Batten did concede that there must have been an error in their reckoning, and that the allowance made for the drift of the current was at fault, carrying them further north than they anticipated. Even so, there was no negligence by Captain Thomas, he stated.

After three days sitting, the Inquiry was adjourned until 12 June, during which time the mails contract was to be examined. This must have been approved, for no further reference was made to it. In spite of Mr Batten's pleas on the 3rd, when the Magistrate and nautical assessors finally reconvened on the 12th they placed the blame for the wreck squarely on Captain Thomas. In their published report they concluded that the assumed position at noon on the 7th was incorrect and the *Schiller* much further north and to the east of where their chartwork indicated them to be. Yet if the lead had been cast at 8 or 9pm, before the course was altered, they had no doubt that the error would have been discovered and the wreck averted. By not using the lead-line, Captain Thomas had neglected the on-board instructions for the safe navigation of the English Channel and the recommendations of the Eagle Line's own captains' manual. The wreck was, they stated:

> *Attributed solely to neglecting to guard against a northerly set when approaching Scilly and not using the lead in thick weather.*[9]

The 'entire neglect' of these precautions was 'the sole cause of the terrible calamity'.

NOTES

[1] *The Times*, 2 June 1875.

[2] as above.

[3] *The Times*, 3 June 1875.

[4] as above.

[5] as above.

[6] Trinity House had already tested a steam fog-horn similar to the one at Sandy Hook at the South Foreland lighthouse. It consisted of two discs with radial slits, one revolving against the other, through which steam was forced at a high pressure. The sound made was then amplified by a 20ft-long, cast-iron trumpet and could be heard for three miles. Trinity House had ordered some made with a view to establishing a complete chain of fog signals around the British coastline.

[7] On 19 May, the *Hamburgischer Correspondent* reported that on the 13th loud cannon shots and the whistle of a steamer had been heard on Scilly during thick fog. Many people there thought it was another wreck. When the fog lifted the whistle proved to have been from a steamship coming dangerously close to the north of the islands. The cannon shots were from a warship, taking no account of the recent disaster and local confusion over signals with cannons.

[8] Opposition to the idea of such improvements had already appeared. At a meeting of the United Services Institution, Sir Frederick Arrow, head of Trinity House, said that connecting lighthouses to the mainland by telegraph was 'absurd'. His first reason was, 'It would not pay.' His second was that lighthouse keepers would have no time to attend their proper duties if they were busy using the telegraph.

[9] Abstracts of Wrecks, Casualties and Collisions; Returns to Board of Trade (1875).

CHAPTER 18

•◆•

Salvage

Captain Thomas was not alone in having mistakenly relied upon dead reckoning and arrived at the Isles of Scilly totally unexpectedly. It was an error made by some famous forebears. Rear Admiral Sir Clowdisley Shovell's fleet of ships had done just that after encountering thick and cloudy weather in October 1707, when the Captain of the *Torbay*, one of the surviving vessels wrote:

> *We were much to ye Northwards of what was expected… and likewise more to the Eastward.*[1]

Fourteen years prior to this disaster, Sir John Narborough, commanding a squadron of ships returning from Cadiz, had narrowly escaped the same fate among the 'Bishop and all his clerks', having not made allowances for Rennel's current.

> *Our being more Northerly than expectation….. is by the current that do constantly set Northerly…* he wrote.[2]

By the nineteenth century, navigators had far more accurate instruments and charts to work with. The nautical sextant had long since replaced the cross-staff and quadrant of Shovell's era, and by the late eighteenth century the marine chronometer enabled mariners to work out their longitude with a degree of reliability unknown in former times. From 1821 carefully surveyed hydrographic charts of all parts of the world were available to merchant shipping from the British Admiralty, giving data of depths and sea-bed deposits for comparison with results from the lead-line. Yet wrecks still happened frequently through navigational error or neglect.

On the same night and in almost the same locality as the *Schiller*, another wreck occurred. The ship was a barquantine, the *Abadour*, of London, carrying a cargo of rum and sugar from Demerara. At noon on the 7th the vessel was to the north of Scilly but later that night ran on to rocks at Pendeen, north of Land's End. Two of the crew were drowned in an attempt to swim ashore, but one succeeded and raised the alarm; and the rest were taken off when a line was fired across to them by coastguards. An Inquiry held at Greenwich in late May found that the captain had neglected to take 'the necessary precaution during thick and foggy weather', having not used the lead-line at all. This neglect caused him to suffer the suspension of his master's certificate for six months.

Captain Thomas's neglect had been the same, but his responsibilities and the result of this neglect were more terrible by far. Of all passenger shipwrecks on or adjacent to the British coastline up to that time in the nineteenth century, *Schiller*'s total of 341 casualties were eclipsed only by those of the auxiliary steamship, *Royal Charter*, in which 459 died when she was wrecked off Anglesey on a passage from Australia in October 1859. The *Schiller* was the 62nd Atlantic steamship to be lost in 37 years of regular steamship services across the Ocean since their beginning in 1838, and was one of the worst. Only the disappearance of Inman Line's iron screw pioneer *City of Glasgow* with 480 on board in 1854, the fire on the Hamburg-Amerikan *Austria* in which 471 perished in 1858, and the wreck of the White Star liner *Atlantic* in 1873, had cost more lives. *Atlantic*, the worst wreck of them all, accounted for 562 of the numbers of lives lost in Atlantic steamships – totalling more than 4500 and said to be as many as 5776. Fortunately, the majority of all wrecks were without loss of life.

The wreck of the *Schiller* almost paralleled that of the *Atlantic*. The shipping line owners of both vessels arrived on the Atlantic scene in the early 1870s to run against established rivals – Eagle Line with Hamburg-Amerika, the Liverpool-based White Star with Cunard. Each line aimed to outdo the competition with a combination of passenger comfort and speedy crossings. Both *Schiller* and *Atlantic* were wrecked on rocks due to navigational error and their captains subsequently deemed to have been guilty of negligence. Yet the behaviour of the two captains had been vastly different.

When the *Atlantic* encountered heavy weather and ran short of coal on a passage from Liverpool, her captain, James Williams, decided to make for Halifax, Nova Scotia, instead of New York. Observing a light which he mistakenly took for a lighthouse west of Halifax harbour, but which was another 19 miles east of it, he then retired to his cabin without once consulting his charts. None of the officers on watch consulted the charts or took soundings, and the *Atlantic* continued through the night at a speed of 12 knots – right until she ran on to rocks at Mars Head.

Captain Williams survived the wreck of his ship, and at an investigation held in Canada was judged to have been negligent; the main charge against him being his failure to take soundings. Apart from that, he had failed to consult his charts and retired to sleep as his vessel entered waters unfamiliar to himself and his officers. Such conduct called for 'severe censure'. He had, however, shown courage and done his utmost to save life in the aftermath of the wreck. Taking this into account meant that his licence was revoked for only two years, after which he once again commanded transatlantic steamships.

By the standards of Captain Williams of the *Atlantic*, George Thomas's 'entire neglect' seems mild, despite the calamitous wreck and the many casualties. He had, as Mr Batten said in his defence, slept in the chart room for several days when they experienced thick weather, such was his conscientiousness. Unlike Williams, he had not left the bridge at a crucial time and was cautious enough to slow the ship and change course in an attempt to take his vessel further out into the English Channel, away from potential danger. Like Williams, in trying his best to retrieve the situation by saving life afterwards, he had done so, in his case, to the point of losing his own.

In not taking soundings with the lead-line, Captain Thomas contravened advice in the Eagle Line's instruction manual which mentioned as an example the wreck of the *Atlantic*. Yet culpable though he was in this omission, it is probable, as Mr Batten hinted during his defence, that he would have done so had he not thought he was well clear of the Isles of Scilly. Believing from his own and his officers' reckoning that the ship was much further south and west of where she actually was, and totally unaware that he was close in among rocks to the west of the islands, he had no reason to think it essential to do so.

Perhaps Captain Thomas's greatest fault was over-confidence. Like many a man who has worked his way up in through the ranks, he was intensely proud of his abilities and achievements. He had gained high repute as an officer of the P & O Line, whose own reputation for reliability and punctuality was a byword, and through it the command of the *Schiller* had been offered him. Ever since joining the Eagle Line he had maintained these standards, almost invariably keeping to the scheduled sailing times. Even in spite of the setbacks at the onset of his seventh and final return passage across, he was about to arrive at Plymouth almost on time. This pride in his ability and reputation comes across in his words: when Polemann first became concerned over the thickening fog, Thomas had said, 'I will make Scilly, I always do.' No doubt he was as confident in the correctness of his chartwork; the position at noon and the ship's true heading being almost unquestionably 'right' because he always was. Only for once, he was not, and many others would suffer the consequences of his error.

Within two years, Captain Thomas's reputation had been salvaged to some degree. As early as two weeks after the wreck, the Hamburg journalist conducting his rather flawed newspaper inquiry into the wreck of the *Schiller,* which totally exonerated the Captain, had queried:

Do we not bear ourselves part of the guilt for accidents at sea?[3]

Demands for more and more speed by ships came from the public, who also lauded the captains making the fastest journeys. Seafaring, he wrote, had become 'a hunt and a chase,' but it was through no fault of the seafarers themselves. Concluding his article, the ex-mariner asked himself, 'Would we have acted differently?' It was a pertinent question, and others were asking the same.

Three weeks after the wreck, an editorial in *Harper's Weekly*, the American illustrated journal, baldly stated:

Let the blame rest where it belongs. The public is itself largely responsible for these dire events.[4]

It was the public as ever, it claimed; impatient of delays by railroad trains or ferry boats alike – always bursting with impatience at the slightest delay. They were the people responsible; it was their impatience which dictated the instruction for swift passages. The Post Office was also awarded some scathing comments, selecting only the fastest ships for their contracts and encouraging a contest of speed between shipping lines.

These were certainly the main external pressures working on transatlantic steamship lines. Punctuality and speed were not just matters of a captain's pride and reputation. Since the days of sailing packets people had favoured those with a reputation for the quickest crossings, regardless of the tremendous risks taken by their captains. In the steamship era it was Blue Riband liners and others with a record of speed and punctuality, or else the attractions of the latest in on-board luxury, which attracted the most passengers. Staid but safe lines lost out to rivals who were able to better them on these counts – as Cunard had found when Collins liners took their trade in the 1850s and again when White Star came along in the early 1870s. The public demanded speed, the post office encouraged it and because of this, shipowners insisted upon it. It was good for business. The old sea adage, 'The more days, the more dollars', applied especially to the considerable day-to day expenses of running a fully laden passenger vessel. Any delay, even of a few hours, cost vast amounts of money, could eat into the owner's profit and might reflect badly on the line, causing a fall-off of passengers and freight or the loss of a mails contract.

With time a main consideration in the cut-throat competitiveness between German lines of the mid-1870s, safety may have been compromised. The regularity with which Eagle Line ships ran aground in the difficult-to-negotiate River Elbe, suggest an over-anxiousness to make headway. Schnellenberg's observations indicate that the operation of *Schiller*'s main lifeboat davits or the signal guns were seldom, if ever tested – possibly through lack of time. And though, as Mr Batten implied, Captain Thomas may have intended to heave-to and take soundings with the deep-sea lead-line, it is equally plausible that with *Schiller* behind timetable for arrival at Plymouth, this safety proceedure would also have been overlooked.

The effects of such intense pressure to keep to a timetable was ultimately recognised. A writer on shipwrecks commenting on the *Schiller* disaster in 1877 stated:

A loss of three hundred lives was primarily due to the unwillingness of her captain to prolong his voyage by only a few hours. Yet no special blame ought to be thrown on his memory, for he was unquestionably thinking of the interests of his owners.[5]

Captain Thomas had good reason to impress shipowners, especially those of the Hamburg-Amerika Line. With the Eagle Line's demise imminent he would be looking for employment, most likely with the company about to take them over. His record would be under scrutiny, and as the writer commented:

It is notorious that owners do not regard with favour those captains who lengthen their passages by what they are apt to consider unnecessary caution.

Yet having absolved Captain Thomas from blame, this same writer was not about to condemn owners for losses such as that of the *Schiller* and concluded in much the same vein as had *Harper's Weekly* two years beforehand:

Are the owners then at fault? Not entirely; they depend on the patronage of the public for interest on their capital, and in these days of competition, pleasure and feverish excitement, ships which are reported to make slow voyages soon find their cargoes reduced and their berths empty.

Sadly, on the night of 7 May George Thomas and 340 others paid a heavy price for such competitiveness.

No one would seriously claim that the unfortunate passengers on *Schiller* were personally the architects of their own destruction for having booked passages on a vessel with a reputation for punctuality. Yet when the *Schiller* struck upon the terrible Retarrier Ledges, the behaviour of so many of them certainly worsened the plight of all aboard her. Panic was only to be expected, but had most cleared the decks and gone below as Captain Thomas ordered them to, the lifeboats would have been launched more readily and more might have been got away before the sea worsened. The actions of those who commandeered lifeboats, disregarding the needs of women and children in their desperation to save themselves, further hampered the crew's efforts to launch them. Only this disorderly and frantic behaviour in that first crucial hour after striking prevented many more people from being saved. But is that the whole story?

The *Schiller* was certainly well-equipped with lifesaving apparatus at a time when almost all ships carried far too little. She was near-new and, according to the Board of Trade's nautical assessors, in exemplary condition, unlike some older vessels with lifeboats rusted in place or unseaworthy through neglect. There was space in her lifeboats for everyone on board – having less than a third of her total capacity of 1000 passengers – and they all had designated lifeboat stations to go to in an emergency. There were also life-jackets enough to spare, even if few knew or could remember in the panic where they were situated.

Yet two survivors, Franz Schnellenberg and Louis Reiderer, contended that a thick coating of paint on the davit ropes hampered the crew when launching the lifeboats. They claimed that for over an hour after the wreck, when the sea was 'quite calm', all the boats could have been launched and most people saved in them but for this problem. Officially-taken statements from the surviving crew and other passengers mention no such difficulties with painted ropes, and these two passengers may have seriously underestimated the power of the waves. Schnellenberg added that thick paint had stuck the signal gun trigger and kept closed a hatch door where life-jackets were kept. If all this is true, there is a possibility that the delay in raising lifeboats in their davits due to paint, worsened the panic on board, which in turn hampered the crew's efforts. Yet for a nearly new ship to have had such a thick coating of paint, particularly on ropes, seems unlikely. Repainting may have taken place when in March 1874 the *Schiller*'s stern was repaired – but to that extent? It is a mystery that must remain unanswered.

Why more women did not survive is more easily addressed. It was probably because of their comparative helplessness in the awful situation. The better-off 'ladies' particularly were conditioned to think of themselves as the 'weaker sex', and acted accordingly; some resigning themselves to fate, sitting mute and white-faced in the saloon, others crying out continually for male assistance. Their clothing, tight corsets, bustles and long heavy dresses, or even the flowing nightgowns which so many wore, would have inhibited movement enough to make clambering into a lifeboat or climbing the rigging extremely difficult. Physical acts which could have saved them, like being lowered into a gig, proved impossible for some 'ladies' who insisted that steps must be provided. Yet Christine Joens, the only woman survivor, thrown into a lifeboat by her husband John, whose prompt action almost certainly saved her life, proved the stronger in the aftermath, for unlike him she could recollect the details of their long ordeal.

The rumours, said to be prevalent on St Mary's, that women were locked in the pavilion, were utterly denied both by Hillers and by Polemann. Yet Schnellenberg added another twist to this story, later claiming to 'have heard' that it was the second cabin passengers who were locked below. It was when they finally broke out that the number 5 lifeboat was commandeered, with passengers themselves attempting to lower it, he wrote. The main evidence from men like Sterne and Hexter refute this story completely, for they and others seem to have had free access through the pavilion doors and companionways to all sections of first- and second-class accommodation. As for women being locked in deckhouses, several were seen with Captain Thomas on the bridge and others climbed the rigging. No purpose could possibly have been served by treating other women, however hysterical, in such a manner.

Yet it is plain that for most women on the ship, male assistance was essential to their survival – and not nearly enough was forthcoming. Some men did help, as did Henry Sterne and others in distributing life-jackets to women in the saloon. Leo Weste tried desperately to get his wife and daughter to leave their stateroom and climb into the rigging with him, though as he barely survived this himself and five other women died there, the chances that they would have lived is remote. No doubt others unknown, who did not live to tell the tale, performed valiant acts to save women and children; and remained with them to the last when they might have saved themselves. Yet significant numbers sought only to save their own skins, never once considering the women and children who might have easily been helped into the lifeboats.

Should Captain Thomas have been more resolute in ejecting the selfish men crowding the number 5 lifeboat? Had he fired at them rather than over their heads, as Sterne said he would have done had he been in the Captain's place, would the boat have been cleared for women and children? Perhaps not. In January 1873, the sailing ship *Northfleet*, run down and sunk by a steamship off Dungeness, had her lifeboats commandeered by emigrating navvies after the many women among the 379 emigrants on the ship refused to climb down into them. The *Northfleet*'s captain fired his pistol directly into the navvies, wounding one in the leg. In spite of this, they stayed there, shouting in defiance:

Shoot us would you? We might as well be shot by you as drown with you.[6]

In that very similar situation on the *Schiller*, such men may equally have felt that death by drowning was far worse than being shot.

On Tuesday 11 May 1875, a regular contributor to *The Gentleman's Magazine* received through the post a large official envelope. It was marked OHMS in one corner and 'Saved from the Schiller' in the other. Inside was a stained and torn letter from a friend in Philadelphia. This was just one letter from the 250 mailbags loaded on to the ship at New York. Most were eventually recovered but a lot of the letters inside were reduced to pulp.

Later that Saturday, the fishing boat *Robert,* returning to Mousehole from Scilly on Saturday and passing about 200 bodies off the island of Samson, brought another three mailbags ashore along with some bundles of circulars and passenger luggage. Among the luggage was a large cylindrical kitbag, similar to those used by man o' war sailors. On the outside it bore the name 'D.W. Percival, Barnstable' in one-inch high lettering; inside were a pair of boots and some clothing. Much other passenger luggage and odd items from the ship's cargo, bags of feathers, bales of cotton, casks of flour and the boxed parts of an agricultural mower among them, were to be recovered by small boats over the next few days.

Salvage from the *Schiller* itself was to prove more difficult. On the Saturday afternoon, the naval steam tug *Carron* with a gang of riggers aboard was despatched from Devonport for Scilly by order of Admiral Sir H. Keppel, in the hope of salvaging part or all of the steamer. Finding the task was impossible, the riggers returned to Devonport. Salvage of a sort would be possible in time; some fishermen who had visited the wreck said that the ship, though badly broken up, was firmly embedded on the rocks in around two or three fathoms at low tide and was unlikely to slip off into deeper water.

On the Monday, John Banfield's steam-launch, *Will o' the Wisp* took representatives of the underwriters and consignees, Captain Page, Captain Lodge and Herr Bech from Hamburg, all newly arrived in St Mary's on the *Lady of the Isles* that morning, out to the wreck. Although the *Schiller* and her cargo were fully insured, they wished to find how much could be salved. The weather was by then just calm enough to allow them to make a cursory examination. Banfield's little steam launch ran close to the wreck, but though it was low tide, a high sea was running and the only parts of the *Schiller* visible above water were the stumps of the masts and the cylinders of her engine showing its brass lubricators and copper piping. Still attached to the vessel but floating beside her in the water were the main boom, topgallant mast and a couple of spars.

Captain Page rowed a small boat right up to the wreck and noticed that her upper deck was gone completely, her stern was lower than her bow and there was slight list to starboard. Prospects of salvage seemed gloomy, though they were fairly certain that the barrels of specie aboard would present little problem to divers in fine weather.

In this kind of situation the other captain in the party, Captain Lodge, had experience that was second to none in salving treasure, having been engaged in such work all over the world. It was his expertise and perseverance which had finally procured almost all of £320 000 in Australian gold dust, spread over the seabed after the wreck of the Liverpool-bound auxiliary steamship *Royal Charter* off Anglesey, when on a passage from Melbourne in 1859. He had also successfully fought off armed Yankee adventurers in salving gold from a wreck in South America, and more recently recovered a large quantity of silver from the China seas in the face of constant threats from Chinese pirates. Around the Isles of Scilly, his foe would be the weather.

A second trip out to the wreck on the Wednesday by the same men, accompanied by two experienced divers, provided a more positive opinion on prospects for salving. The sea was still high so nothing was then done, but two days later the divers spent four hours searching the wreck. The once 'elegant, Clyde-built steamship' was broken in pieces, all in one confused mass, they reported. Her lower decks could be made out, suspended from rock to rock, but the bottom of the vessel, including her keel and engine shaft, were gone altogether. There was no cargo or corpse to be seen, nor could they locate the specie. In searching, one of the divers got his boot jammed irretrievably in a rock crevice, but keeping his presence of mind, drew his knife and cut it away so that he could withdraw his foot and so rise to the surface. All that was recovered that day were two passengers' portmanteaux and six sewing machines.

The divers spent another four hours searching the wreck on Saturday, but their efforts were rewarded only with the discovery of a one dollar piece. All the cargo was dispersed and there was no sign at all of the treasure. For the next two weeks no salvage work could be undertaken as the weather worsened. By the end of the month, all that had been retrieved from the wrecked ship was about two tons of copper piping from her engine.

Meanwhile, a large amount of wreckage from the *Schiller* was being washed ashore or brought into ports all around west Cornwall by fishing boats. Beams, deck planks, portions of her cabins and their furniture were commonplace items, but most were so smashed up as to be of little value. The schooner *Jamie* of Padstow, when ten miles north-east of Cape Cornwall, picked up a piece of bulkhead from a cabin with a plated salver attached. On it was engraved an eagle and 'Deutsche Transatlantische Dampfschiffahrts Gesellschaft in Hamburg'– the symbol of a shipping line which was by then as extinct as its once proud liner *Schiller.*

June and July proved to be a very unsettled months for the salvors, with gales and high seas to hinder or halt their efforts on many days. When the divers did descend to search the broken mass of iron and lumber for the lost specie, it was mostly more bodies that were discovered. On 12 June two male passengers' bodies were brought to the surface; one a rather tall man in grey cord trousers, the other wearing a small gold scarf pin with a Masonic-like emblem. They were later identified as Ferdinand Kreuter, the New York optician, and Edward Mannheimer, a Philadelphia shoe dealer. Both were buried on St Agnes. In the next few weeks two more bodies of men were recovered from the wreck, one of them with his feet wrapped in a shawl as if asleep when he drowned.

Salvage work on the Schiller *wreck, c.1875.*
GIBSON OF SCILLY

Below: *A gold 20-dollar piece salvaged much later and still attached through concretion to part of a bulkhead from the Schiller.*
GIBSON OF SCILLY

By the end of July results of the salvage operation were disappointing: on the 27th the divers' haul was two bales of cotton and a ton of old iron. But the new month proved to be kinder, both in weather and fortune. The first two of the six kegs of specie aboard the *Schiller* was brought to the surface on 3 August, and they were followed by two more on the 6th. The last two kegs were raised three days later – a haul of gold totalling £40 000 in value. During the wreck, one keg had split open and some of the coin – gold 20-dollar pieces – had been scattered throughout the ship's engine room. Between 21 August and 8 September, 1499 of these were recovered during three dives upon the wreck. The weather was by then usually, as reported on the 21st, 'remarkably calm'.

Salvage work continued during the following year. On 31 March, Captain Lodge reported that £10 000 had been recovered during that single day. Another £1000 worth was brought to the surface on 2 and 3 May. When operations were concluded on the 6th, £57 712 from the £60 000 total value of the specie aboard had been recovered.

Rewards for people of the Isles of Scilly and others who had worked on behalf of *Schiller's* survivors or victims came in a variety of forms. On the recommendation of John Banfield, the Eagle Line paid £1 to every seaman involved in the recovery of a body. They also paid, at their own instigation, £10 to the Overseers of the Poor on Scilly to help islanders in need. Thomas Jones Stevens, the Eagle Line's Plymouth agent, thanked Dorrien-Smith by letter on behalf of the Company.

In August, the German Ambassador in London contacted the Chancellery at Berlin recommending the presentation of decorations and other rewards to a number of people who were considered to have been of particular help in the aftermath of the disaster. Bernard Von Bulow, Foreign Secretary of the Imperial German Empire, then wrote to the Senate of Hamburg to find out how best to do this and to discover what had already been done by the Eagle Line themselves. In answering the Senate queries, the Eagle Line's managing director recommended John Banfield, their agent on St Mary's, for his diligent work in the rescue, organising funerals for the dead, ensuring that their personal effects were sent on to their heirs and dealing with tremendous amounts of correspondence.

The first announcement of official rewards from His Majesty the Emperor Wilhelm to those connected with the *Schiller* disaster came in September. Head of the list was John Banfield, who was awarded the Royal Crown Order, fourth class. Two others, James Handley, the Head of Customs and Receiver of Wreck at St Mary's, and James Bulley the chief coastguard there, were presented with inscribed telescopes. Coxswain Alfred Hicks of the St Mary's lifeboat, was rewarded with a gold watch inscribed with the Imperial German crown. The crew of the lifeboat on Scilly were awarded £20 between them while crews of the Sennen luggers, the St Agnes gigs and other boats in which survivors had been rescued, plus those of the *Lady of the Isles*, shared between them £40. Others who had done 'helpful acts' according to John Banfield were to receive a written commendation in which they were mentioned by name above the Imperial signature.

Somehow overlooked at first it seems was Algernon Dorrien-Smith. In late November Von Bulow wrote to the Senate of Hamburg informing them that the Emperor had agreed to grant Dorrien-Smith the Order of the Imperial Crown, third class – one grade higher than Banfield's. Also overlooked for a while had been three women workers at Matthews undertakers in Penzance, who were especially recommended for having dealt with the female corpses washed up there. In December it was decided they should each receive from the Empress a present of an Imperial Cross on which was the symbol of the Red Cross.

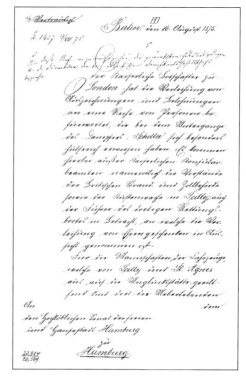

First page of a letter from Bernard Von Bulow to the Hamburg Senate, 16 August 1875, stating that the Ambassador in London has sanctioned the awarding of decorations and money to Scilly islanders and requesting their help and that of the Eagle Line in deciding who to recognise.

HAMBURG STAATSARCHIV

Right: *First page of the Eagle Line's reply to Von Bulow, 23 August 1875, stating that £10 has been awarded to the Overseers of the Poor in Scilly and mentioning the parts played by Dorrien-Smith and John Banfield.*

HAMBURG STAATSARCHIV

Far right: *Letter from Von Bulow to the Hamburg Senate, 20 November 1875, stating that Dorrien-Smith has been awarded the Order of the Imperial Crown, third class.*

HAMBURG STAATSARCHIV

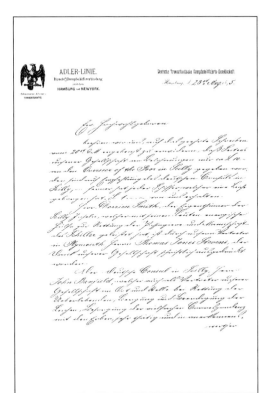

NOTES

[1] *Dead Reckoning and the Ocean Voyages of the Past.* C.V. Solver and J.G. Marcus: *Mariners Mirror;* Vol 44.

[2] as above.

[3] *Hamburgische Correspondent*, 21 May 1875.

[4] *Harper's Weekly*, 29 May 1875.

[5] Nelson, *Great Shipwrecks*, 1544–1877, Thomas Nelson, 1877.

[6] as above.

CHAPTER 19

·◆·

Postscript

The wreck of the *Schiller* had a considerable effect on the German populace, having suffered no terrible disaster to one of their own steamships since the loss by fire of the Hamburg-Amerika *Austria* in September 1858. Such was the impact of the wreck that it was incorporated into the repertoire of Moritat singers.

Moritat singers were itinerant folk entertainers in a tradition which had origins hundreds of years old. They visited rural market places and set up their boards on which were illustrations for the song they were to sing, mostly lurid tales of murder and robbery – rather in the style of English broadsheets of the eighteenth century. Apart from the entertainment value, they served to inform the illiterate of newsworthy events, albeit of the more ghastly kind. As the Moritat singer went through his song, he would point out the illustrations which went with it. Most, as does the following Moritat, owe more to artistry than accuracy:

THE SONG

From America's far shores
Sailed to Hamburg's home port,
Sped with joy the steamer 'Schiller'.
Many passengers report
That to their homeland they hurried,
Far too long abroad had tarried,
Sailed they now with restful ease
To their home across the seas.

Peace, contentment quietly reigned
On the steamer, ocean's pride.
Yet they felt a gentle yearning
Soon to be on that far side.
Then, quite near unto the land,
On the rocky island strand,
Came disaster overnight,
That the lives of all did blight.

All wrapped up in densest mist,
The so proud and beauteous ship,
As it drifted through the surf,
Struck against the sharpest reef,
Fast against the rocky shore.
We see the proud ship move no more.
Then the wild, wild waters burst,
Showed that they could do their worst.

Frantic terror seized them all,
Passengers as well as crew,
All did try to save themselves;
No one knew what they should do.
Many, many sadly drowned,
Sank so deep were never found.
Down into the water black,
That never gave its victim's back.

Husbands wept about their wives,
And the mother sought her child,
That the mighty waves devoured
Like a lightning flash so wild.
Many a man once bright and gay
By the waves was swept away.
Even, yes, the Captain brave
We see him sink beneath the wave.

And if many a one is saved,
As we hear, we are not sure,
Yet the most of them were drowned,
Never saw their homeland's shore. [1]

After the loss of the *Schiller*, Hamburg-Amerika paid 11 400 000 marks for the Eagle Line instead of the 12½ million first agreed. Many German people lost large amounts of money over the failure of the line; shareholders received only one-third of the value of their shares.

Once the takeover was complete, the six remaining Eagle Line ships, together with their Elbe tender *Hoboken*, were repainted in Hamburg-Amerika livery with all black funnels. *Gellert* and *Wieland*, having not seen service with their original owners, left Hamburg for New York on their respective maiden voyages in late May and July of 1875. *Herder* and *Klopstock* resumed service on the North Atlantic during June that same year. *Lessing* was not put to work until she sailed for New York in March 1876 and a further month was to pass before *Goethe* set off on her first voyage for the new owners.

It was to be *Goethe*'s last voyage on the North Atlantic route, and her swansong was not without some drama. Leaving Hamburg on 12 April, she ran into a hurricane nine days later in longitude 41° W, mid-Atlantic, during which she lost her screw. Captain Meyer decided to turn for home under sail only, but on reaching the Isles of Scilly while beating up Channel against the wind, took her in and lay off St Agnes overnight to await a tug from Plymouth. That evening, 3 May, was just four days short of the first anniversary of the *Schiller*'s wreck on the nearby Retarrier Ledges. It was by sheer coincidence that this visit to the vicinity from *Goethe*, her Napier-built, twin- funnelled, identical sister ship, should occur at such a time – but somehow fitting.

Goethe was soon repaired at Plymouth and, having been re-coaled, left once more for New York on 10 May. After this one voyage she was transferred to the company's South American routes to run in conjunction with *Germania II*. The arrangement was short- lived: both ships were wrecked near Bahia, Brazil, in late 1876 and the service was withdrawn.

Klopstock had only a brief career with Hamburg-Amerika, being sold by them to the French CGT line in 1876 after six Atlantic voyages. The four remaining vessels were rebuilt with twin funnels and triple-expansion engines during the early 1880s. *Herder*, the first to be altered, was wrecked off Cape Race in October 1882; *Lessing* was sold off to the French Messagieres Maritimes in 1888; *Gellert* and *Wieland* remained with Hamburg-Amerika until broken up in the late 1890s. Eagle Line's Elbe tender, *Hoboken*, was sold to the General Steam Navigation Company in 1877 for service between London and the Isle of Thanet; and from 1887 sailed on their East Coast run to Yarmouth. She was still in service as late as 1898.

Eagle Line's ex-Chairman, Rob M. Sloman junior, still headed the Sloman Line in the late 1870s, with six sailing ships and four steamers in service on Mediterranean routes. In 1881 he opened up a new line to Australia, but withdrew five years later to join forces with his nephew Edward Carr, whose Carr Line ships had since 1881 competed against Hamburg-Amerika in a steerage only service on the North Atlantic. The Carr-Union Line continued this rivalry until 1886, when the two lines operated their services jointly. Carr was bought out by Hamburg-Amerika two years later, but their collaboration with the Union Line lasted until Sloman's death in 1900. Seven years later Hamburg-Amerika bought out the Union Line altogether but the service was referred to as Sloman-Union until the onset of the First World War.

Three and a half years after the wreck of the *Schiller* and the death of his Eagle Line friend, George Thomas, Captain H.F. Schwensen still commanded the *Pommerania*, as he had since her maiden voyage in November 1873. Just before midnight on 25 November 1878, when coming up the English Channel in thick fog and heavy rain on the return passage from New York to Hamburg, the *Pommerania* was in collision with an iron barque. With only the briefest warning of the sailing ship's approach, Schwensen ordered his ship turned to port – but too late. The barque, *Moel Eilian*, having just left Rotterdam loaded with coal for Bombay, struck amidships with such a blow that her stem came well into the *Pommerania*'s engine room, while her bowsprit knocked away the German liner's funnel and bridge and then carried three lifeboats overboard as she passed aft.

Schwensen stood on the remains of his bridge as the *Pommerania* heeled over to starboard, ordering blue lights and rockets to be fired and the remaining five lifeboats to be quickly launched. The first to leave was so overcrowded she sank, but others were successfully lowered with Schwensen himself helping at the davits. The last boat to leave did so 20 minutes after the vessel had been struck and just as the vessel began to circle slowly around in her final whirlpool before going under. From this lifeboat, the first mate called out to Schwensen, still standing on deck with a lifebelt worn over his greatcoat, to ask if he was coming with them. He replied,

'Are you full? Can you take another one?'

When the first mate said he could, Schwensen asked him to wait awhile, but as the *Pommerania* was about to sink the lifeboat left without him. She sank when they had rowed about 15 yards away from her side. Schwensen and about 60 others were eventually picked up from the sea by the *City of Amsterdam* and taken to Maasluis, Holland, while further survivors were taken aboard a steam tug towing the Middlesboro' steamship, *Glengarry*. Of the 220 aboard the Pommerania, 44 died. It was to have been Schwensen's 126th successfully completed voyage.

Obadiah and Mary Hicks's gig, the *O & M*, which had rescued some survivors of the *Schiller* wreck, was said in 1887 to be 'the best known gig in Scilly'. In that year another lighthouse was built on Round Island, north of the Scillies, and the gig was used to relieve the keepers there as it did those on Bishop Rock. It also figured in two more wrecks, though fortunately none was as serious as that of the *Schiller*. In 1887, when the S.S. *Castleford*, bound for London from Montreal with 450 head of cattle aboard, ran on to Crebewethan, the *O & M* was instrumental in bringing steers off the island – and had her bow knocked in by one angry bull. It was still in use in 1903, taking the captain's wife and child off the barque, *Queen Mab*, which, damaged by striking rocks, was being towed into St Mary's.

One of two lads in the gig *O & M*, who – as Henry Sterne praised them, 'pulled with a bravery that could not be excelled' – was Billy Cook Hicks. On the afternoon of 14 December 1907, islanders were signalled by rocket fired from Bishop Rock lighthouse – there was still no telegraph link from the lighthouse to the shore, although the islands had cables laid between them in 1893–4. The American seven-masted steel schooner, *Thomas W. Lawson*, the largest sailing vessel ever built, had come inside the lighthouse and was anchored in a dangerous position. A storm was gathering, but the huge schooner's master was complacent about the danger his vessel, loaded with 2½ million gallons of paraffin oil, was in. When lifeboatmen from St Agnes pleaded with him to seek a safer anchorage, all he asked was that they look out for his riding lights overnight. Billy Cook Hicks, a Trinity House Pilot, was put aboard to assist if need be. Overnight, the wind blew up and drove the huge steel vessel, rigged and equipped with motor winches so she could be manned by a tiny crew of only 18 men, onto the rocky isle of Annet. Watchers on St Agnes saw her lights go out as she turned over and could smell oil in the wind. The gig *Slippen* quickly went to her and the pilot's son, Frederick Cook Hicks, swam through the boiling sea, taking a line to the

The American schooner Thomas W. Lawson; *in which Billy Cook Hicks lost his life.*

overturned vessel. Her master and engineer were the only ones rescued. Sixteen crew and the pilot, Billy Cook Hicks were lost. *Slippen*'s crew were each awarded gold medals from the United States Government.

The decorations and rewards given to the islanders by the German Emperor in 1875 were not quickly forgotten. During the First World War, it was commonly reckoned by Scilly islanders that the Kaiser (grandson of the Emperor) had instructed his submarine commanders not to attack the islands' packet steamer on its regular run to and from Penzance. This was supposedly because of German gratitude for the kind manner in which the people of the Islands had treated the survivors and dead of the wrecked steamer *Schiller* in 1875. The story has some credibility; the Kaiser had after all instructed Zeppelin crews not to bomb Buckingham Palace for fear of killing his cousin King George and the Royal Family. Strangely, in March 1915, when the German submarine U29 sank a merchant steamer off the Scillies, having first allowed her crew to take to the lifeboats, she then towed them all towards St Mary's so they could reach safety. Such old-style courtesy and respect for fellow mariners was not to last much longer however. On 7 May that year, by coincidence exactly forty years to the day after the wreck of the *Schiller*, another German submarine, U20, sank the *Lusitania*.

At the churchyard in Old Town, St Mary's, a few reminders of the unfortunate victims of the *Schiller* disaster can still be seen. The most prominent is the large, railed-in stone obelisk, situated in a position higher than the little church itself on a raised terrace to the rear of the churchyard. It is dedicated to the young wife of the Broadway, New York, kid glove importer Lewis V. Holzmaister. An inscription reads:

In memory of Louise Holzmaister, born at New York, 15 May 1851, who lost her life in the wreck of the S.S. Schiller on the Scilly Isles, 7 May 1875. Her body rests in the deep. This monument has been erected to her memory as a mark of affection by a sorrowing husband.

There is also a Holzmaister memorial window at the east end of the little church, which was placed there in 1899.

Of the actual graves there is now little evidence, in spite of the vastness of the long trenches dug in the rocky soil. A headstone of one of the individually buried victims was still readable in 1948, but its wording was fast weathering away even then. It stood over the last resting place of another young woman from Broadway, New York,

Clara Just, the wife of shirt manufacturer Edward Just. Beside her was laid her two year old son Edward. Else, her five-year-old daughter, was not recovered or was unidentified. The inscription read:

Ruh sauft mit deiner Kindern, du edles treues Weib, du gute leibrieche Mutter. (sic) – *Rest gently with your children, noble, faithful wife, good, loving mother.*[2]

The only headstone still readable beneath its thick covering of sickly-green lichen stands between the little church and the bay, where one of the long trenches was dug during those grim May days of 1875. Beneath it and for many yards on either side are buried innumerable *Schiller* victims in layers two deep. But the stone records the dead wives and children of only two families – both of British origin. Susan Duckfield and Fanny Evans, the good friends and neighbours from the same Bleecker Street, New York, apartment block and whose husbands were both shoemakers, have their memorial here. It reads:

Modern view of the Schiller *mass graves at Old Town Church. The lichen-covered gravestone in the centre is the memorial to Susan Duckfield, Fanny Evans and their five young children.*

Sacred to the memory of Susan Hill of Barnstaple, aged 28 yrs. wife of Geo Duckfield of Bristol – and of Georgina their daughter aged 4 years. Also of John Evans a dear friend aged 4 years who were lost in the Schiller off the Scilly Islands 7 may 1875. Also in memory of Elizabeth Ann aged 8 years, Mary Matilda aged 7 years and Edward France aged 2 years whose remains rest in the deep. Also to the memory of Frances Mary Evans aged 28 years mother of the above John Evans whose remains rest in the deep.

One other gravestone on the islands is that of Ferdinand Kreuter, the rather tall optician from New York who, like so many on board, was going to Europe for his health. This is on St Agnes, where his body was taken after recovery from the wrecked ship by divers several weeks afterwards. Other relics from the *Schiller* herself that can still be seen on the islands: at Valhalla, the shipwreck museum on Tresco, are a signal gun and part of a bulkhead with an eagle insignia upon it; at the museum in Hugh Town, St Mary's, there is another signal gun, a sunseat from her deck, a brass kettle, some cutlery and a seaman's knife. Some furniture recovered at the time of the wreck which is in private hands includes two or three tables and a sideboard.

Above: *The gravestone in close-up. The word 'Schiller' is just visible under the lichen.*

Left: *St Agnes Church, where Ferdinand Kreuter's grave can still be seen.*

There are several memorial stones and tablets further afield in the many cities and towns in America or Germany from which the victims originated. One in Cobb Hill Cemetery at Barnstable, Massachusetts, is inscribed:

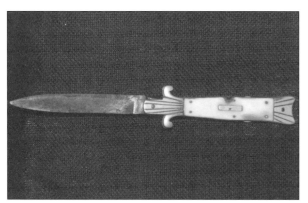

Various items retrieved from the Schiller, *Left to right:*
First row: *Deck seat. Brass kettle. Fish slice and cutlery.*
Second row: *Seaman's clasp knife. A porthole. Barrel staves. Salt spoon.*
Third row: *Broach. Corroded toast rack and tiles. Brass escutcheon from the ship's Chubb safe.*

ISLES OF SCILLY MUSEUM ASSOCIATION

Percival, Daniel W. – Died 1875. Born 1841. To the memory of him who died at sea.

Captain Daniel W. Percival, the master mariner from a town renowned for its sea-faring Percival family was not forgotten there. He deserved to be remembered for his valiant assistance to others on the night of the wreck. Acknowledgement of this by Henry Sterne formed part of his obituary, published in the *Barnstable Patriot* on 18 May . This concluded with a poem, the first two verses of which read:

> *Another true heart lulled to rest by the waves*
> *Of the sea he loved to roam;-*
> *Other hearts filled with mourning, and ready to break,*
> *In the saddened and desolate home.*

> *'Tis the same old story of life in its prime*
> *Cut down like a flower of the field;*
> *Why, we know not yet, but by and by*
> *The reason shall be revealed.*

Sterne thought that Percival died when the mainmast fell overboard. The real reason for his death was the chain falling upon him from above: he may otherwise have lived.

Yet by far the longest lived and almost universally known name from among the dead passengers of the *Schiller* is that of the business mogul from Milwaukee with interests in banking, insurance and, above all else, brewing. Before leaving home, Joseph Schlitz, married but childless, had a new will drawn up which provided that, should he die, his brewery would continue under the name 'Joseph Schlitz Brewing Company'. On his death, control of the Schlitz Brewery passed to the four Uihlein brothers. Curiously, the largest stockholder among them, August Uihlein, had as a boy of eight survived the sinking of Rob M. Sloman senior's ill-fated steamship *Helena Sloman*, when in 1850 he was travelling to the United States. Under the Uihleins, the Schlitz Brewing Co. flourished and by 1947 was the world's top producer of beer, though decline set in during the 1970s when the brand lost some of its popularity. Schlitz beers are now produced by the Stroh Brewery Company of Detroit, who purchased the Milwaukee brewery in 1982. The beer remains popular to this day and is marketed all over the world under the name 'Schlitz'.

Right: *Schlitz beer bottles: the smaller of the two dates from the 1870s when bottled beer was first introduced.*

COURTESY STROH BREWERY CO.

Far right: *The modern beer can still bears the Schlitz signature.*

COURTESY STROH BREWERY CO.

NOTES

[1] Arnold Kludas, *Die Geschichte der Deutschen Passagierschiffahrt*, Vol. 1 (Die Pionierjahre von 1850 bis 1890). Ernst Kabel Verlag, Hamburg, 1986.

[2] Geoffrey Grigson, *The Scilly Isles*, Duckworth, 1948.

∙◆∙

The Crew of the *Schiller*
27 April–7 May 1875

<u>Known members, saved or lost</u>

Note: Schiller's crew was said variously to number 101, 118, 120 or 124. In Germany it was stated that 91 crew died in the wreck, and as 28 lived and one was left at Hoboken, the number of 120 given by the first and second officers appears to be correct. But there were at least 13 men working their passage – whether they were included in the 120 or not is unknown.

* denotes more details in main text.

<u>SAVED</u>

SHIP'S OFFICERS
Heinrich Hillers,* first mate. (p 81, 85, 87, 91, 103, 116, 118, 173, 184)
Erwin Polemann,* second mate. (p 81, 85, 87, 93, 135, 151, 152, 161, 173, 188)
Richard Heintze,* fourth mate. (p 81, 88, 89, 105, 108, 110, 114, 116, 120, 129, 130, 135, 136, 151, 157, 160, 170, 183, 190)

STEWARDS
Christian Adamson.
Wilhelm Blohm,* boy steward. (p 89, 93, 94, 110, 155)
Theodore Hoffmann,* first cabin. (p 106)
James Juergen Jansen.
Claus Mahler.
Auguste Rheburg.
Hans Peterson.* (p 116, 129)
Frederick Wermke,* steerage. (p 94)

SAILORS
Hans Beck, able seaman.
Friedrich Waldemar 'Fritz' Beckhaus.* (p 89, 94, 102, 190)
Frederick Blusinger.
H. Dan.
Max Goldberger,* able seaman. (p 93, 94, 105, 106, 113, 116, 120, 126, 155)
Heinrich Heitmas.
Simon Jensen,* chief boatswain. (p 81, 89, 91, 96, 102, 106, 107, 117, 118, 132, 183, 192, 195)
W. Packendorf, boatswain.
Henry A. (Andrew) Wallis,* able seaman. (p 117, 126, 155)
Claus Wick.

STOKERS & OTHERS
Hans Balling, stoker.
Carl Ernst, stoker.
Charles Henicke, stoker.
Wilhelm Hinsch,* sailmaker. (p 93. 94, 100, 102)
Hugh Pierson, coal-trimmer.
Augustus Peal, storekeeper.
Johann Schwermske, boilermaker.

LOST *(and if recovered where buried)*

SHIP'S OFFICERS
G. Freese,* third mate. (p 81, 101, 108, 114)
Leonard Fahrig,* chief engineer. *St Mary's.* (p 82, 99, 107, 116, 172)
F. Conrad, second engineer.
H. Roenne, third engineer. *St Mary's.*
J. Kundel,* fourth engineer. (p 116)
Dr A. Boll,* physician. (p 80, 83, 107, 116)
E. Schmettan,* purser. *Mousehole.* (p 79, 172)
C. Putfarken,* first-cabin chief steward. *Penzance.* (p 79, 103, 171, 172)
Augustus Felkstow,* second-cabin chief steward. *St Mary's.* (p 79, 125)

OTHER KNOWN CREW MEMBERS *(unless otherwise stated buried at St Mary's)*
Heinrich Blackwas, steward.
Erling, first carpenter.
H.D. Erks, seaman.
Holm,* second-cabin steward. *Penzance.* (p 172)
Krender, chief baker. *Mousehole.*
Maria Felkstow,* stewardess. (p 79, 125)
P. Luschner, steward.
Henry Martin, first fireman.
Annie Milsner, stewardess.
D Ohlsen, sailor.
Auguste Thomas, steward. *At sea from fishing lugger* Tempus Fugit.
C.F. 'Fritz' Thomas, messroom steward.
Schroeder, assistant cook.

UNIDENTIFIED CREW MEMBERS *(unless otherwise stated buried at St Mary's)*
Ship's butcher.
2 quartermasters.
Third cook.
5 firemen.
3 sailors.
1 sailor lad.
Second carpenter. *Penzance.*
Unknown stewardess (or steerage passenger). *Penzance.*

OTHERS, ACTING CREW MEMBERS
Godfred Altmann.* Aged 27, an artist from Mannheim. *St Mary's.* (p 80, 170)
Herman Baumgarten and Richard Nautch.* Working as deck-hands. (p 80, 148)
Heinrich Machaur. Born Spiers, Germany, lived at 6th St New York. Working as a steward.

Mr Osquorn.* Of Vienna, marine artist employed by Eagle Line. (p 80)

Dr W.A. Sanders.* Ship's surgeon of the *W.A. Scholten* but acting ship's surgeon on the *Schiller*. *St Mary's*. (p 80, 83, 160)

[Compiled from British, American and German newspapers.]

The Passengers of the *Schiller*

Note: *Schiller*'s second officer gave evidence that there were 264 passengers. A telegram from Philadelphia gave figures of 268. John Banfield stated there were 266. The list of passengers and the accommodation they booked compiled in this Appendix makes the total 261. Yet there were several unlisted passengers, as many as 12 or more, whose bodies were recovered and identified after the wreck – and possibly more still who were not found.

<u>**FIRST-CABIN PASSENGERS. 59 total: 25 men, 23 women, 11 children**</u>
All *lost* and bodies not recovered or unidentified unless otherwise indicated.
* denotes more details in main text and page number(s).

<u>**FROM NEW YORK**</u>
Herman Bachmann.* 117 East 40th St; aged 45. (p 59, 60)
Mr and Mrs N. (or A.) Becker.* 56, West 56th St. *Mrs Becker embalmed and returned to U.S.* (p 60, 103, 159, 175)
John Jacob Brunner.* 80 Leonard St. (business). *Buried at Penzance.* (p 57, 143, 174)
Mrs Caverly and daughter Amy.* Lowell, Massachusetts. (p 57, 60, 61, 64, 116, 121, 143, 148)
Mrs Clara Gregory and Master Frank Gregory.* Staten Island. Wife and son of George Gregory, a book-keeper. (p 52, 148)
Mrs Marie Hesse and child. 191 State St., Brooklyn; aged 22. Wife of Dr Richard Hesse. Her child was aged two. Bound for Saxony.
Mrs Clara Just, two children and a female servant.* 613 Broadway. *Mrs Just and Edward buried together in a single grave, St Mary's.* (p 59, 159, 170, 218)
Mr and Mrs Michael Kornblum, three children and a female servant.* 6 Howard St. (business). *Mrs Kornblum embalmed and returned to U.S.* (p 58, 64, 104, 143, 145, 175)
Mr E. Kuhn – or Carl Kuhn.* *Saved.* (p 116, 117, 126, 136, 143, 154)
Paul Reiff. Garden St., Hoboken. Had been only a few years in America and worked in the silk trade. Returning home to Switzerland where his father was a wealthy silk manufacturer.
Mrs Ridgeway and her maid.* 15, East 43rd St., New York. Widow of George Joseph Ridgeway of Newbury, Massachusetts. (p 57, 61, 116, 121, 148, 159)
Mr and Mrs Carl and Catherine Schmidt.* Carl a partner of Fox & Co., jewellers of 2 Maiden Lane. Born at Burginfeld, Oldenberg and came to the U.S. as a child. *Carl Schmidt embalmed and returned to U.S.* (p 57, 145, 168, 175)
Arnold Schwarzenbach. New York.
William T. Smith.* Resided at Plainfield, New Jersey, with wife and three-year-old son; aged 38. Manager of hosiery importers, P. Schuloff Dry Goods, 477 Broome St. (p 98, 100)
Henry Sterne.* Jewish commission agent of Jonas Sonneborn & Co., of 120 Pearl St. *Saved.* (p 90, 95, 100, 103,

108, 116, 119, 126, 135, 136, 143, 151, 154, 177, 179, 183, 184, 186, 195, 204, 205, 512, 221)

Mr Charles W. Walter and his two little girls.* Walter was English by birth; aged 32 (or 40). Owner of the Laurel Hills Chemical Works, Greenpoint. *Charles Walter embalmed and returned to U.S.* (p 57, 61, 100, 116, 121, 148, 170, 175)

Mr M. Wasserman.* Originally from Posen, Prussia, but had been in the U.S. about 35 years; aged 60 or 67. Retired about ten years. (p 60)

BOSTON

Susan Dimock MD* Boylston St. *Embalmed and returned to U.S.* (p 56, 57, 149, 150, 159, 175)

Miss Bessie Greene.* Daughter of Colonel William B. Greene and Anna Shaw Greene of Parker House. (p 56, 149)

Captain Daniel W. Percival.* Son of Captain Nathanial (1812–1882) and Rebecca C. Percival (D. 1852) of Barnstable; born 12 April 1841. (p 48, 76, 77, 78, 116, 119, 125, 146, 205)

MILWAUKEE

Henry Friend and wife Frances.* Henry born Autenhausen, Bavaria, 1821. Emigrated to U.S. with brother Elias in 1840. Another brother, Mayer, joined them in 1848, when they became H. Friend & Bros. Married Frances Samuels of New York in 1850. One of their 11 children was married and lived in New York. *Henry and Frances Friend both embalmed and returned to U.S.* (p 58, 168, 174, 175)

Jacob Lamfron.* A merchant from Oconomowac. (p 58)

Joseph Schlitz.* Born at Mayence (now Mainz), 15 May 1831. Emigrated to U.S. in 1850 and was taken on as a book-keeper at August Krug's brewery in Milwaukee. Married Krug's widow Anna Maria in 1858 and changed the name of the brewery to the Schlitz Brewery Co. (p 58, 59, 145, 146, 221, 222)

Marcus M. Stein.* Friend of Jacob Lamfron, above. *Embalmed and returned to U.S.* (p 57, 58)

Hermann Zinkeisen, wife Celine and daughter Annie.* Four young sons aged ten to 17, were left in the care of brother-in-law Oscar Mohe. *Celine and Annie Zinkeisen buried together in mass graves, St Mary's.* (p 58, 64, 103, 145, 168, 172, 173)

PHILADELPHIA

Miss Frederica Mann. Born in Philadelphia, where her father was once in the wine trade, but had since moved with them to Europe. Was on a return visit to the city where she was welcomed by many friends in the society set.

Leo Weste, wife Hermine and their daughter (or step daughter).* Leo Weste *saved. Hermine Weste buried in single grave, St Mary's.* (p 60, 111, 116, 119, 126, 136, 151, 155, 159, 204)

WASHINGTON

Miss Caroline M. Crane.* (p 56)

FROM OTHER CITIES AND TOWNS

Mr M. Kahn. A businessman from Mattoon, Illinois; aged 35. Originally from South Germany.

Dwight Klink.* Fruitport, Michigan. *Embalmed and returned to U.S.* (p 50, 116, 121, 148, 168, 175)

Sigmund Stern. From Greenville, Illinois; aged 28. Jewish and unmarried. Previously from Wurtemburg. Travelling companion of M. Kahn, above.

Herman Stoelting, Mrs Ida Stoelting and Master George Stoelting.* Georgetown, Colorado. *Herman Stoelting buried in mass graves, St Mary's.* (p 58, 168)

HAVANA, CUBA

Gustav Woltman.

Frederick William Zach, wife Johanna and daughter Margarethe.* Frederick born Cosswig an der Elbe, 30 December 1824. Studied law in Berlin 1846–9. Worked for the Prussian Justice Ministry 1850–8; the subaltern service at the Prussian Embassy, Brussels, 1858–60; the Prussian legation at Hamburg, 1860–5; and was attaché at the Prussian Legation in Washington, 1865. Married Johanna Grüne, daughter of a Berlin manufacturer in

1860. Mrs Zach, aged about 37. Daughter Margarethe, aged about ten. *Johanna Zach buried in a single grave, St Mary's.* (p 49, 64, 145, 167, 168, 170)

•◆•

SECOND-CABIN PASSENGERS. 80 total: 32 men, 34 women, 14 children
All *lost* and bodies not recovered or unidentified unless otherwise indicated.

FROM NEW YORK
Catherine Bonath. 56 West 56th St., servant to Mrs L. Becker of same address (in first cabin).
Mrs Pauline Forster and infant.
Mrs Ernestine Furst and little girl aged three.* 106 South 5th Ave. Originally from Prussia. Not on any passenger lists but said to be a second-cabin passenger. (p 70, 145)
Mrs Catherine Hering.
Mrs Louise Holzmaister.* 106 East 14th St. Wife of Lewis V. Holzmaister. Daughter of John and Suzanna Thomass of 72 East 4th St. (p 4, 5, 70, 71, 145, 217)
Mr Ferdinand Kreuter.* 166 East Houston St. Optician for fifteen years. Left behind a wife and three children of his own plus three step-children. *Recovered from Schiller wreck and buried on St Agnes.* (p 71-72, 207, 219)
Mr and Mrs Augustus Munte (or Munter).* *Buried together in mass graves, St Mary's.* (p 48,159)
Mr and Mrs Louis (or Ludwig) Reiderer and child.* Louis from Ellewangen in Wurtemburg. Child either a daughter, 'Lulu' (*Times*), or 'a fine little boy about six' (*Cornish Telegraph*). Louis Reiderer s*aved. Mrs Reiderer and child buried together in a single grave, St Mary's.* (p 134, 136, 143, 151, 155, 158, 159, 162, 165, 187, 203)
Mrs Maria Schuhr and Miss Bertha Schuhr.* 377 East 23rd St. Husband Charles Schuhr (or Schulor) owned a barber's shop at 54 East 23rd St. (p70, 143, 149)
Miss Louise Veitenheimer. Had lived in the U.S. only two or three years with her uncle Charles, an insurance agent of East 114th St., Harlem. Aged 22, she was in delicate health. Parents said to be poor people in Heidelburg (or Frankfurt) where her father was a railway baggage man, and she could bear to be away from them no longer. She had made many friends in New York and intended to return in two or three years.

HOBOKEN
Mr Louis (Levi) and Mrs Elise Selig.* Had kept a dry goods store at 145 Meadow St. An order for Selig's arrest dated 16 Sept 1874 was issued by Judge Joschmisen on suit of Morris A. Tynberg for an unpaid invoice when Selig was a fancy goods merchant in New Jersey, but had never been executed. (p 70, 148)
Mrs M. Wilkes.

AUGUSTA, GEORGIA
George C. Leonhardt, **Mary Leonhardt and Jenny Leonhardt.*** George born in Hanover but was a U.S. citizen. Employed by F.A. Brahe & Co. at Telfair, Augusta. Mary, aged 30, born in New York of foreign parents (née Bosag). Jenny, aged eight, born in Georgia. George's brother Charles lived at 64 Nassau St., NY. *George C. Leonhardt buried in mass graves, St Mary's.* (p 71, 145, 159, 160, 172)

BALTIMORE
Mrs Lina 'Minna' Kirchmayer.* Possibly stayed at home of Mr and Mrs Jacob Greisch, 1002 Myrtle Ave., Brooklyn, while in N.Y. as it was Mr Greisch who brought Charles Kirchmayer's telegram to the Eagle Line offices. (p 70, 145-146)

BROOKLYN
Herman and Augusta Deckritz.* Court St. He was aged 60 or 65. Mrs Deckritz said to be aged 65 and previously widowed. The couple had adult children – one was a book-keeper at a well-known German house in Ducene St. *Mrs Deckritz buried in mass graves, St Mary's.* (p 71, 168, 175)

CHICAGO AND ILLINOIS

Mrs R. Cutlow (Lutlow, Butlow or Ludlow). Shelbyville, Illinois. Booked passages for four persons, one of whom possibly Miss Flachs (below).

Miss Anna Eisner. Division St., Chicago. Daughter of Maurice Eisner of the grocery firm, Kohn & Eisner. *Buried in mass graves, St Mary's.*

Mrs Elizabeth Len and Miss Christine Len. Chicago Ave., Chicago. Wife and daughter of John Len.

Miss Ella Flachs. Quincy, Illinois.

Silas Hexter.* Ashland, Illinois. German by birth. *Saved.* (p 89, 94, 100, 103, 104, 105, 106, 108, 117, 121, 133, 136, 154, 156, 204)

Michael Hurlemann. Highland, Illinois.

Christian Hurst. Ashland, Illinois.

J. William Metzger.* Chicago. *Embalmed and returned to U.S.* (p 72, 170)

Gottfried I. Schmidt. North Wells St., Chicago. Of Schmidt & Laverenz, flour and feed dealers. Left a wife and four children at home.

Mr and Mrs John Suppiger, Miss Adeline Suppiger, Master John Suppiger, Mr Louis G. Suppiger. Highland, Illinois. *Adeline Suppiger buried in mass graves, St Mary's.*

Mr and Mrs Henry Wohlers and two children. North Wells St. Chicago. Mr Wohlers was aged 37 and worked for the provision firm Gualier & Co. Wife aged 31 and children six years and six weeks.

DAVENPORT, IOWA

William and Charles Frahm.* Charles Frahm only s*aved. William Frahm embalmed at Penzance and returned to U.S.* (p 44, 45, 76, 93, 98, 121-122, 133, 136, 147, 156, 169, 175, 185)

Carl F. Haase, his wife and two children.* Main St., of Haase, Bielefeldt & Co. Married a Miss Albert about four years previously and had a girl aged three and boy aged 18 months. (p 44, 147)

Mrs Emma Hansen and child. Wife of one of the leading farmers in Liberty township.

Otto Kircher.* Born 1842. Emigrated to U.S. in 1865. Was a book-keeper for a Chicago wholesale jewellers then a salesman by sample for the same employers. Met Fred Goos when on the road and together set up firm of Goos & Kircher, taking over established business of Rutenbeck & Co., Davenport, in 1869. Married Tillie Steinhilber of Blue Grass Town in December 1872. (p 45, 146, 147)

Mrs Margaretta Klemme. A widow aged over 50 who lived with one of her daughters, Mrs Henry Priest, at the St Louis House. Five of her children lived in the U.S., one in Germany.

P.A. Paulson.* Jeweller and widow. Father of five daughters aged six to 20. *Buried in mass graves, St Mary's.* (p 43, 45, 46, 145)

DETROIT, MICHIGAN

Mrs Johanna Beyer. *Buried in mass graves, St Mary's.*

Mrs C. Klonhammer.

Mrs Xavier, or Maria Reichlin.* Aged about 38 and mother of four children (not on any passenger lists but said to be on board the *Schiller* with her by Polemann). *Enbalmed at Penzance and returned to U.S.* (p 171, 175)

Mr Alois Stockmann.

MILWAUKEE, WISCONSIN

Mrs Marie Miltner and her infant child.*

OHIO

C.E. Aulig. Columbus, Ohio.

Richard Feederle.* Akron, Ohio. Born in Baden 1833 and emigrated to U.S. when aged 18. Married with one daughter. While in Germany was to stay at 'Hufengen Bd. Schwarzald'. (p 72, 103, 145)

Mr and Mrs Edward Schrier (or Schirmer). Columbus, Ohio. *Mr Schrier embalmed and returned to U.S.*

C.T. Stephen. St Mary's, Ohio.

Frederick Uhlmann.* Columbus, Ohio. *Embalmed and returned to U.S.* (p 72, 170, 175)

SHENANDOAH, PENNSYLVANIA

Dr F.J. Kern.* Born at Hennfield, Prussia in 1825. Married with three grown up daughters and a ten-year-old son. Director of Shenandoah Savings Bank. (p72)

ST. LOUIS, MISSOURI

Mrs Auguste Ziegler, her infant child, Miss Dora Ziegler, Mrs Dora Cohrs and Mrs A. Mayer. These three married ladies, plus Miss Dora and the infant, were travelling together, possibly sharing the same stateroom on *Schiller*. They may have all been related.

OTHER PLACES

Mr Marx Cohen. Montezuma, Georgia.
Edward Ball.* Not on any passenger list but said to be a cabin passenger. *Buried at Penzance.*
William Kohl. From Buffalo, N.Y.
Mr M. (Michael, Morris or Morrison) Harrison.* Hawkinsville, Georgia. *Embalmed and returned to U.S.*
Mr Herman Spritz. Macon, Georgia. A youngish man. Was a prominent merchant and accompanying Mr A. Waterman for a short tour abroad. Both men stopped over at the French's Head Inn from 22–26 April while in New York. *Buried in mass graves, St Mary's.*
Mr A. Waterman. From Kittery, Hawkinsville, Georgia. A wealthy merchant.
John Williams. From Newburgh, N.Y.

•◆•

STEERAGE PASSENGERS. 123 total: 70 men, 29 women, 24 children

All *lost* and bodies not recovered or unidentified unless otherwise indicated.

NEW YORK

Mr & Mrs Oscar Cramer.* 330 East 18th St. (p 68, 143)
Mrs Susan Duckfield and four children, Elizabeth Ann, aged eight, Mary Matilda, seven, Georgina, four and Edward France, two.* 129 Bleecker St. Susan born Susan Hill in Barnstaple, Devon, 1847. *Georgina (possibly Susan also) buried in mass graves, St Mary's.* (p 68, 93, 143, 160, 218, 219)
Mrs Frances 'Fanny' Evans and her only child, John, aged four.* 129 Bleecker St. Frances born Leeds 1847. *John possibly buried in mass graves, St Mary's.* (p68, 93, 143, 218, 219)
Carl Jahns.* 132 Leonard St. Had had been in the U.S. for 14 years; aged 32. Was a grand-nephew of Professor Jahns, the founder of 'Turnverien' (gymnastics). (p 68, 69)
Carl Jantzen and wife.* Carl Jantzen. *Saved.* (p110,136)
Edward Oscar Knock. *Buried in mass graves, St Mary's.*
Charles Henry Percy.* From London. *Saved.* (p 133, 136, 151)
Marcus Powitzer.* *Saved.* (p 50, 90, 104, 105, 106, 136, 154, 156)
Johannes Rink.* *Saved.* (p 93, 94, 133, 115, 134, 136, 154, 155)
Christian Roach and wife. *Christian Roach buried in mass graves, St Mary's.*
Franz Otto Shellenburg.* Travelling to visit his native village of Ebersbach near Glauchau, Saxony. *Saved.* Later wrote an account of the wreck. Died 26 May 1900.
Friedrich Sopper. From Switzerland. *Buried in mass graves, St Mary's.*
Richard Williams.* From Chacewater, Cornwall. *Saved.* (p 108, 109, 100, 136, 151)
Sophie Winser (or Winter) and two children. 36 Eldridge St. Came to U.S. at age 19, married Franz Winser. Travelling to see her father in Germany.
Carl Schneider, wife and two children.
Carl Schilling, wife and one child.

Joseph Holler and wife	**Wilhelm Schmidt & wife.**	**Louis Armbruster.**
Louise Broschwitsky.	**Albin (or Allein) Buhmer.**	**Michael Detta**
William Dopheide.	**L. Eckstein.**	**Christian Esser.**

Kathy Funck.	Herman Hansen.	M. A. Horst.
Henry Jerome.	George Johns.	S. Koppel.
Thomas Lynsol.	Richard Mitchell.	E. Nelson.
Auguste Polezoch.	Thomas Rimmer.	Philip Santo.
William Santo.	Henry Saupe.	Ludwig Schneider.
Alexander Tobin.	Theo Zopfel.	

HOBOKEN

Mrs Elise Neo and two sons, Henry, ten, and Walter, eight* 154 Garden St. *Mrs Neo buried in mass graves, St Mary's.* (p 68, 142, 168)

Emiline Steinmetz. Aged 23. Had been residing with Mr Oeder, a butcher in Hoboken, for about a year. Was returning to Germany to live.

JERSEY CITY

Henry Forster. Union St., Old Bergen. A ship's carpenter by trade.

Mrs Anna Meisner and two children, Sophie, ten, and Charles, six.* Essex Street. Husband was a night-watchman at Mattheissen & Weicher's sugar house. *Mrs Meisner buried in mass graves, St Mary's.* (p 68, 145, 168)

TROY, N.Y.

Fredericke Brenecke Jnr and Doris Brenecke. 177 Fourth St.

Brother-in-law to Fredericke. Not on passenger list but mentioned in *New York Times* report.

Mrs Sophie Holzhauer and child.* 136 North 2nd St. Aged 26. Had come to U.S. five or six years before from Glessen, Germany. A sister and three brothers lived in N.Y. (p 68)

Frederick Katzenberger with wife and three children. 45 Franklin St. Frederick only on passenger list, others in *New York Times* report. Family were going home to Hessen, Darmstadt for good.

PHILADELPHIA

Edward Mannheimer, wife and two children.* South 2nd Street. *Edward Mannheimer recovered from Schiller wreck and buried on St Agnes.*

CHICAGO AND ILLINOIS

John Becherle.

John Bundick.

Carl Burghard, wife and two children. Returning to Germany for good.

Frederika Fluentze. A young lady going to visit friends.

Henry Mohr. Superior St., Chicago. A cigar manufacturer. A single man and member of Chicago's 'Turngemeinde' (gymnastics club).

F. Zimmerman. Highland, Illinois. *Buried in mass graves, St Mary's.*

DAVENPORT, IOWA

John Bohnsack. (or Bohnhoff). Liberty St. A young man travelling to visit his parents in Germany.

Mr Henry Goettsche. Unmarried cabinet maker. One of the oldest settlers of Davenport, having lived there for over 20 years. Intended to visit relatives and bring some of them back with him.

G.W. Gutsche and wife.* He was a carpenter and both were returning to Germany to retire.

Mr and Mrs John and Christine Joens.* Luzerne, Benton County, Iowa. John Joens the son of Hennings and Margaret Joens of Hollingstedt, Schleswig. His brother Peter (1855–1918) also emigrated to America in 1868 and lived at Luzerne. *Both John and Christine saved.* Returned to Luzerne in early August 1875. (p 45, 93, 109, 110, 117, 118, 133, 136, 147, 151, 152, 154, 156, 204).

John Nissen. One of the old settlers of the city having lived there for over a quarter of a century. Was a wagon maker by trade. A widower, he had a married daughter, Mrs John Specht, living in Durant.

P.C. Roschmann.* A resident of the city for ten or 12 years. His wife was visiting friends in the country while

he travelled to Germany. (p 45)
Aug. Stracke.

WILLIAMSBURGH
Carol Fell and two children.
Mrs Sophie Haacke. *Buried in mass graves, St Mary's.*
Elizabeth Henning.
John Jlg.

OTHER PLACES
Franz Daner (or Dauer). Syracuse N.Y. **A** tailor by trade who left a wife and three children at home.
I.F. Diewohl and wife. Scranton, Penn.
T. Goldsmith. Newark, New Jersey. Aged 22. Worked in liquor business at Froelich, grocers, corner of Mulberry and Canal streets. Intending a brief visit to his parents in Germany.
William Kock. Rockport, Illinois, an ex-artillery man. Travelling to Hanover.
Joseph Legenore (or Leyenbein). From Kentucky and travelling to Cherbourg – ultimately for Havre. *Saved.* (p 93, 94, 98, 113, 114, 118, 134, 136, 155, 157).
Mrs Louise Wercher* (or Wenchen) Baltimore (or Detroit). A recent widow. (p 69)
J. Ahrens. Terre Haute, Indiana. **F. Conntrei.** Columbus, Ohio. **M.T. Galmbacher.** Brooklyn.
F.H. Grunberg. Germany. **John Harter.** New Albany. **M. Manguen.** Detroit.
B. Mulot. San Francisco. **T.L. Roell and wife.** Brooklyn. **Wilhelm Sailer.** Highland, Illinois.
Frederick Sauerbier. Columbus, Ohio. **Mr Joseph Wiel.** Greensboro, N. Carolina.

•◆•

<u>Not on any passenger lists</u>
Seven persons who stayed at the Eagle Hotel, New York, before joining *Schiller*. (*New York Herald* report). These were:
George Gambach. Tosanta. On a business trip to Europe.
John Hecker. Lexington. On a business trip to Europe; aged 25.
Mr Winter, wife and three young children. Chicago; aged 45. Was widely known in Chicago, where he kept a large saloon. Before joining *Schiller* the family promised to return to the Eagle Hotel after their voyage.
'Henry' the well known headwaiter at Monquins Restaurant, frequented by New York's literati. (probably under his real, full name on the lists)

<u>Passengers whose bodies were recovered but not on passengers lists</u>
(buried in mass graves at St Mary's unless otherwise indicated).
Mrs Ackermann. An elderly lady identified by a label in her boots.
S. Black. M. Bottger. Mrs Jacks. Peter Jennings. E. Kasek. Ellen Little, buried at sea from Porthleven fishing lugger *Victory*. **Andre Petersen. Henry Rohrs and wife. M. Rosnowski.** Army, 74th Regiment. **F. Sayer. Miss Wagner,** aged about 18 (could have been the lady's maid of either Mrs Just or Mrs Kornblum

Passenger trunks recovered with unknown names: Mrs Auguste Tegier, S.J. Jensen, Frederick Krittien.

[This passenger list is as complete as possible, having been drawn up from the slightly different and incomplete passenger lists published in the *New York Times* and *Hamburgischer Correspondent* newspapers, May 1875, with additional information from other American and British newspapers]

◆•◆

The Cargo Manifest

Julius Jungbluth order
Herman Brothers & Co., order
Herman Brothers & Co., order
E. Benedict, E.Rudenberg & Co.
E. Benedict, E. Rudenberg & Co.
E. Benedict, Elkan & Co.
E. Benedict, Andre & Markerling
H. Koop & Co., H.V. Fischer, Bremen
H. Koop & Co., H.V. Fischer, Bremen
H. Koop & Co., Hettel Brothers

P.W. Kriege & Muir, C. Voermann
S.S. Hatch, order
American Clock Co. –
    Christopher Christopherson, Christiana
Tiedman & Gafney, order
Stroher & Reitzenstein, Jules Sandtman & Co.
Edward Unkart, C.H. Jordan
Sinclair & Marvin, order
Barclay & Co., G. Voso
New-York Knitting Machine Co. –
    Berland, Tangwall & Co.
Knauth, Nachod & Kuhne, Brenstakie & Co.
L.P. Rose, Uhlman & Co.
Albert Bohme, Albert Bohme
P. Elmenhorst, A. Teadopf & Co., London
Mason & Hamlin Organ Co., Ullman & Co.
Halcket & Co., H.F. Kirsten
F. Probst & Co., H.J. Blume
F. Probst & Co., C. Brothean
F. Hertz & Co., order
Merchants' Dispatch Line, account of –
    R.M. Warger & Co., Doubleday & Son
Arnson & Wilezynski, M. Wilezynski
Jacobowski & Hart, I. Newfeld

60 packages merchandise. (butter valued at $700)
14 bales merchandise
21 bales merchandise
35 reapers in 35 packages
32 reapers in 70 packages
2 barrels wheat
10 boxes mowers and 10 poles
14 cases leaf tobacco
36 cases leaf tobacco
72 cases leaf tobacco (total 112 cases valued at $3100)
2518 barrels resin
7 boxes clocks

47 boxes clocks
200 barrels flour (valued at $1000)
50 cases leaf tobacco
500 boxes starch
600 staves
5 cases merchandise

1 case machinery
25 cases knitting machines
10 cases merchandise
35 pieces casings
293 barrels honey
10 cases cabinet organs
150 barrels beef
25 boxes nails, 10 cases blacking
88 packets sundries (mostly hardware)
4000 barrels corn in 1386 ship bags and 1 sample

103 cases sewing machines
21 barrels shoe pegs and 1 sample
2 cases machinery

W.A. Wood, James R. McDonald & Co.	33 mowers in 66 packages (valued at $36 030)
Marks & Co., L.J. Wordell & Co., Stockholm	4 cases hardware
Marks & Co., P. Berghans, Gothenberg	26 cases merchandise
Marks & Co., Marks & Co.	1 case forks
A.C.L. & O. Meyer, J.G. Schlondorf, Bremen	174 barrels shoe pegs
F. Alexander & Sons, account of –	
City of New York. J. Arthur, F. Meyer	29 cases cigars
F. Alexander & Sons, account of –	
City of New York. G.I. Strych, Antwerp	1 case cigars (total 30 cases valued at $15 578)
J.H. Rosebach, order	264 packets merchandise
J.H. Rosebach, order	5 casks bark extract
Saxton & Seabury, M. Wilezynski	4 boxes machinery
Lewison Bros, order	20 bales and 6 packages packages merchandise
Lehmann Bros., order, Amsterdam	300 bales cotton
Lehmann Bros., order, Amsterdam	500 bales cotton. (total 800 bales valued at $65 000)
Union Line, account of Glick Bros	10 barrels casings
E. S. Ballin & Co., E.S. Ballin & Co. Paris	6 kegs containing $300 000 gold
I.P. Rose, Jno. G. Rollins & Co.	5 cases merchandise
I.P. Rose, F. Naumann	19 reapers in 119 packages
I.P. Rose, A. Gunther	24 reapers in 144 packages
I.P. Rose, P.A.V. Essen	28 reapers in 168 packages
I.P. Rose, A. Gunther	10 harvesters in 66 packages, 30 packages shut out
I.P. Rose, Russian Agricultural Agency –	
St Petersburg	40 reapers and 6 mowers in 220 packages
I.P. Rose, A. Gunther	18 mowers in 54 packages, 30 packages shut out
Parcel receipt No. 81, Henry Edye, A. Edye	1 mower in 2 packages

TOTAL WEIGHT OF CARGO, over 2000 tons
TOTAL VALUE OF CARGO, EXCLUDING GOLD, $ 107 148

[From the *New York Times*]

APPENDIX D

•◆•

The Rescuers

<u>St Agnes gigs: the men who manned them</u>
O & M
Obadiah Hicks, Stephen Hicks, William Mortimer and three youths, Richard Legg, William Cook Hicks and Stephen Hicks* (from *The Scillonian*, June 1944, No. 78). * This Stephen Hicks was more likely Osbert Hicks, aged about 22 (from Osbert Hicks of St Agnes – his grandson).
Bee and *Thomas* – no names of crews.

<u>Sennen fishing luggers: the men who manned them</u>
Rapid and *Shade of Evening*
Jacob Deason of St Agnes.* John, Thomas, Joe and William Trenery; William Barnes Sen. and Willaim Barnes Jun.; W.H. George; Henry Nicholas; Thomas Williams and John Gillis – all from Sennen (from the *Cornish Telegraph, 12 May, 1875).*

*Jacob Deason (story told by Richard Legg) while fishing off one of the islands was captured by a French privateer and taken to South America, where he jumped ship and eventually got back to the Isles of Scilly.

Bibliography

Archibald, E.H.H. M.A. *Travellers by Sea*. London (1933)

Blake, George. *Down to the Sea; the romance of the Clyde, its ships and shipbuilders*. (1937)

Blake, George. *British Ships and Shipbuilders*. (1946)

Bonsor, N.R.P. *North Atlantic Seaway. Vols 1–5*. Brookside Publications (1978)

Boulay, Juliet de. *Wrecks on the Isles of Scilly*. Mariners Mirror Vol 46 (1960)

Bowley, R.L. *The Fortunate Islands*. Bowley Publications (1990)

Box, Peter. *All at Sea*. Rushmere Publishing (1992)

Brinnin, John Malcomb. *The Sway of the Grand Saloon*. Arlington Books (1986)

Bunnell, Paul J. F.A.C.G., U.E. *Cemetery Inscriptions of the Town of Barnstable Massachusetts and its Villages, 1600–1900*. Heritage Books Inc. (1995)

Carrol, Peter N. & Noble, David W. *The Free and the Unfree*. Penguin (1988)

Coleman, Terry. *The Liners*. Allen Lane (1976)

Cornish Times and General Advertiser. 15 May 1875

Daily Bristol Times and Mirror. 10–12 May 1875

Dessoff, Ulbert. *Kunst und Künster in Frankfurt am Main*. Frankfurt (1909)

Dickens, Charles. *American Notes and Reprinted Pieces*. Chapman Hall (1894)

Evening Standard. 8 May 1875

Fletcher, R.A. *Travelling Palaces: Luxury in Passenger Steamships*. Pitman (1913)

Fry, Henry. *History of North Atlantic Steam Navigation*. Sampson, Low, Marston & Company (1896)

Gardiner, Robert. (Ed.) *The Advent of Steam*. Conway Maritime Press (1993)

Gentleman's Magazine. June 1875

Gillis, R.H.C. *The pilot gigs of Cornwall and the Isles of Scilly*. Mariners Mirror Vol 55 (1969)

Gillis, Richard. *The Last Voyage of the Schiller*. (unknown) 21 March 1970.

Grigson, Geoffrey. *The Scilly Isles*. Duckworth (1948)

Hamburgischer Correspondent. 9 May–1 June 1875

Harper's Weekly. 29 May 1875

Haws, Duncan. *Merchant Fleets in Profile. Vols 1 and 4*. Patrick Stephens Ltd. (1978)

History of Benton County. (Iowa) (late-nineteenth century)

History of Milwaukee. (1881)

Hoff, Jon Freidrich. *Ein Künsterhiem ror 70 Jahren*. Frankfurt (1902)

Hope, Ronald. *A New History of British Shipping*. John Murray (1990)

Hoppin, Augustus. *Crossing the Atlantic*. Boston (1872)

Howarth, David and Howarth, Stephen. *The Story of P & O*. Wiedenfield & Nicholson (1986)

Illustrated London News. 15 & 22 May 1875

Isles of Scilly Museum. *Shipwrecks around the Scilly Isles*. Publication No. 3 (1988)

Johnson, Howard. *The Cunard Story*. Whittet Books (1987)

Katcher, Philip. *The American Civil War Source Book*. Cassell (1992)

Kittredge, Henry. *Shipmasters of Cape Cod*. Boston (c.1939)

Kludas, Arnold. *Die Geschichte der Deutschen Passagierschiffahrt, Vol 1. (Die Pionierjahre von 1850 bis 1890)*. Ernst Kabel Verlag, Hamburg (1986)

Larn, Richard. *Cornish Shipwrecks; the Isles of Scilly*. David & Charles (1979)

Larn, Richard & Bridget. *Shipwrecks Index of the British Isles. Vol 1.* Lloyd's Register (1995)

Liverpool Weekly Mercury, 15 May 1875

Lloyd's List, March 1859 & Sept 1873–May 1876

Manchester Evening News, 10–12 May 1875

Manchester Guardian, 10–12 May 1875

Mark, David & Oakland, John. *American Civilisation.* Routledge (1995)

Milwaukee Daily Sentinel, 10 May 1875

Nautical Magazine, 1875

Nelson, T. *Great Shipwrecks 1544–1877.* Thomas Nelson (1877)

Paasch, Captain H. *Illustrated Marine Dictionary.* (1890)

Parliamentary Papers. 1875, Vol 70; & 1876, Vol 67.

Parker, Captain H. and Bowen, Frank C. *Mail and Passenger Steamships of the Nineteenth Century.* Sampson, Low, Marston & Company (1926)

Royal Yachting Association. *Navigation an RYA Manual.* David & Charles (1991)

Schnellenberg, Franz Otto. *The Shipwreck of the 'Schiller' on May 7, 1875 Near the Scilly Islands off England.* Personal record.

Solver, C.V. & Marius, J.G. *Dead Reckoning and the Ocean Voyages of the Past.* Mariners Mirror Vol 44. (1959)

The Argus (Jersey City), 8–12 May 1875

The Augusta Daily Chronicle and Sentinel, 9–19 May 1875

The Baltimore Sun, 10 May 1875

The Barnstable Patriot, 24 May 1870, 18 May 1875, 4 April 1940

The Belle Plaine Union (Benton County, Iowa), 10–13 & 27 May, 12 Aug 1875

The Boston Post, 10 May 1875

The Boston Evening Transcript, 10–11 May 1875

The Chicago Daily Tribune, 8–10 May 1875

The Cornish Telegraph, 12, 19 & 26 May 1875

The Daily Constitutionalist (Augusta, Georgia), 9–13 May 1875

The Daily Sentinel (Milwaukee), 10 May 1875

The Davenport Democrat, 8 & 10 May 1875

The Evening Journal (Jersey City), 8–15 May 1875

The Graphic, 22 May 1875

New York Herald, 9–11 May 1875

The New York Times, 8 May 1872, 1 Oct 1873–23 May 1875

The New York Tribune, 10–11 May 1875

The Observer, 9 & 16 May 1875

The Scillonian, Nos 31 (Sept 1932), 33 (March 1933), 41 (March 1935), 46 (June 1936) and 78 (June 1944).

The Standard, 10, 14 & 15 May 1875

The Sunday Times, 9 & 16 May 1875

The Times, 10–24 May, 2–14 June 1875, 27 Nov 1878

The World (New York), 9–11 May 1875

The United States Biographical Dictionary. (1877)

The Weekly Despatch, 16 May & 6 June 1875

The Western Morning News, 10–13 May 1875

Trayser, Donald G. *Barnstable, Three Centuries of a Cape Cod town.* F.B. & F.P. Goss, Hyannis Massachusetts (1939)

Tute, Warren. *Atlantic Conquest.* Boston (1962)

Verne, Jules. *Round the World in Eighty Days.* (1873)

Vernon Gibbs, C.R. *Passenger Liners of the Western Ocean.* Staples Press (1952)

Western Daily Press, 13 May 1875

Whitman, Walt. *Specimen Days in America.* Walter Scott, London (1887)

Winchester, Clarence (Ed.). *Shipping Wonders of the World.* Amalgamated Press, London (1938)

Index